# EUROPE IN THE WORLD

# Europe in the World

## The Persistence of Power Politics

Maurice Keens-Soper
*Fellow*
*Centre for the Study of Diplomacy*
*University of Leicester*

First published in Great Britain 1999 by
**MACMILLAN PRESS LTD**
Houndmills, Basingstoke, Hampshire RG21 6XS and London
Companies and representatives throughout the world

A catalogue record for this book is available from the British Library.

ISBN 0–333–71921–2

First published in the United States of America 1999 by
**ST. MARTIN'S PRESS, INC.,**
Scholarly and Reference Division,
175 Fifth Avenue, New York, N.Y. 10010

ISBN 0–312–21851–6

Library of Congress Cataloging-in-Publication Data
Keens-Soper, H. M. A.
Europe in the world : the persistence of power politics / Maurice
Keens-Soper.
p.   cm.
Includes bibliographical references and index.
ISBN 0–312–21851–6 (cloth)
1. Europe—Politics and government—20th century.   2. Europe–
–Foreign relations—United States.   3. United States—Foreign
relations—Europe.   I. Title.
D443.K38   1999
320.94—dc21                                              98–35014
                                                              CIP

This book is printed on paper suitable for recycling and made from fully managed and
sustained forest sources.

10   9   8   7   6   5   4   3   2   1
08   07   06   05   04   03   02   01   00   99

Printed and bound in Great Britain by
Antony Rowe Ltd, Chippenham, Wiltshire

To Wendy Earle

# Contents

# List of Abbreviations

**Main List**

| | |
|---|---|
| APEC | Asia Pacific Economic Co-operation |
| ASEAN | Association of South East Asian Nations |
| CBR | Chemical Bacteriological and Radiological |
| CCTV | Closed Circuit Television |
| CFSP | Common Foreign and Security Policy |
| CIS | Commonwealth of Independent States |
| COREPER | Comité des Représentants Permanents |
| ECJ | European Court of Justice |
| ECSC | European Coal and Steel Community |
| EDC | European Defence Community |
| EEC | European Economic Community |
| EMU | European Monetary Union |
| EPC | European Political Co-operation |
| ESDI | European Security and Defence Identity |
| EU | European Union |
| GATT | General Agreement on Tariffs and Trade |
| GDP | Gross Domestic Product |
| G7 | Group of Seven leading industrial nations |
| IAEA | International Atomic Energy Agency |
| IGC | Intergovernmental Conference |
| ICBM | Inter Continental Ballistic Missiles |
| IMF | International Monetary Fund |
| NAFTA | North American Free Trade Area |
| NATO | North Atlantic Treaty Organization |
| NGO | Non-Governmental Organization |
| NPT | Non-Proliferation Treaty |
| OAS | Organization of African States |
| OECD | Organization for Economic Co-operation and Development |
| OSCE | Organization for Security and Co-operation |
| QMV | Qualified Majority Voting |
| SACEUR | Supreme Allied Commander Europe |
| SEA | Single European Act |
| UN | United Nations |

| WEU | Western European Union |
| WTO | World Trade Organization |

## Abbreviations in Chapter 5

| CE | Candide's Europe |
| ERE | Exemplary and Radiant Europe |
| FNUs | Feisty National Unities |
| FUN | Fantasizing the United Nations |
| HE | Houdini's Europe |
| MAMEE | Mighty America in Europe |
| RDE | Recidivous Europe |
| SPE | Salus Populi Europe |
| TASTIE | Taxonomically and Acronymously Stupefying complexities of Europe |

# Introduction

## I

Europe plays havoc with rounded argument. When it fails to be a killjoy the topic spoils the idea that argument is a venture in completeness of reasoning within or towards an ordered design. What can be meant by 'Europe' and what sense is there in speaking as if 'it' had a presence and future that mattered to the citizens of states and nations? Can anything intelligible be made of claims that Europe's composition and place in the world may sooner rather than later affect the well-being of people more than the nations and states to which many remain attached?

When argument over Europe flares the independence of reason is among the casualties. Pressed to make explicit the assumptions on which one's arguments rest, it is hard to deny their dependence on a mixture of historical interpretation and more wayward beliefs whose ultimate foundations remain stubbornly unyielding to exposition. If, among other things, Europe embodies a civilization, how is one to name and uphold its attributes in a world where there exist companion and perhaps incompatible examples of human worth? How can one *organize* a civilization that may form only one portion of the broader assemblage of 'western civilization'? For what purposes is the question even put? Did not Europe flourish best during the times of its most fragmented diversity?

If argument rests on opinions for which there are seldom adequately persuasive foundations, it is accompanied by a flanking hazard that can also be counted upon to ruffle. Having advanced a fulsome argument, feelings aroused by the force of reasoning then threaten to impassion one's judgement. If Europe is or should be more than the sum of its parts, are not delays in recognizing and acting on this conclusion culpable? Or if, on reflection, 'Europe' is baloney should not those who traffic in mischievous nonsense get their desserts? Instead of providing an occasion for dispassionate enquiry governed by the light of reason, argument over Europe is caught between beliefs lodged in inaccessible assumptions, and opinions sparked by tumbling into their consequences.

Europe illustrates so well how argument cohabits in hyphenation with foundations and feelings that it is wasteful to deny or conceal their association. Labour as one does to persuade by dint of argument and weight of reasoning, it is perhaps better, or at least more prudent, to allow at least partial expression to the tone of one's thinking. The attempt to inter a standpoint is unlikely to survive its exhumation by others.

## II

Europe is what it has become. This was as true in 1914 and 1945 as it is towards the close of the century. One difference between the onset of ' the great war for civilization' and now is that in 1914 Europe's 'form and fate'[1] lay in the hands of its fratricidal states. By 1945 this was no longer so. Yet a widely accepted view of Europe's more recent past and impending future has us believe that whatever is to become of Europe is once again entirely its own business. Its 'matter and form'[2] are said to be for its governments and peoples alone to determine. This confident opinion is held by advocates of a united Europe as well as by those whose sympathies rest wholly with its individual states and yet more numerous nations. They agree that in whatever direction decisions are taken they will be made by Europe's rulers and ruled. With appropriate democratic insistence it is said to be a matter for them alone to determine whether Europe becomes a substantial political unity, reverts to its long practised plurality, remains as at present a hybrid of perplexing and nameless typology, or discovers as yet untested ways of living together in and around the western extension of the Eurasian landmass. Whatever the choice it belongs of right to the peoples of Europe.

A contrary interpretation of Europe's prospects is outlined in what follows. No quarrel is picked over matters of right. The line of argument adopted does, however, question whether Europe and its states possess adequate might and means to govern their futures solely according to their wishes. It reasons instead that the formulation of Europe is inextricably bound up with the fate and form of the world at large. Over the world beyond itself, composed of states, nations and religions that are home to the bulk of humanity, Europe's influence is confined, and its room for independent manoeuvre thereby limited. This appears true whether one thinks of Europe acting and speaking with a single voice or persisting as individual states co-operating on occasion to further their separate interests. Viewed from this cautionary angle, Europe's increasing exposure to external events will do more than tug attention away from its own affairs. How Europe succeeds or fails to adapt itself to the diplomatic system of the world, and the measure of influence it thereby exerts on foreign affairs in general, may play an important, perhaps decisive, part in shaping its own development. How 'Europe' acts towards the world is inseparable from what sort of entity, if any, it becomes. Europe's future lies in its own keeping only if it adjusts to what Burke called 'the dominion of circumstances' over which, even under the most favourable conditions, its influence will be constrained by the powers and passions of other peoples.

III

The exposition opens with the post-war plight of western Europe's weakened states that obliged them to seek assistance from the USA and renounce war among themselves. This provided the opportunity for what forty years on can be seen to constitute an incomplete but notable political reformation. It then proceeds to an outline of the diplomatic system which Europe bequeathed to the world and which continues to supply the basis of foreign affairs and the setting of power politics. Claims that globalization is producing a world economy whose market forces are pulling the carpet from under states and establishing a new world order divested of power politics are considered and rejected. Discussion of this issue is followed by the suggestion that the new powers generated by globalization play into the hands of the already powerful, or are promoting changes that only a concert of great powers seems fitted to order and restrain.

Attention is directed next towards Europe's standing in foreign affairs where the inadequacies of the European Union(EU), the tenacity of independently minded states and the fraught question of relations with the USA are examined. In connection with Europe's dependence on the US it is suggested that the good habits of the Atlantic alliance, necessitated by the Cold War, risk becoming slothful reflexes in the altered circumstances that have followed the end of that particular conflict. The concluding portion of the discussion dwells on Britain's position in relation to the rest of Europe, the USA and the world; it is to be approached as a heartfelt addendum. Like the country to which it refers, it is perhaps detachable from the main body of the script.

Forewarning is due to those in search of prescriptions. If by this is meant policies designed to meet prevailing events they will find none.

This is not because attention to the 'practicalities' of public affairs is unworthy of close attention. The justification for seeking to elucidate the general features of Europe's position and account for the persistence of power politics is that without an extended effort to see what they are, why they matter and above all how they are related, it is misplaced to call any policy or institutional development important. The reasons for adopting one 'practical' choice rather than another – in connection, for example, with making the EU's Common Foreign and Security Policy (CFSP) more effective – can be established only by reference to considerations of a wide-ranging kind; of necessity these ultimately refer to the question why a common or single European foreign policy is thought necessary, desirable, implausible or perverse. Argument, sometimes of a tiresomely unrounded kind, is, or should be, required to establish policy on defensible if not rational grounds. How else are governments to find instruction or the governed be consulted? Hence the attempt to envisage a line separating the exposition of an argument from the 'concrete' actions necessary to further policies is falsely conceived. It is a *trompe-l'oeil* beloved of pragmatists. As with arguments, policies are no more reliable than the assumptions upon which they rest.

## Notes

1. Burke writes of 'the form and the fate of Europe': Edmund Burke, *Burke's Writings and Speeches* (London: The World's Classics, 1907), I Vol. VI p.172.
2. The full title of Thomas Hobbes' *Leviathan* is 'Leviathan or the matter, form and power of a Commonwealth Ecclesiastical and Civil'. Thomas Hobbes, *Leviathan*, Introduction by Michael Oakeshott (Oxford: Basil Blackwell, 1946).

*'He said that history was a nightmare during which he was trying to get a good night's sleep.'*

— Saul Bellow, *Humboldt's Gift*

# Part I

# The Matter and Form of Europe

# 1 Renunciation and Reformation

At the close of the Second World War western Europe was notable for the weakness of all its hitherto great powers. France ceased to be a Great Power in 1940 and Germany in 1945. Mussolini's ambitions to raise Italy to that status ended in disaster. At Yalta, Churchill became aware that the price Britain had paid in remaining unconquered was a loss of power that left Roosevelt and Stalin with the preponderant say in re-drawing the map of Europe. The leaders of the USA and the USSR were backed by the unrivalled capacities of their states to wage war and make peace in their own interests. As a result of military victories, the power of their two countries marked them off from all other states. They were shortly to be labelled superpowers.

The USSR was of course a European power, whose exhausting victory over Germany left the Red Army in sole command of central Europe. Whereas the Second World War enhanced the position of the Soviet Union in Europe, it made the USA the strongest power in the world. In 1945 the Pacific as well as the Atlantic and the Mediterranean were American lakes. The USA accounted for more than half the world's manufacturing output. Among the great powers only it emerged richer from the war. In the aftermath of wartime alliance, the USA and the USSR interpreted each other and the shifts in their respective fortunes in ways that prevented the co-operation that Roosevelt had hoped would ensure world-wide peace. The result was the Cold War, whose centrepiece was a new division of Europe. Stalin was determined to reinforce military strength with political control of central Europe, while the weakness of western European countries induced the USA to add its weight to the task of counter-balancing the position of its Soviet rival. This policy included Marshall Aid for the reconstruction of Europe's battered economies and in 1949 the creation of the North Atlantic Treaty Organization (NATO). The USA made clear that support for western Europe depended upon forthright co-operation between countries that in some cases had been at war with each other twice in a lifetime. Most notably, West Germany was to be accepted as essential to economic recovery and the collective defence of 'the West'. External pressure by the USA on its European dependants provided powerful and perhaps decisive stimulus to the search for means by which German rehabilitation would promote rather than threaten the stability of western Europe. Many remembered Keynes' strictures on the failure to achieve this after the First World War. The solution inscribed in NATO, and made necessary by the imbalance between western Europe and the USSR, was for the USA to become a European power. Within the American embrace, Adenauer's Germany could play its part in containing Russia without rekindling fears in France. This double reassurance, against the prominence of the USSR and a revitalized Germany, was the great contribution of the USA to post-war Europe. In the cause of 'Western' interests, Washington spent half a century persuading its European allies to put their historically riven house in order. Because in American eyes western Europe was a fragmented and fractious whole whose disarray was a cause of weakness, the USA wanted its separate states and nations to act upon what they had in common and keep before their eyes the common dangers to the east to which they were exposed. How many in Europe then saw themselves as Europeans or believed in a universal communist conspiracy is unclear, but since the Congress of the country that funded their recovery and committed its arms to their safety proclaimed the truth of both, that sufficed. If the moral scourging of the USSR was necessary to arouse the USA to action, then the 'ideological' struggle was indeed for the soul of humanity, and only incidentally about the balance of power in post-war Europe. Whatever reservations were harboured over the wisdom or veracity of moral crusades, their own recent experience prevented continental Europeans from publicly describing their predicament in the discredited language of power politics and the balance of power.

The crippled states of western Europe were not well-placed to belittle American interest in the reform of foreign affairs. When their own co-operation in NATO, made necessary by fears of the USSR, was represented as compatible with the United Nations (UN) they were in no position to demur. Many in Europe agreed with the American view that Europeans had brought upon themselves the calamities of the twentieth century, and that the principal culprit was the precepts and practices of power politics that spawned two world wars. There was widespread acceptance that responsibility for the collapse of Europe's position in the world, which in 1900 it had dominated, rested with the great powers and their inveterate conflicts. If their own disaster was the result of alliances, 'secret diplomacy' and the 'balance of power', and if these were the expression of 'power politics', a prudent as well as pious conclusion after 1945 was to wish them all good riddance. The willingness of the USA to save part of Europe from the consequences of noxious practices, and to put its strength and virtues behind a better ordering of the world, was not therefore something to be scorned. Reservations about the zeal with which Americans approached the Cold War took second place to Europe's dependence on the might of the USA. Assurance could be found in the way that in spite of its principled abhorrence of power politics, Washington managed to practise them. The USA may have been led astray in Korea and Vietnam, but its NATO commitment to counterbalancing Soviet power in Europe remained constant.

The post-war recovery of western Europe rested on the security provided by America's nuclear power and the stationing of armed forces in and around the continent. The position thus arose in which, from the point of view of its allies, the USA was engaged in power politics against the USSR, although itself declining to see matters in that light. For their part, western Europe's enfeebled states were forced to recognize the failures of power politics while finding succour in the protection of a great power whose moral traditions and historical experience were affronted by a world activated by the balance of power. Amid confusions of this kind it is not surprising that few can say with certainty what the Cold War was about, other than that it was not a war. The 'hard and bitter' peace of post-war Europe was kept by two superpowers whose enmity divided it. Under these conditions the foreign policies of western Europe's states were reduced to being either better or worse allies of their overseas protector. Whereas Britain sought to make a virtue of this necessity and bound itself tightly to the USA, Gaullist France resented it, and dreamed of a Europe standing on its own feet. In both cases however, western Europe's Cold War dependence on the USA relieved them of primary responsibility for their own security.

Safeguarded by the superpower of the USA from the consequences of their own weakness *vis-à-vis* the USSR, the countries of western Europe were both exposed to and insulated from power politics at the highest level. Armed force of unprecedented power was assembled on both sides of the iron curtain that divided Europe, yet decisions of war and peace were lodged in Washington and Moscow. If the security of western Europe's states was not in their hands, this did not imply that they had lost all interest in foreign affairs. Many post-war governments were embroiled with overseas possessions in various stages of disaffection with rule by Europeans. Until well into the twentieth century, Europe's empires were seen as embellishments of power, but their unscrambling in the decades after 1945 drew attention to the underside of the story. The larger effect of colonial disengagement was to make plain the reduced powers of western Europe's countries. As with the Cold War division of their continent, about which either individually or collectively they could do nothing, the end of imperial rule redirected interest nearer to hand; to issues that lay within their diminished compass.

II

For all the governments of western Europe, the most urgent task after 1945 was the re-establishment of their states and economies. When it became clear they were unable to achieve this without American help, they were obliged to submit to a condition that lay at the heart of Marshall Aid. The requirement of detailed co-operation among recipients went beyond the inclusions of the western zones of occupied Germany. It meant the adoption of new methods of diplomacy. American Cold War interests in a less bitty western Europe were influenced by a wider sense that bilateral relations were part of the failure to secure peace. In place of one to one dealings and the rival alliances to which it was believed this gave rise, Americans argued that multilateralism obliged the governments of many countries to work together. In keeping with the spirit of liberal internationalism, it was believed that the experience of jointly manned institutions would break the cycle of distrust which had been for so long the principal feature of Europe's power politics. After half a century of bloody turmoil many in Europe were ready to agree. In some cases, such as the forerunner of Benelux created by three governments-in-exile in 1944, there was no waiting upon promptings from the USA. The result was a wash of organizations designed for various purposes but at one in the belief that they represented an improved way of conducting foreign affairs. International organizations set up in western Europe to administer Marshall Aid and encourage co-operation in other directions thus formed part of a wider picture of the post-war world notable for the burgeoning of multilateral agencies. In addition to the UN, the most important included the International Monetary Fund (IMF) and the World Bank. These all reflected American power and thinking and were in turn influenced by the onset of the Cold War.

Once Soviet-American conflict had riven Europe into hostile camps, by far the most important organization in western Europe was one so old in style that Thucydides would have recognized it. Once responsibility for the communist coup in Prague in 1948 was traced to Stalin, the countries of western Europe sought support more urgently fundamental than even economic aid. The result was NATO. The test of wills illustrated by the Berlin airlift was a further reminder of the inability of western Europe's states to fulfil the primary purpose of securing their citizens against external dangers. Only the USA had the means to remedy their vulnerability. Despite its wealth and monopoly of atomic weapons, the USA feared that a western Europe at the mercy of the Red Army would tilt the global balance of power against it. In China, Mao's armies were threatening to gain power. Yet although it was made to chime with both the Charter of the UN and the diabolism of the Cold War, NATO was a recognizably old fashioned alliance of states. Its purpose was to redress a regional imbalance of power by organizing a counter-balancing combination of allies. There was nothing novel in countries of unequal power being drawn together for mutual protection, or that one of their number was also the world's most powerful country. It was therefore no surprise that ultimate decisions in the Atlantic alliance rested unequivocally with the President of the USA. In the event of attack, the armed forces of NATO countries were to come under the command of the Supreme Allied Commander in Europe (SACEUR), whom no European complained was always an American.

Just as economic aid to western Europe was made to include West Germany, so the rearmament demanded by the USA of its Cold War allies required German participation. The largely American creation of West Germany and its expected economic resurgence had already led to the Schuman Plan. The essential purpose of this unorthodox scheme was to reconcile the unequal powers of France and Germany in two war-making industries, but having applauded the creation of the European Coal and Steel Community (ECSC), the USA waited to see whether plans for a European Defence Community (EDC) would issue in the German contribution to Cold War defence it considered urgent. When France rejected EDC, the result was German rearmament within NATO. While the three Benelux countries, together with France, West Germany and Italy, were thus able to agree on how jointly to manage coal and steel, France could not bring itself to accept the recreation of German armed forces or the subordination of its own military to authority beyond national control.

The Cold War division of Europe which produced an Atlantic alliance under US command and control bore two lessons. It illustrated the ability of external events, represented by Soviet power in central Europe, to promote co-operation among states. At the same time it suggested that but for the Red Army and American cajoling, the European members of NATO would have remained unwilling to combine among themselves in matters of defence. Over matters of war and peace, governments proved willing to trust the power and decisions of the USA when they remained unable to rely upon each other. Of equal significance was the gap separating issues of economic betterment on which European states were able to combine on their own, from those affecting national security that remained beyond them. This bifurcation became institutionalized in two separate organizations both now with their headquarters in Brussels. On the one hand is the Atlantic alliance in which European states figure as dependent allies of the USA, while on the other are the bodies established by the Treaties of Rome and their emendations, which embody the partial organization of part of Europe for certain purposes. The USA played an important part in both developments. From the Schuman Plan onwards Washington encouraged developments in continental Europe designed to integrate economies, even where this meant proceeding without Britain. Yet however much it blessed efforts among some of its NATO allies to put their civil affairs in order, the USA took no controlling direction of the European Economic Community (EEC). America provided the essential buttress of military security and cheered on the undefined end of European integration, while leaving to the states concerned the formulation of means and the gradual discovery of what it was they were busy producing. Although the Cold War provided the USA with reasons of its own to value a less distempered western Europe, neither it nor anyone else was in a position to foretell what use the members of the EEC were to make of their plans to create a common market.

By the time the Cold War in Europe was ended by the collapse of Soviet power in central Europe, the EEC had become established as the magnet of both economic and political development. While one Brussels organization represented prosperity, the other signified peace. With peace seemingly assured by the disintegration of the Warsaw Pact, it was open to suggestion that NATO might be replaced by either the more inclusive though toothless Organization for Security and Co-operation (OSCE), or by a European defence organization based on the hitherto lame Western European Union (WEU). It soon became evident, however, that despite French advocacy of a refurbished WEU, both NATO's existing members and the countries of central Europe continued to regard the USA as vital to their security. From the reorganization that followed the demise of Soviet power, the emergence of a united Germany, and plans to include new members, NATO's character as a military alliance of armed states emerged unaltered.

Within this steadfast fold, western Europe has for nearly half a century been at liberty to experiment with its recomposition. Although not all EU members are signatories of the Atlantic treaty, those that belong to the alliance are members of a well-known species of foreign affairs. Few other alliances may compete with NATO's peacetime longevity, but its duration has not been accompanied by changes that make it difficult to know by what name to call it. The same cannot be said of the EU. The entity that developed from the ECSC, via the EEC and the Single European Act (SEA), into the EU of Maastricht and Amsterdam, is more awkward to classify. Largely because of NATO, it is not of course a military alliance, and for that reason the EU has thus far had little to do with those aspects of foreign affairs that rely on the backing of force. Even so, in seeking to decipher the significance of the EU's preceding acronyms it would be false to imagine that it has at any time been hermetically sealed off from events taking place outside Europe. In addition to terminating imperial rule, western European countries had important stakes in overseas trade. On several occasions too, the impetus to consolidate the common market came from places far away from Brussels. The Yom Kippur war of 1972 and the Iranian upheaval of 1979 cautioned that if they wanted to withstand the shock of external events, western European countries should look more to their own devices. Favoured throughout the 1950s and 1960s by the longest known period of continuous economic growth, EEC countries were thereafter faced with the wavering position of the USA as the hub of western prosperity. The slackening of their own rates of expansion and the rise of the Asian 'tiger' economies also demonstrated that Europe's good fortune was not a gift authorized by providence. The single market was part of the response. Although western Europe's internal development has been safeguarded by NATO, the world external to it has not therefore been a tapestry or passive stage-setting. The actions of statesmen, politicians, officials, businessmen, bankers and diplomats whose manifold exertions have produced the EU and paved the way for European Monetary Union (EMU), should not disguise the extent to which they were often responding to events set in motion elsewhere.

## III

Necessary as it is to recall that actions are sometimes more accurately described as reactions, NATO and the wider setting of the EU's genesis do not explain what has been created. While NATO has remained an alliance designed to keep the peace, under its guardianship the EU has become something unmistakably distinct from a gathering of separate states intent on reaping the rewards of a jointly run single market. The appropriate way to take the measure of what has come into being is not to consult the intentions of the 'founding fathers' of European integration in the hope of discovering how far they viewed economic collaboration and inventive institutions as stalking horses for political aims. Plans are misleading guides to events. Nor is it helpful to rehearse here the steps, side-steps and false steps taken over the past five decades. What needs emphasis is the storyline that emerges from the traipse of events. For this purpose two related developments demand attention. In both cases their effects have outdistanced anything initially plotted.

The most encompassing change that has come about in western Europe is a reformation based upon renunciation. Relations between members of the EU have ceased to assume that war as well as peace is likely to occur between them. In no longer being geared to this eventuality, the states affected have revised one of the conditions that for centuries has lain at the heart of Europe's foreign affairs. The military establishments of EU members are no longer maintained because of each other. Their common borders are no longer military frontiers. With the completion of the single market and the absorption of the Schengen accords, lines that once divided states are ceasing to have business or even civil significance. After generations of conflict, the Rhine is of commercial rather than strategic importance. Only the slightest feeling for European history is necessary to appreciate the meaning of this shift in outlook and activation. That peaceful relations in the second half of the twentieth century are now taken for granted does not make their enjoyment banal. Various explanations of this decisive turnabout are naturally available, many of which dwell on the effects of two world wars followed by a cold war. Hence the importance of not overlooking the part played by the USA in welding NATO together, fostering a return to constitutional government and promoting widespread co-operation among its European dependants. Yet even if necessity is frequently the mother of invention, it is what her offspring choose to devise that eventually makes the difference. What is noteworthy from the standpoint of the present is how the assumption of peace, above all between France and Germany, has become so securely grounded as to be unworthy of comment. When expectations have taken such hold that their fulfilment goes unnoticed, it suggests that relations based upon them depend on more reliable material than the official undertakings of treaties. Habit has sealed what contract began. It is therefore one thing to relate the historical circumstances that induced France and Germany to stop eyeing each other as enemies, and another to capture the effects of this renunciation some forty years later.

Once the belief has taken hold that states have renounced war as an instrument of policy it transforms relations between them. The example of Canada and the USA comes readily to mind. Without ceasing to be states, the assumption of undisturbed peace puts dealings on a different footing. It is as if one of the poles between which foreign affairs move has been dispensed with. Peace is no longer shadowed by gnawing fears and precautions that it may be only a pause in the oscillations of a pendulum, at the other end of which lies war. The hovering uncertainties of armed peace are a reminder that foreign affairs are invested with mistrust and that the existence of mutual suspicion explains why the first promise of governments is to protect citizens and their homelands from external dangers. The business of states, Hobbes wrote in the introduction to the *Leviathan*, is 'salus populi, the people's safety'. It thus appears risky to the point of treasonous irresponsibility to take peace with one's neighbours for granted. Where this is no longer a gamble, rulers and ruled are relieved of formidable burdens. *Si pacem para bellum* (if you want peace, prepare for war) may provoke ills it is designed to avert, but few states are willing to entrust themselves to a heavily armed world without first looking to their own powers of defence.

It is because foreign affairs are the meeting ground of self-reliant political bodies who forearm against each other and accept the commands of no higher authority that they acquired the name 'power politics'. This also helps explain why foreign affairs are an unstable mixture of peace and war, and why diplomacy is confined by the circumstances that give rise to it. The arts of negotiating cannot be separated from the readiness of states to safeguard their interests by brandishing force where needs must or opportunity beckons. The art may lie in persuading mutually suspicious states to bargain rather than brawl, but where they stand in relation to each other as potential adversaries, no mystery is attached to why they value power and why armed force usually forms a prominent part of it. However much open to abuse, the justification of *machtpolitik* in external affairs is 'the people's safety' and domestic tranquillity. In the absence of power, diplomacy would, as Frederick the Great said, be like music without a score. He may have underestimated sources of power other than force, but his forthright recognition of enmity between states and resort to the judgement of war can hardly ring false as a commentary on Franco-German relations in the century after 1870.

In drawing attention to the renunciation of war between EU members, it is therefore necessary to emphasize both its singular nature and how much of the world's power politics it leaves unaffected. No longer being armed against each other is a novel experience for the states of Europe that stands out against their own pasts but also contrasts their revised circumstances with conflicts that stretch from the Aegean via the Gulf and central Asia to the straits of Taiwan. Many of the EU countries who no longer fear each other remain armed members of NATO because they are exposed to the hazards of global power politics. Membership of NATO during the Cold War may have helped school European states in the disciplines of co-operation. The existence of the Soviet 'enemy' persuaded Europeans that allies could proceed to becoming 'friends'.

Although impressive, the assumption of peaceful relations between members of the EU is not sufficient to abrogate foreign affairs or put paid to power politics. The recurrent disorders of foreign affairs do not prove that power politics are synonymous with war or even conflict. Lack of regulated order does not imply chaos. If power politics were everywhere disorderly to the point where war always prevailed over peace, continuous and purposeful foreign affairs could hardly occur. The diplomatic history of Europe would be foreshortened to accounts of uninterrupted armed conflict. It does not therefore follow that where war has been renounced its sequel must be the advent of some wider reformation. Open and unarmed borders between states are doubtless a prerequisite of political union, but the achievement of the former does not bind states to the more arduous business of proceeding further. Close as relations are astride the forty-ninth parallel, they remain foreign. Unprecedentedly close ties within NATO have not transformed the constitutional independence of its members or turned an alliance into a body politic. The renunciation of war leaves the authority of states intact.

IV

Within the EU, states that no longer contemplate war against each other have not thereby renounced their national interests. Accompanied by hesitations, delays and occasional refusals, they nevertheless pursue their ends in ways no longer describable as foreign affairs, diplomacy or power politics. Even where conflicts of interest are acute, 'wars of words' in the Council of Ministers where representatives 'fight their corners' and 'do battle' on behalf of their countries are misleadingly so described. Resort to military metaphor is an eerie reminder of the past, and perhaps unselfconscious testimony that part of it has been successfully lived down. When EU business reaches stalemate it is mercifully unlike the lines of parallel trenches that between 1914 and 1918 pockmarked the landscape of Europe from Belgium to Switzerland. A hard-fought campaign in the Council of Ministers is not orchestrated by the withdrawal of ambassadors and a summons to arms.

The EU has come instead to acquire features familiar to the *domestic* and *internal* workings of the public affairs of a political body. The reformulation of the common life of a significant part of Europe thus constitutes a *political* reformation. Although this has not abolished the EU's member states or conflicts of national interest, it extends well beyond renunciation of war. In doing so the re-formation of western Europe has generated *politics*. Politics feature alongside diplomacy and increasingly in place of diplomacy. The EU has given rise to a version of politics one is prompted to describe as politics properly so-called: politics as the public affairs of a polity or *res publica*. Hence the politics to be observed within the EU is markedly unlike the *power politics* that prevail in foreign affairs. Politics properly so-called have emerged in the EU as its components have taken to sharing government, to making and abiding by laws enforceable against themselves, and to accepting the authority of institutions whose authors they are. Thus understood, the term 'politics' in the expression 'power politics' is misleading. Derived from the German *machtpolitik*, 'power politics' is a blunter rendering of the more courtly *raison d'état*. Both call attention to the pursuit of external interests by means largely ungoverned by constitutional constraints. What is striking in relations between states is their resolve *not* to share government or be bound by laws and authority not of their own making. The *power* in power politics at least has the merit of highlighting the pervasive arbitrariness of relations between political bodies insubordinate of higher rule. The sovereignty of states expresses the widespread recognition that states belong to a species that falls under no more compelling jurisdiction. They do not belong to a world-wide *res publica* whose public or common affairs constitute 'world politics' or 'international politics'. It is just because the assertion of power by states is not subject to lawful authority and a universal morality that politics in the full and adequate sense cannot arise in foreign affairs. Politics flourishes only where the activities associated with it are incorporated in a wider realm, body or whole, constituted in large part for that very purpose. The idea of a 'body politic' hints at this. The ultimate point of reference of local and even family politics is national politics.

There exists no global body politic composed of states. Were the former to exist the latter would not. It would thus be more truthful to the setting of foreign affairs to describe the external relations of states as *power diplomacy*. This would at least permit one to underline the unique oddities of EU affairs, that are so unlike those that take place among more than 150 states. In deference to Wittgenstein's caution to stick to accustomed usage rather than attempt to fix indelible meanings to words, power politics will, somewhat ruefully, be allowed to keep its place. Transferring to the more recondite but less familiar *power diplomacy* would not in any case resolve all misunderstandings that like limpets attach themselves to misdescriptions. 'Power diplomacy' is itself something of a pleonasm. As the articulation and mediation of relations between states, whose relative and separate powers are of the essence, diplomacy stands in need of no adjectival uplift. Power is already subsumed in diplomacy.

The reason for pausing to toy with the distinction between politics and diplomacy has nothing to do with splitting hairs. The need to mark their different characters is directly related to the emergence of the EU and the need to consider Europe's place in world affairs. The political activity exemplified in the EU, between its states and their institutional creations, can no longer be adequately represented under the nameplate of diplomatic relations between foreign countries. Nevertheless, impatience with fussing over distinctions is not easily quelled by recalling Aristotle's dictum that all thought relies on classification. Not every difference that can be drawn is worth making. Does it much matter whether one labels the internal affairs of the EU 'politics' while reserving 'diplomacy' or 'power politics' for the external relations of states? Do they not share the common coinage of power, compared to which all other features that differentiate them, pale in significance? Machiavelli is sometimes thought to support the argument that since power is present in both politics and diplomacy, it is otiose to shuffle about trying to distinguish between them. The author of *The Prince*, who insisted that whatever the ends of political action, power was its instrumental component, did not however wish to fore-shorten action to its means. He would not have approved of the destination to which a levelling cast of mind leads. If power is all pervasive and all important, to the point where it is a synonym for politics and diplomacy, both the domestic activities of political bodies and their foreign relations become indistinguishable from Darwinian nature, where the only law that matters is that survival favours the most fittedly powerful. Where this reductionist line of argument is given intellectual licence it becomes futile to mark one field of action off from another, or single out human endeavour from the activities of impersonal physical matter. Human action, which along with others Machiavelli looked upon as the sole antidote to human disorders, is allowed to become a sub-division of biology. History subsides into Evolution.

As a consequence of their fatal flirtation with the idea that science vindicates the unscrupulous use and pursuit of power, Europeans in particular have good reasons not to obliterate or downplay their redeeming ability to act politically. The totalitarian regimes of twentieth-century Europe appealed to the urge to replace the pussyfooting decadence of politics with rule that saluted unmitigated power: the power of class or the power of race. If all action that involves the use of power is said to be much of a muchness, it becomes impossible to make clear why a voluntarily created, law-governed and representative Europe is preferable to one marshalled into unity by the jackboot of the strongest.

In so far as the EU is a political enterprise upholding the civil, civilized and civilizing virtues of politics, it is dangerous as well as indolent to ignore their distinctiveness. The alternatives to the frustrations of politics are anarchy, tyranny or reversion to power politics. Were all manifestations of power to be regarded as 'essentially' the same, there would be nothing to choose between them. The difference between politics properly so-called and power politics would be only a matter of words, of interest to the fastidious but otherwise unimportant. Much of foreign affairs is indeed distressingly similar to the unremitting strife of nature, but that provides strong reasons for marking off the EU both from the power politics of Europe's past and from the world about it. A political understanding of the EU is therefore necessary to placing Europe in its diplomatic setting.

## V

In its beginnings the sixteenth-century Reformation of western Christendom aimed to correct abuses. The Church had become a scandal.
By the end of the Second World War, the ferocity of Europe's unrestrained power politics also cried out for reform. As the Reformation
sought at first only to rid the Church of Rome of shameful practices,
and only later found its adherents had created new orders of piety, so
the chastened states of western Europe who pledged themselves to
'ever closer union' did not intend to disown or replace themselves.

The six states who formed the nucleus of the reformation were
aware that something more binding than exhortation was needed if
their relations were to be regrounded in lasting peace. After the First
World War the Kellogg-Briand Pact outlawed war while omitting to
say what was to prevent its recurrence. In the years following 1945
there was much talk of co-operation between states as a necessary
complement to their re-establishment, but the international organizations created to secure this mostly lacked the means to bring this
about. Hopes that economic recovery would promote more effective
co-operation were also haunted by the fear that prosperity as well as
depression is capable of arousing conflict. Monnet's experience of the
League of Nations warned against expecting too much from treaty-
based promises of co-operation that states were able to withhold at
will. So long as relations between states went unreformed, renunciation of war was not alone sufficient to prevent its recurrence. The need
was for means by which states could bind themselves together without
retaining an interest in unbinding themselves.

The method eventually discovered was the result of neither philosophical enquiry nor pragmatism, but derived from the need of countries to prevent the prospective benefits of renewed prosperity from
turning into a curse. Propelled by the need to improve on exhortation
and diplomatic co-operation, the six original members of the ECSC
decided to experiment with shared government. Although the High
Authority was the creation of six governments it was designed not to
remain entirely their creature. Authority was peremptorily set up
which required all signatories to abide by its decisions. Although
treaties are mostly signed on the general understanding that they
will be kept, the rule of thumb derived from history is that they are
likely to be held to only for as long as the circumstances and the
interests of the participants do not alter. The institutions of
the ECSC were therefore intended to short-circuit this dilemma

while recognizing that the best chance of keeping governments to their word lay in appealing to their interests. The modest powers of state relinquished by members of the ECSC were set against the common desire to solve problems of economic management that none could achieve separately or by means of diplomacy. The agreement to endow an executive with supranational powers of decision sought to prevent paralysis and national conflict in two industries whose importance straddled war-making capacity and peacetime prosperity. The wager tucked into the ECSC, and running threadlike through the treaties of Rome, the SEA, Maastricht and Amsterdam, was therefore intensely political. Governments gambled that however gingerly they proceeded, stepping beyond the safety lines of diplomatic co-operation that allowed all parties to call a halt should they get cold feet, would by and by implicate all in sharing government. Were this to work, success would germinate confidence and trust would thrive upon what nourished it. As common policies were adopted and a common market became established, some of the habitual distrusts of power politics would be eroded.

To an unexpected extent this has happened. In bringing about a single market and furthering plans for EMU, the EU has enlarged the substitution of 'domestic' for 'foreign affairs'. With the exception of Gaullists on both sides of the English Channel, members of the EEC and its successors embraced the political nature of their undertaking. If it was never made clear exactly where 'ever closer union' was designed to lead or what would signal the journey's end, it was surely evident that in leading away from foreign affairs, decisions to share government were turning those who made them in the direction of domestic politics. The practice of sharing government was chiefly responsible for putting flesh on the bones of a skeletal body politic. Although the European Commission had fewer powers than the High Authority of the ECSC, it retained the right to urge governments into action and nudge them towards making policies in common. The existence of a body composed of neither diplomats nor active politicians encouraged those who remained instinctively attached to the pursuit of national interests to interpret their responsibilities in a wider public setting. The Commission helped persuade states who in war and peace had for generations existed in external relation to each other, to turn about and accustom themselves to treating their mutual affairs as internal.

To the repeated dismay of those baffled by its ramshackle appearance, the EU has emerged from the experience of its forerunners with a constitution. Or rather, it has acquired a constitution in two senses. Although without a juridical document of the kind enjoyed by all but one member state, and made famous by the founders of the USA, the EU is nevertheless saturated in law. Attachment to lawful government and law abiding life is traceable as far back in European history as the preoccupation with rightful rule. Modern ideas that link state and law are informed by the towering legacy of the Roman Empire, whose captivation with law was perpetuated in the religious institutions and practices of western Christendom. From this inheritance Europeans derived the sense that the most solid expression of rightful rule is to be found where government itself is subject to law. Disregard for law was one of the principal abuses of power that the re-established states of post-war Europe wished to rule out. Constitutional government and civil rights were everywhere expected to be the antidote to arbitrary or lawless dictatorship. With the dangers of populism to mind, it was recognized that democracies too needed to protect themselves in law from their unthinking selves. Following the events of the first half of the twentieth century when law was often subordinated to the will of the strongest, even the sovereign will of the majority had to be vested in law. In order to safeguard their otherwise limitless authority from abuse, nations trussed themselves up in constitutional law.

It is not therefore surprising that countries who wished to proof their public life against the return of arbitrary rule were equally determined to surround an experiment in shared government with the virtues of law. Vital as it is to economic life and the functioning of markets, the importance of law reaches beyond the regulation of wealth to the foundations of good government. The absorption of law into all levels of life was therefore part of the reformation of post-war western Europe, made all the more poignant by the Soviet imposition of party-states on the far side of the iron curtain. The European Court of the EU is consequently of larger importance than a mechanism whose purpose is limited to clearing impediments from the path of fruitful economic activity. In matters covered by the EU, the European Court of Justice (ECJ) stands at the apex of law, where it frames the political undertaking of 'ever closer union' in civility. Rulings of the Court are not complied with because its officials or their backers can mobilize a 'monopoly of the legitimate use of force'. The ECJ has no such coercive powers. Its decisions are generally complied with for reasons that are inexplicable to those who see in the EU only the veiled continuation of power politics. The Court's decisions rest not on force of arms but weight of authority, and in this crucial sense the EU appears as an entity alongside other constitutionally ordered political bodies. The achievement of the rule of law, to which the unequally powerful states of the EU are equally subject, stands in remarkable contrast to the unimpeachable position of states within diplomacy. Between states standing fast on their 'sovereign equality', the corpus of international law they often abide by is unable to oblige states to submit disputes to the jurisdiction of the International Court of Justice. In foreign affairs, law is subject to the veto of power politics. Peace in the Aegean, in the Balkans, and perhaps in the nuclear-armed subcontinent of India, rests less on the authority of international law or the mediating resources of diplomacy, than on US power to browbeat.

Even though the EU is a constitutional order pervaded by law, it remains in telltale ways incomplete. Not all relations among its members come under law or are justiciable by the ECJ. Although Gibraltar is unlikely to lead to the refloating of Armadas, or Ulster to war between London and Dublin, the settlement of these disputes is in the hands of foreign ministries rather than EU institutions. The advent of politics within the EU has not removed all elements of foreign affairs. Some issues between members are so sensitive that they are absent from the Council of Ministers. National interests remain the material out of which shared government has to be formed. Yet the EU is noteworthy less because it awakens memories of Pufendorf's description of the Holy Roman Empire after the Thirty Years War as a 'political monster,' than because it constitutes a unique political order salvaged from the wreckage of Europe's twentieth-century power politics.

In the absence of a fully-fledged written document the EU possesses a constitution in a somewhat different though connected sense. Just as a person's physical constitution is healthy or otherwise, so the EU has acquired body. Its separate parts work together as a whole. This appears true irrespective of whether one favours its actions, bewails its presumption, profligacy and inefficiency, or concentrates on the tasks it has set itself with EMU and enlargement. In human affairs, as in the rest of nature, bodies hang together by virtue of the way their constituent parts are related. The EU is no exception. Alongside the ECJ, its principal organs are the Council of Ministers, the Commission and the European Parliament. Although Commission members are appointed by national governments they are not accountable to them. The ability of this bodily part of the EU to initiate policies and administer laws, and of the European Parliament to deliberate and amend legislation, comes to fruition only in the willingness of members states to be governed together. For a while, the Commission was poised to become the governing centre of the EEC, but in more recent years that position has been claimed, or reclaimed, by the Council of Ministers. This is the law-making quick of the EU. It is here, and in the European Council which twice yearly assembles heads of government and state, that the authority of states is most in evidence. This has led to the conclusion that because the Council of Ministers convenes the representatives of states, without whose co-operation little else can function to much effect, in all but name the EU is a system of diplomacy. Padded as the Council is with ample bureaucratic upholstery, this should not, it is urged, disguise the fact that it is a meeting ground for states, whose responsibilities are to their own governments and to the national interests they exist to uphold. The presence of fifteen ministers or officials around the same table does not demonstrate that they constitute a whole that subsumes its parts.

As its acronym suggests, the body (or limb) that does much of the routine work of the Council of Ministers, COREPER (Comité des Représentants Permanents), is composed of diplomats accredited to the EU in Brussels. It is these ambassadors and their stand-ins who meet twice weekly to consider the entire range of EU affairs. Their task is to reach agreed decisions by means of negotiations. Where this succeeds, the Council of Ministers has usually only to register the outcome of their deliberations. Where COREPER falters, matters are directed to the Council. The business of the six-monthly European Council is mostly taken up with issues to which neither COREPER nor the Council has found answers. To those who see only the diplomacy of states at work, the clinching feature of this multiple and routinized activity is that no matter what the topic, states are dealing with one another on much the same footing of independence and equality as first became the practice with the advent of resident diplomacy in sixteenth-century Europe. The Council of Ministers may function as a legislature in ways made familiar by envoys accredited to the UN, where 'delegates' 'debate' 'resolutions' in something called a 'general assembly', but this is whimsically misleading. It is similarly urged that constitutional appearances notwithstanding there exists at the hub of the EU only an updating of foreign affairs that reiterates the undiminished importance of states. The Council of Ministers is therefore said to substantiate the most fundamental precept of relations between independent states. Where agreement is forthcoming it is ascribed to the outcome of successful diplomacy rather than as evidence of the ways of government.

From this perspective not even the introduction of weighted votes, and the practice of qualified majority voting in connection with the single market, is permitted to obscure the diplomatic nature of the EU. Allocating and counting votes may, it is said, be indicative of modern representative government, but its selective introduction into dealings between states is hedged about on all sides. Most revealingly, where conflicts of national interest go deep, issues are seldom put to the vote. Blocking minorities serve as a warning not to push too hard when states appeal to the sanctity of vital national interests. The secretiveness of the Council's workings is also said to illustrate its character as a forum of diplomacy. It is recalled from earlier times, and from the experience of foreign affairs elsewhere, that closed doors are as vital to the confidential give and take of diplomacy as publicity is to the raucous and quite different business of drumming up support where politics are practised.

Portraying the EU as a modernized version of diplomacy is nevertheless misleading, and for countries who see in Brussels only the continuation of foreign affairs by other means, a source of damaging confusion. Myopia not only fails to register the desire to reform foreign into domestic affairs, but ignores the effectiveness of the institutions whose purpose is to achieve this. The elaboration of a legal order, with a court, commission and representative body testifies to more than a collusive desire to obscure power politics. From the standpoint of power politics, the ECJ, the European Parliament and the Commission must appear wasteful as well as wantonly cynical. To persevere in seeing the last forty or so years solely through the eyes of the half century that preceded them is, however, to mistake change for continuity and miss the significance of what has intervened. Discounting evidence that the EU is a political undertaking makes it all but impossible to do justice to its development and the capital accumulated through perseverance to proceed further. Whereas alliances like NATO usually specify carefully the obligations of mutual support, among the interesting features of the EU is that most of its members have demonstrated a willingness to strive towards 'ever closer union' without taking precautions to set down in advance what this means. Although to some this is further evidence that the EU lacks credible substance, to others it is a sign that those who have learned to trust one another do not have to put everything down in writing. What led from the ECSC to the EU and a single market, has now set its sights on EMU and enlargement. There is nothing, for example, to prevent the EU conducting foreign affairs with other countries. In matters of trade 'Europe' already speaks and acts as a single body, and perhaps of even greater significance is increasingly expected to do so by other states and international organizations.

Even where it continues to be argued that the innovations made since the creation of the ECSC and the EEC have revolved around the actions of states, this overlooks the content of what daily passes through and is decided by the Council of Ministers. What the officials of states accomplish in combination matters as much as their representative status. Having willed a single market it was, for example, found necessary to introduce qualified majority voting in order to make progress: no shared government, no single market. In the range and density of its business, the work of COREPER and the Council exceeds anything to be found in the records of even the most byzantine diplomacy. What perhaps most concisely illustrates the political complexion of the EU is the nature of the topics that now fall within its purview. They not only mirror the concerns of rulers and ruled within states where politics are practised; decisions taken in Brussels increasingly determine the extent to which elected governments are able to fulfil their promises. The professional diplomats of COREPER have before them examples of the entire conspectus of political life as it has taken shape in recent times. Employment, business reorganization, competition, civil, occupational and personal rights, welfare provisions, town and country life, transport and the environment, are randomly listed items that are as much deliberated within and determined by the EU as they are in the domestic politics of member states. According to *The Economist*, the Council of Ministers 'now meets in some 23 gatherings of national ministers, from foreign affairs and finance to education and environment ... Every day 1,000 delegates attend some 20 council or group meetings. About 90% of council decisions are taken before ministers ever get entwined.'[1] Foreign Ministers and their resident COREPER envoys in Brussels are thus immersed in, if not deluged by, large numbers of civil servants and politicians schooled not in diplomacy but in government, party politics, business, pressure group activities and public relations. Specialists from fifteen countries are likely to have more in common with each other than with other parts of the governments they may represent. Peopled as they are by officials from all departments of state, the myriad committees of the Council of Ministers also have dense working relations with the Commission, the European

Parliament and the ECJ. COREPER may have the job of summoning all this unwieldy activity together, but what they sift and order, negotiate over and eventually lay before the Council of Ministers is better described as constitutional and committee politics rather than power politics and foreign affairs. Marshalling their labours into agreed decisions on behalf of 375 million citizens, or surviving failures to do so, no doubt demands all the 'tact and intelligence' identified by Earnest Satow as the hallmark of diplomacy, but these negotiating attributes are also required for the successful conduct of many-sided politics.

## VI

Conflict is the lifeblood of politics. The renunciation of war by once bellicose neighbours means however that conflict within the EU is no longer armed with force. The clash of powerful national interests has ceased to be life threatening. In order to safeguard the peace between them and to further a more encompassing reformation, six west European states established first the ECSC and then the EEC. The progression, from six to fifteen, from customs union to single market and EU, illustrates a reverse movement from that taken by the ever wider disunion of the previous 300 years or so of European history. The reformation housed in the EU is intended, if not perfectly designed, to replace the abuses of power politics with a union in which constitutional politics, politics properly so-called, can prosper.

Even so, the turnabout from external to internal relations, from foreign affairs to domestic politics, should not be too blithely drawn. The body politic of uncertain pedigree and resilience that has come into being remains partial, contested, reversible, and in part misdirected and poorly managed. With EMU, budgetary reform, revision of the Common Agricultural Policy and regional funds all pending, and with enlargement also in the offing, the busy body politic of the EU will have to be overhauled and adapted. This exacting task will test the political character of the EU as much as it will reveal it.

The laudable effort of learning to trust others with powers of government has produced an EU with discernibly narcissistic tendencies. Yet in becoming a body politic, the EU cannot expect to be ignored by the power politics of the diplomatic system, or left unaffected by its developing relations with all parts of the world. In the scales of global power, the individual states of Europe who continue to conduct their own foreign policies are of diminished consequence. Foreign affairs thus mark the threshold at which Europe's experiment with shared government stops short at diplomatic co-operation. The plurality of the EU's national voices in foreign affairs registers the dissonance of disunion.

**Note**

1.    *The Economist*, 18 March 1997.

# 2 The Diplomatic System

If little is more useful than experience, Europe's long familiarity with foreign affairs is an asset of considerable worth. Even the smallest of the EU's fifteen countries conducts active foreign policies throughout the world. Its principal members have elaborate diplomatic dealings with nearly all of the 180 or so bodies recognized as states, as well as envoys accredited to the growing numbers of international organizations. Two countries (and if Russia is counted as European, then three) are permanent members of the UN Security Council. Like the other states charged by themselves at the close of the Second World War with 'primary responsibility for international peace and security' Britain and France possess nuclear arsenals. Germany has the world's third largest economy, whose exports amount to nearly 10 per cent of the world total. Along with Italy, these four countries belong to the G7 group of leading economic powers. Taken together EU members account for a third of foreign trade and for about the same measure of world output. The governments and businesses of the EU invest and dispense aid wherever they can gain access. Although the population of the present EU is only $5\frac{1}{2}$ per cent of humanity, its citizens are to be found living and working in every part of the globe. If it is true that much of this activity is connected with individual states, in matters of trade the Commission of the EU conducts a common external policy on behalf of all its members. While in some instances EU states share diplomatic representation in third countries, the EU has developed its own official relations with more than 123 countries as well as with numerous international organizations.

In matters of defence and security it remains true that Europe's WEU plays second fiddle to NATO and the USA, but wherever UN peacekeeping operations are dispatched, EU countries usually contribute to and receive public support for their often disinterested actions. Further evidence that Europe does not overlook the world might be catalogued by listing the numbers of non-governmental organizations (NGOs) to which its broad-minded citizens contribute. While Europe therefore still speaks officially through the separate, though often co-ordinated actions of its individual states, seen from many of the capitals to which they are sent, the representatives of France, Britain,

Italy and other EU countries are increasingly cast together as diverse parts of a single if singular entity. From the standpoint of Washington and Beijing 'Europe' has already ceased to be a handy though misleading précis and become a body with substantial if indeterminate powers. Diplomatic, business and private activities of this extent might therefore be thought to give the lie to the accusation that in putting its own house in order, Europe has turned its back on the wider world and failed to acknowledge how far the internal affairs of the EU and their members are caught up in foreign affairs that now gird the earth. With this corrective in mind, it is then suggested that the EU's further internal development, and above all the consequences of EMU and enlargement, are not likely to leave it indifferent or unprepared in the face of diplomatic crises. In case of need, European countries are said to have well-cultivated relations with many states and, in the USA, the reassurance of a steadfast and mighty guardian. This sanguine exposition can then be capped by noting that in spite of turmoil in the Balkans, the Mediterranean and the Caucasus, and even more alarming conflicts in the Gulf and central Africa, the world is notably at peace. Following the Cold War, the arms races generated by it have subsided. The peace of the world may remain armed and many states continue to spend lavishly on military equipment, but the great powers no longer glower at each other. The rivalries of the two nuclear superpowers have been replaced by a single power policing the world. Because it is a democracy the USA will not, it is said, abuse its dominant position. Although the trading regime supported by the USA is subject to bouts of turbulence and excites divisions, the pursuit of economic development expresses cohesive as well as universal desires.

Europe's chances of well-being depend on whether this wholesome prognosis holds good. As a pointer to the impending future, it is attached to but one interpretation of the present. And as Europeans have better cause to remember than most, little is more transient than the present. The summer of 1914 did not feel like the prelude to the great caesura of modern Europe. Until teenagers scrambled on to it, clad in jeans and making merry, the Berlin Wall epitomized a superpower conflict seemingly anchored in weapons of ferocious power. Although the past offers no surer yardstick to the future than the present, the experience deposited by it may be salutary. It counsels against presuming that favourable conditions can be relied upon to perpetuate themselves. 'A common failing of mankind', Machiavelli wrote, 'is never to anticipate a storm when the sea is calm'.

## II

The foreign affairs of the world's approximately 200 states compose a diplomatic system whose essential features owe much to the emergence in Europe of numbers of self-governing states. This legacy that the rest of the world has absorbed and which Europe needs to recall, does not imply that foreign affairs were invented or first practiced in the sixteenth and seventeenth centuries. The origins of foreign affairs are as remote as the successful assertion of independent interests by several rulers, and their consequent dealings with each other. The place to look for beginnings is apparently in Asia Minor and ancient Mesopotamia. More generally still, it is plain that relations between states arise as much by political default as by diplomatic design; the world is a multiplicity of self-governing fragments because its hitherto unruly diversity has not once been subordinated to a single government. Even the largest, most 'universal' of empires, including all recent examples, have found their ambitions stubbed by the opposition of rivals. If the world is these days subject to government, it is to the government of numerous states. The superpower of the USA, which enables it to influence other states, confers no authority.

Although Europe is not responsible for the plurality of the world, the form taken by its twentieth-century composition into states of bewildering differences derives directly from the history of Europe's own experience of political individuation. It was the successful assertion by rulers of their own authority within and then against a previously consumated whole, to which for long they had pledged themselves as dutiful parts, that first made it imperative to bring some 'system' or order to their increasingly independent, 'foreign', warlike and ungoverned affairs. Just as many contemporary states began as European colonies, so the kingdoms of early modern Europe detached themselves from the remnant unity of Latin Christendom with its twin organizing principles of the Holy Roman Empire of the German Nation and the Papacy. By the end of the Thirty Years War in 1648, even the contested religious complexion of Europe had become secondary to the foreign affairs of secular rulers. All the Christian 'powers' of Europe, whether Catholic or Protestant, were included in the treaty of Westphalia, though the Ottoman Empire was not party to the proceedings. Papal protests against the settlement were ignored, as were its by now disregarded claims to represent a unified 'universal' Christendom. The Emperor was henceforth recognized as but one ruler among many, circumscribed and challenged by rival sovereigns.

Rulers of even modestly sized states claimed to be emperors within their own realms, denying thereby submission to higher earthly power. As proclamations of independent rule were made good by the exertion of power, Europe was gradually confirmed in its unplanned course as the story of its states. Its line of development was from a pre-existent if tenuous and much contested unity casting back to Charlemagne, towards an ever greater disunion of contiguous states. While most rulers acknowledged that their own authority descended from the author of creation, in mundane matters Europe's monarchs whittled away at internal as well as external restrictions on their powers.

The non-interference of foreign sovereigns in each other's domestic affairs was adumbrated as the principle and condition of co-existence between independent states. In twentieth-century guise this remains the basis of official relations. The Charter of the UN reiterates that 'peace and security' depend on mutual 'respect for the principle of equal rights and self-determination of peoples'. The 1961 Vienna Convention on Diplomatic Relations is even more forthright about the importance of 'sovereign equality' as the basis of 'friendly relations among nations'.

Perhaps nothing was of greater importance in establishing the authority of states than recognition by fellow rulers of each other's powers. It provided valuable support for their claims to marry right and might and to reject foreign interference. Recognition by other states and admission to the UN remain crucial to membership of the diplomatic system. A further feature that once greatly complicated the affairs of Europe's monarchs has also become the common experience of states adapting to a globalized world. Europe's seventeenth-century rulers inhabited a geographically congested as well as a much contested area. Because they were bound to live cheek by jowl in involuntary proximity, the actions of one ruler continuously set off reverberations that attracted the attention of others. As the territory of Europe was repeatedly fought over, kings became schooled in the life and death maxim that eternal vigilance was the price of secure rule. The consequence was an unslakeable craving for political news and intelligence. This was the necessity that stimulated diplomacy. Because the penalties of learning too late what other states are about remain dire, foreign ministries the world over consume yet more information than did their predecessors.

The diplomatic system that emerged in the seventeenth century, and received the explicit blessing of its members at the Congress of Westphalia, was an attempt to square a circle whose dilemmas continue to represent the root of power politics over three centuries later. On the one hand an assortment of rulers asserted claims to be ungoverned by external or higher authority, and did so with whatever civil and military powers they could muster. Although costly and notoriously inconclusive, war in particular was a favoured instrument of foreign affairs. It was the sport of kings from which even republics were unable to absolve themselves. The funding and organization of military power by law, officials, taxes and loans contributed much to the character of states, as they continue to do in more collectivist times. Far from being extraneous to states, foreign affairs go far to shape their internal as well as external actions. On the other hand, the propinquities of sovereigns and the objects disputed by their soldiers and envoys condemned the states of Europe to continuous dealings. The density of foreign affairs and the need to be well-informed about them led to their tentative systemization. Then as now, in order to enjoy the fruits of independence, rulers were obliged to submit the conduct (if not the content) of their foreign affairs to a minimum of regulation. By the time enough of Europe's monarchs accepted the need for at least procedural rules in foreign affairs, and reciprocated in choosing to observe them, the rudiments of a diplomatic system were established.

The sending and receiving of envoys between rulers is no more a European invention than government or foreign affairs. Ambassadors made their appearance in areas of the world where foreign affairs were first developed. They were official missives whose purpose was to represent authority, convey messages, perhaps negotiate and gather information, and then return home. Because this sounds familiar, the origins of modern diplomacy are often traced to the journeying of envoys in Asia Minor and Mesopotamia. This is, however, to deprive diplomacy of its most signal ingredient. The peripatetics of officials do not amount to diplomacy because what disinguishes it is the routinized or system-like nature of its activities, that go beyond itinerant comings and goings for isolated purposes. Diplomacy may have developed from much older practices, but from the standpoint of present-day foreign affairs, the decisive shift which occured in early modern Europe was the movement from fitful to continuous exchanges based on the resident envoy.

The device of sending ambassadors to reside at the court of a foreign ruler, sometimes for lengthy periods, occured first among the city-republics of fifteenth-century Italy. There too it was the volatility of close-knit relations that persuaded Renaissance Princes that the best way to keep abreast of events and form alliances lay in the use of

resident envoys to glean and despatch news. The centuries-old precedent of Papal nuncios lay instructively to hand. By the early sixteenth century, the practice of accrediting resident envoys had spread
north of the Alps from where it gradually became the custom throughout much of Europe. At first the privileges and legal immunities
granted to envoys living sometimes for years on end at the court of a
foreign ruler aroused suspicion. What interest did a monarch have in
safeguarding, and often paying for, the licensed espionage of rival
sovereigns? By the time of Westphalia, however, 'honourable spies'
were fast becoming a systematic feature of foreign affairs. Richelieu
noted the worth of negotiations conducted, 'ceaselessly, openly as well
as secretly, in all places and even when no immediate gain is apparent'. In his view diplomacy properly so-called, based on the watchful
activities of resourceful envoys, was an invaluable instrument of statecraft. *Raison d'état* recommended diplomacy. The advantages prized
by Richelieu could, however, only be secured through reciprocity: by
according the same privileges to the envoys of foreign rulers as, for
similarly interested motives, were sought for oneself. This required the
use of one's own authority to protect the rights of foreign envoys
during their residence. To a surprising degree even inveterate enemies
complied with the dictates of mutual interest. The outcome was that
Europe's fractious rulers formed amongst themselves what Burke
called 'the whole college of the states of Europe'. Within this collegial
setting, the disorder of constantly changing alignments in war and
peace acquired a framework of regularized continuity. The lattice-
work of interweaving envoys radiating from and between the courts
of rulers knit Europe together at the same time as it attested the
rivalries of its wilful parts. With time, the practices engendered by
resident diplomacy produced a unique version of mitigated disorder,
that included both the 'balance of power' and its own version of
'international' law. Although diplomacy neither prevented war nor
guaranteed 'peace and security', its usefulness to the states of Europe
was that while it made order in foreign affairs possible, it set few limits
on power politics.

Diplomacy flourished as the handmaiden of its authors. The system
of reciprocities grounded in the institution of resident envoys has
endured and spread throughout the world. In so far as the foreign
affairs of dozens of states have come to be at all 'constituted' or
collegial, the rules of their formal ordering are to be found updated
in the 1961 Vienna Convention. This is a more reliable guide to the
official ground-plan of foreign affairs than the exhortations and sus-

pect constitutionalism of the UN Charter. The principal function of the Vienna Convention is to emphazise the interests of states in upholding the obligations that allow diplomacy, but also power politics, to proceed. Violation of the rights of embassy is still liable to cause a furore, because most states realize what they stand to lose should one of the few props of order be knocked away. When the American embassy in Tehran was seized in 1979, even diplomatic opponents of the USA were careful to avoid condoning it. Preserving the inviolability of embassies is in the interests of nearly all states who value the element of order maintained by safeguarded communications. In the absence of a diplomatic system, foreign affairs would be yet more chaotic. Even were one to argue that cyberspace has rendered embassies and envoys obsolete, the interest of states in protecting the means of confidential and continuous exchanges would reinforce the same logic of reciprocity.

As Latin Christendom fragmented into the states of Europe, its improvised diplomatic system appeared paradoxical. While centring on conflict between independent rulers it simultaneously demonstrated their ability to make use of inheritances of law, religion, language and administration that continued to draw them together. At the same time as Habsburgs and Bourbons vied for primacy, the intermarryings of royal houses ensured that 'the republic of Europe' as it was sometimes called, expressed a wry sense of family. In 1797 Edmund Burke noted that 'peace and war' were 'the great hinges upon which the very being of nations turn' while in the next breath observing that all Europe's bellicose states belonged to 'the Christian world and the republic of Europe'.[1] In his opinion it was the mass of 'similitudes' shared by Europeans that, even when its member states were disputing the balance of power in blood, supplied an undertow of unity to the diplomatic system. By contrast, even though the Ottoman Turks figured often in Europe's power politics, official relations with Constantinople were antipathetic. Nowhere perhaps could one better glimpse the way in which a Europe of fractious rulers periodically assembled to heal its familial wounds than at the great peace congresses. From Westphalia, via Ryswick and Utrecht, and later from Vienna to Berlin and up to the First World War, these gatherings of diplomats and their vast entourages, punctuated, illustrated and temporarily re-ordered the workings of the diplomatic system. These public occasions revealed that in spite of warfare, external relations within Europe, though not in connection with colonial peoples, fell short of the 'total wars' of 'unconditional surrender' and liquidation made notorious in the twentieth century. For 300 years before the advent of 'wars to end wars', the diplomatic system maintained the belief that Europeans had too much in common to allow their power politics free rein.

With an eye on the present-day diplomatic order that connects states with widely differing historical antecedents, it is instructive to recall how much Europe's foreign affairs were once grounded in custom and manners rather than contract and organization. Between political bodies that were in practice unaccountable for the legally binding treaties they entered into, and who justified disregarding them by reference to what would now be called 'national interests', the power politics of *raison d'état* were restrained by a generalized interest in mutual forebearance. The diplomatic system of Europe was for much of its existence a set of understandings whose prescriptive rules enjoyed much of the force of law. 'Men are not tied to one another with papers and seals' Burke argued:

> They are led to associate by resemblances, by conformities, by sympathies. It is with nations as with individuals. Nothing is so strong a tie of amity between nation and nation as correspondences in laws, customs, manners, and habits of life. They have more than the force of treaties in themselves. They are obligations written in the heart ... [they possess] a strong tendency to facilitate accomoda- tion, and to produce a generous oblivion of the rancour of their quarrels. With this similitude, peace is more of peace, and war is less than war. The writers on public law have often called this *aggregate* of nations a commonwealth. They had reason. It is vir- tually one great state having the same basis of general law, with some diversity of provincial customs and local establishments. The whole of the polity and economy of every country of Europe has been derived from the same sources ... From this resemblance in the modes of intercourse, and in the whole form and fashion of life, no citizen of Europe could be altogether an exile in any part of it. When a man travelled or resided for health, pleasure, business or necessity, from his own country, he never felt himself quite abroad.[2]

Although this may indicate that the EU is a re-embodiment of a much older 'Europe without frontiers', from the point of view of foreign affairs, its wider significance lies in the fact that the global diplomatic system of the twentieth century (which grew out of Europe's experi- ence) can boast no comparable 'correspondences' of the kind described by Burke. It is at once more organized and less homogen- eous. In spite of abundant international law, covenants and charters, the world-wide setting in which diplomacy now takes place is more like an 'aggregate' of states than a 'commonwealth'. Foreign affairs may have acquired more explicit system, but plentiful procedures do not ensure order among powerfully independent states.

Despite Burke's forebodings that the French Revolution had ruptured what he christened 'the diplomatic system', it survived both its violent suspension by Napoleon, and the nineteenth-century replacement of cosmopolitan 'habits of life' by the unyielding clamour of Europe's brittle nationalisms. The industrialization of Europe that swept much of the *ancien régime* into musuems left the essentials of foreign affairs resolutely in place. The resources of industry made states more formidable and enhanced both their internal organization and their external reach. Perhaps because newly enfranchised electorates showed more interest in home affairs than in the balancing activities of states, until 1914 the diplomatic system was manned largely by aristocrats who conversed in French. The *esprit de corps* among Europe's *corps diplomatique* was less hollow than more recent invocations of an 'international community' now said to be manifest in the UN. The Concert of Europe, by which the great powers sought to stage-manage the balance of power, played its part in making the long peace of the nineteenth century so durable.

Before the denouemont of the 'great war for civilization' of 1914–18 damned diplomacy and its pretended system of counter-balancing alliances, Europe's world domination had led to the piecemeal incorporation into its scheme of foreign affairs of states with markedly different histories. This introduced a less convivial meaning of what it was to be foreign. Little difficulty was experienced with admitting the independent states of both Americas, whose 'sympathies' attached them to Europe, but only when the Ottoman Empire became 'the sick man of Europe' was it admitted as an equal. Although for centuries after 1453 the power of the Sultans had troubled the peace of Europe and influenced its power politics, the Porte had declined to adopt Europe's diplomatic customs. Like many European countries before it, Japan forced its way into diplomatic prominence through military victory over an existing great power. Having defeated Russia in 1904–5, Japan was thereafter treated as a power to be feared and an ally to be courted. Lack of 'resemblance in the modes of intercourse' did not prevent Japan from adapting itself to a diplomatic system that afforded it recognition in return for compliance with rules of conduct devised in Europe. At the Paris Peace Conference in 1919, Japan figured in the front rank of powers.

Where a century ago Japan showed the way, numerous other states have since followed. With the dismemberment of Europe's multinational monarchies in 1914–18, and the dissolution of overseas empires after 1945, scores of successor states became members of a world-wide diplomatic order. Although 33 states signed the Treaty of Versailles, nearly twice that many countries were by then in existence. The League of Nations began with 41 members, and out of 75 states that laid claim to recognition in 1945, 51 were founder members of the UN. The break-up of the USSR in 1991, which led to a further population increase in the number of states, may mark something like the completion of the diplomatic system. The achievement of independence is, however, only the beginning of foreign affairs. Irrespective of historical background its first and lasting consequence is to expose states to the hazards of power politics. This remains as much the inescapable corollary of statehood as it was in Machiavelli's Italy. Neither juridical equality, the sending and receiving of resident envoys, nor the development of congress diplomacy into international organizations, can protect states from the inequities and uncertainties of power politics. As critics have often noted, because the diplomatic system enshrines the authority of states, it condones and therefore perpetuates the power politics whose disorders it simultaneously seeks to modify.

## III

The state as a political body and the nation as a collectivity of fellow-feeling are among Europe's most palpable legacies to the rest of the world. They served as idioms by which subject peoples asserted independence and consolidated their separateness. First propagated in Europe and Britain's American colonies, the right of nations to self-government was seized upon in the twentieth century by leaders educated by Europe's last empires. The consequences of this historical and moral boomerang are present in the peopling of the world with states claiming to embody nations, and of nations demanding statehood.

This mimesis of Europe's public life carried far-reaching consequences. In becoming states, the would-be 'national' governments set up to rule them joined a diplomatic system whose rules of conduct had been devised by their recent masters. But just as the state and nation have been adapted to their own purposes by peoples from beyond

Europe, so a universal diplomatic system which is no longer the preserve of European states reflects twentieth-century shifts in the distribution or 'balance' of power. Europeans have not found it easy to reconcile themselves to having spawned a world-wide 'aggregation' of states. Neither have they dwelt sufficiently on the implications of having exported in the baggage of their rule, the methods of power politics. Among the reasons for this averted attention is the sense that power politics were responsible for Europe's attempted suicide between 1914 and 1945, and that everything associated with the failures of its diplomatic system had therefore to be shunned. Given the enormity of the experience, amnesia is not difficult to understand, but the desire to forget, disown, blame, discard and ignore power politics often led to the self-reproachful *non sequitor* that because Europe's diplomatic system licenses power politics, it is therefore responsible for the very existence of power. As if it was plausible to overlook that power is present wherever, and at whatever level, human fears and desires stimulate action to contain and advance them! Although politics were indeed invented in the city-states of classical Greece, the idea that power is only to be found where polities exist, and that war arises only in a diplomatic system designed in part to regulate its incidence and conduct, is misplaced. The histories of civilizations other than Europe's are also the registers of war and peace.

Europe's post-war renunciation and reformation expressed the need to live down the disastrous power politics of the first half of the twentieth century. The delayed effects of this success have, along with the end of the Cold War, been to bring Europe up against the unreformed power politics of an expanded diplomatic system that unashamedly resounds to a past now discredited in its own eyes. In contrast to European regrets, the precepts of *raison d'état, machtpolitik* and 'national interest' have been indigenized with little time for handwringing. From outside Europe its attempted reforms are eyed selectively. While the EU's economic achievment of a single market attracts attention, few states from other continents wish to follow in its political footsteps. There is little desire to curtail national self-government which was often painfully achieved against European states. Despite the imbalances of power politics and the inequities of the international economy, many recently independent countries find in the formal precepts of the diplomatic system tailor-made buttresses for their separate existences.

A penitential view of foreign affairs overlooks the fact that self-governing states recently freed from external rule are unlikely to foreswear their independence merely because a group of European states has come to regret their own past excesses. Rivalries between states in many parts of the world are thus manifestly alive, and accepted as the fateful consequence of statehood. In recently established states, what causes most concern is internal weakness, not the external effects of membership of a diplomatic system. India and Pakistan, or Iran and Iraq, are not about to form political unions modelled on the EU merely because armaments are costly and independence burdensome.

With close to 200 states, each with its own foreign ministry and complement of envoys, the present global diplomatic system resembles the intermingling of a vast spread of spider's webs. At their wakeful centre are nationally inspired states each with its own interests and widely differing powers. Although this conspectus implies neither the inevitability of war nor unresolvable conflict, the uneven and shifting relations of separately organized lethal power makes the containment of disorder an unending task. The yet more arduous business of bringing the interests of states into acceptable alignment is thus the *chef d'oeuvre* of negotiations. Rather than dispel the obdurate features of diplomatic life, international organizations like the UN have only housed them in more eirenic settings. One implication for Europe is that if the EU or its states wish to further their interests in a diplomatic system no longer under their control and containing some states of continental proportions, they must address the outcome of their original creation. Only by taking part in power politics can they be influenced. And the influence that counts for most is the actions of the most powerful.

IV

The most adept exposition of why the independence of states is necessarily accompanied by power politics is provided by the unlikely figure of Jean-Jacques Rousseau. A writer of the eighteenth-century enlightenment, and one of its fiercest critics, Rousseau is more associated with schemes for a perfected political order than with the diagnosis of disorders that arise between states. He none the less took a close interest in the diplomatic affairs of Europe, dominated as they were by its great powers. He was briefly secretary to the French ambassador to Venice, but his summary and commentary on the abbé Saint-Pierre's *Project for Perpetual Peace* expresses a contempt for rulers and the abuse of power that is of a piece with all his discussion of public affairs. He found the actions of diplomats and generals as callously preposterous as the monarchs they served. Europe's rulers had so much in common and were so intimately caught up in one another's affairs that, like Burke a generation later, he noted the 'similitudes' and 'resemblances' that bound the diplomatic system of Europe together. Rousseau believed that the affairs of France, Britain, Austria, Russia, and Prussia were 'so cunningly interwoven as to hold their respective forces mutually in check'[3]. While in his opinion the balance of power among these five great powers prevented the domination of Europe by any one of them, it did not ensure lasting peace. Because the balance of power was unable to maintain an ordered equilibrium, imbalances of power were endemic and ineffectually countered through diplomatic alliances and war.

In laying bare why a Europe of tightly bound states managed by its French-speaking aristocratic elite was so prone to conflict, Rousseau probed beyond the diplomatic intricacies of the times to explain the existence and persistence of power politics. The attempt to predicate peace on the independence of states will, he argued, leave the participants so warily untrusting of each other that all are driven by the necessities of survival to prepare for war. In Rousseau's view, it was the very things states had in common that generated the rivalrous pursuit of power and dominion, wealth and territory, eminence and pre-eminence. The inexorable consequence of this remorseless situation, whose effects are perhaps desired by none but are nevertheless multiplied by proximity, constituted the uniqueness of the diplomatic system. To one side, the resemblances of Europe's self-interested rulers gave rise to practices that moderated their conflicts. These rules included both the customary laws surrounding diplomats, and the conduct of war.

This simulacrum of order was, however, achievable only under conditions that ensured the continuation of a more abiding and pervasive disorder. It was this bleak effect of independence that Rousseau chose to stress. 'But the established order', he observed, 'if indestructible, is for that very reason the more likely to constant storms'. 'Between the powers of Europe' he wrote, 'there is a constant action and reaction which, without overwhelming them altogether, keeps them in continued agitation'.[4] Differences in power between rival states, and the fact that unlike individuals, political bodies can augment their physical powers, ensures that agitations among rulers of unequal powers are relentless. 'Thus the size of the body politic being purely relative', he concluded, 'it is forced to compare itself in order to know itself; it depends on its whole environment and has to take an interest in all that happens ... its very consolidation, by making its relations more constant, gives greater sureness to all its actions and makes all its quarrels more dangerous'.[5]

Rousseau was no admirer of power, politics or diplomacy. He desired with all his turbulent soul to see might dissolved in right. He shared with the abbé Saint-Pierre and his latter day followers a sense of the futility of like-minded states co-operating to sustain a diplomatic system whose purpose was not peace, but the interests of unruly states. Willingness to risk conflict for the sake of their independence ensured general insecurity. Despite his reasoned and impassioned aversion to power politics, Rousseau none the less rejected schemes for lasting peace. In his reckoning only violence would wean states from the self-defeating pursuit of their interests, and while perhaps resolving one issue the enforcement of peace would create fresh dilemmas. If only might would induce states to submit to order, the remedy risked being more terrible than the ill. The transformation of Europe's diplomatic system into a political body capable of providing government would, he believed, have to be imposed by military means against the will of defiant states.

The voluntary reformation of the EU would therefore have only half-surprised Rousseau. That the prolonged catastrophe of 1914–45 was necessary before the states of western Europe were ready to begin sharing government would have confirmed his view that states will go to exorbitant lengths before yielding their powers. On the other hand, Rousseau would have been harder put to explain the willingness of European governments after 1945 to remedy their predicament by *voluntarily* agreeing to share government. He would surely have interpreted the proliferation of self-governing states over the last century as certifying the continuation of power politics. In so far as Rousseau conceived of a release from power politics compatible with the independence of states, it lay in his belief that the less they had to do with one another the better. The diplomatic system was a trap that no state could entirely avoid and in which none could find repose.

Isolation and autarky are not, however, choices for Europe. The effect therefore of taming power politics in much of Europe, and of creating a new centre of power in Brussels by doing so, is to have escaped from one dilemma while preparing the ground for another. In so far as 'Europe' has escaped from its localized past of ungoverned states, it is now exposed to a universalized version of its old predicaments: out of the regional frying pan and into the world fire. One difference between Europe and much of the rest of the world is that whereas the convulsions of twentieth-century power politics felt like death-throes to the states of Europe, in many other parts of the world they are greeted as the birth-pangs of independence.

V

The appropriation by a more organizationally minded century of the amateurish diplomatic system produced by Europe's states led to broadly conceived adaptations. Just as for 300 years the great powers of Europe shaped foreign affairs to suit their interests, so their successors have since 1945 left their own distinctive marks on power politics. Some of the changes introduced after victory over Germany and Japan by the world's mightiest state did indeed appear radical.

The UN was designed by the USA to correct defects of the League of Nations that at the close of the First World War had been presented as an alternative to European power politics. No one at the Paris Peace Conference of 1919 rivalled Woodrow Wilson's principled disavowal of the European diplomatic system. 'Secret diplomacy', alliances, arms races and despotism had issued in the failure of 'the balance of power' to maintain the peace of Europe. The result was a death-toll of 33 million. With biblical zeal and the power of the USA behind him, the diplomatic system was castigated by Woodrow Wilson as a system of war. The League of Nations was intended to replace a catalogue of discredited strategems with the institution of an orderly system of collective security. 'Open covenants openly arrived at' would bring the educative advantages of public deliberation to bear on foreign affairs, inspiring thereby the trust in whose absence shoddy diplomacy flourished. The constitutionalism under which representative government civilized power within states was to be grafted on to the stock of relations between states. Under the League Covenant, nationally self-determined states bound themselves by treaty to rally to one another's aid even though not themselves directly threatened by aggression. Since peace was proclaimed to be indivisible and in the equal interest of all, League members were to act in unison to safeguard it. In order to avoid the need to generalize war in order to keep the peace, states pledged themselves to submit disputes to procedures of mediation, arbitration and international law, without however creating the means of keeping states to their word. This omission ignored the opinion of Thomas Hobbes some centuries earlier that 'covenants without the sword, are but words, and of no strength to secure a man at all'.[6] 'It is no wonder', he added, 'if there be somewhat else required, besides covenant, to make agreement constant and lasting; which is a common power, to keep them in awe, and to direct their actions to the common benefit'.[7] An international organization with powers of compulsory jurisdiction and enforcement would have ceased to be a league of nations and become a sword-bearing governing body. At a time when national independence was in vogue, states were unwilling to exchange self-government for rule by a world authority. Nor was it thought necessary; self-determined states were not only considered compatible with peace, they were said to provide the foundation that would make their leaguing together effective. Nationalism, liberalism and democracy were to be the solvents of power politics. Properly constituted states would transform the diplomatic system without dispensing with its principals.

Hence the class of 'great powers' that dominated the pre-1914 'international anarchy' remained in control of the League of Nations. Even before the Senate rejected the Treaty of Versailles, and with it US membership of the League, the diplomacy of European states was notable for its unreconstructed pre-occupation with the balance of power. Only the victors had the power to enforce or alter the terms of peace they had exacted. Dominated by separate states with their own interests to follow, and armed forces at their disposal, the inter-war years revealed that law-governed power politics were a cruelly misleading contradiction in terms. Had the unifying assumptions of a common interest in peace been true, the League would hardly have been required. Since the interests of states clashed, the League proved too weak to arbitrate or suppress the conflicts of its members. Most damaging of all to the belief that any start to the reform of the diplomatic system was better than none was the League's attachment to the contested peace settlement of 1919. The effect of combining power politics with hopes and procedures for transcending them was to invest foreign affairs with additional confusions. While the merits of 'collective security' and the fecundity of the Geneva organization was propagated to credulous publics, diplomacy of the old sort that the League was meant to replace continued. By the time Hitler gained power, Britain and France lacked the will either to enforce the terms of Versailles, or contain the consequences of appeasement. Without saying so openly, neither great power had transferred its trust from self-reliance and diplomatic alignments to the powerless League of

Nations. While 'secret diplomacy' had become publicly indefensible, the deliberations of the League aroused false expectations. Veiled and distracted by the League of Nations, the broken-backed diplomatic system of Europe lumbered on until overwhelmed by the armies of the Third Reich.

The revised version of international organization agreed by the victors at San Francisco in 1945 held to the belief that an alternative to power politics was feasible Like its predecessor it nevertheless upheld the standing of states. While acknowledging the 'equality of states', the new scheme enhanced and made still more explicit the role of the dominant great powers. The Security Council thus embellished the category of states responsible for taking Europe and the world into twentieth-century war. With the consent of small states, the victors made themselves responsible for what was intended to be a more systematic and law-governed peace. The UN established procedures in the Security Council that entitled its five permanent members to enforce the peace they had won. Unlike the League, its successor was not to be hamstrung by arguments that the equality of states necessitated the unanimous agreement of the entire executive. Rather than all states having the veto, the allied powers who formed the core of the Security Council confined the veto to themelves. In matters of war and peace, only their concurrence was therefore effectively needed. Although the Charter avoided calling its principal states 'great powers', its provisions made explicit that some states were more equal than others. As befitted those with power, the permanent members of the Security Council clothed their might in the rules and procedures of organizational right. They were careful not to circumscribe their own powers too tightly.

The demarcation between great powers and other states was far from novel. Just as the origins of the League and the UN are traceable to the peace congresses and peacetime conferences of Europe's diplomatic system, so the privileged position of the permanent members of the Security Council updated a status long enjoyed in European diplomacy by its principal 'powers'. In other respects as well, the advent of continuous conference diplomacy was less of a break with the past than is sometimes thought. The ability to assemble the entire diplomatic system in one place and on a permanent footing did not lead to the annulment of bilateral relations based on resident envoys. Although the League and the UN carried hopes of differently conducted foreign affairs, the persistence of power politics did not prevent old style diplomacy from taking place in international organizations. For many new and small states that is one of their main advantages. Although its formulation in the language of liberal constitutionalism is deceptive, the effect of international organization is to carry the practice of resident diplomacy to the point where the representatives of large numbers of states are housed under one roof. Along with a new breed of 'international civil servants', professionally trained and ever more specialized envoys from umpteen countries now man large agencies in places like Geneva and New York, whose essential purposes none the less remain largely unaltered. They allow diplomats to inform themselves and their governments about foreign affairs, represent their states, and to engage in negotiations. Although international organizations have not displaced direct relations between states, it is however true that 'standing' or multilateral diplomacy reveals the prolix workings of a world of states foreshortened as never before by ease of communications.

The effect of the Cold War was to paralyse and therefore question the renewed hopes vested in the UN. The USSR saw in the 'world authority' not a decisive break with power politics, but their manipulation by the arsenal of capitalism. Contrarywise, the USA declined to interpret Moscow's resort to the veto as a familiar means of defending interests, and saw instead revolutionary malevolence. As the decolonization of Europe's empires produced a profusion of new states, an organization whose serious purpose was to foster diplomatic co-operation among the great powers became a noisesome sideshow. Before long, non-aligned states saw the advantages of selling their favours to whichever side in the Cold War had most to offer. Disfigured as it was by propaganda, diplomacy at the UN remained the diplomacy of power politics. When the superpowers wished to negotiate in confidence, they usually met well away from international organizations. The conflict between the US and the USSR was called off in Reykjavik rather than in New York.

The Cold War and decolonization illustrated how effortlessly the habits of power politics migrate with their dispersal. If this left unfulfilled the aspirations of the UN's begetters, it was possible to find comfort in a residual justification; in a world compacted with states, international organization provides a usefully refurbished setting for diplomacy. Multilateral agencies are, to a world overcoming time and space, what the resident envoy was to the diplomatic system of Europe when the pace of negotations was set by horse-drawn postillions and sailing ships. Yet for all the continuities linking Machiavelli's Florence and Richelieu's France with the national interests pursued by today's great powers, at least one important difference deserves note. Whereas the earlier systematization of foreign affairs around the resident ambassador could not be portrayed as inhibiting the princely powers of sovereigns, the twentieth-century ramification of international organizations produces just that unfounded suggestion. Although there are agencies dealing mostly with trade, to which states have ceded significant powers, for the most part international organizations amplify the extent to which in becoming universal, foreign affairs have remained forthrightly state-centred. This does not imply that the obligatory disputes procedures of the World Trade Organization (WTO), for example, may not be signs of the future, but thus far the effect of international organization has been to re-house rather than dislodge the authority of states.

To the extent that the UN, NGOs and other varieties of official, business and private agencies have added to foreign affairs without removing states from their animating centre, the world is still most aptly described as a diplomatic system. A states-system does not imply that co-operation in foreign affairs is impossible or rare, or that international organizations do not have important uses. The UN may be of especial help to great powers by enabling them to call their co-operation 'the will of the international community'; or when their conflicts can be diplomatically understated as 'divisions within the Security Council'. The diplomatic utility of the UN cannot, however, be used as evidence that foreign affairs have ceased to be power politics between states. Organizations composed of states, funded by them and answerable to them, are not equipped to transform the diplomatic system into a universal political body.

## VI

'Political reason', Burke argued, 'is a computing principle'. From this it might appear that since diplomacy, like politics, illustrates the artifice of human affairs, it too can be made to yield to precise as well as clear explication. What men fabricate is analysable back into its contstituent parts. It is part of the credo of the modern world, derived from the Enlightenment, that once something has been rendered explicit it is well on the way to being brought under control. Burke's meaning lies, however, in the opposite direction. He reasoned against the belief that public affairs are reducible to exact formulation. 'Political reason', he maintained 'is a computing principle; adddding, substracting, multiplying, and dividing, morally and not metaphysically, or mathematically, true moral denominations'.[8] By a moral denomination Burke had in mind political bodies where 'power and right are the same'[9]. However much this combustible combination can be counted upon to pepper controversy, its principal effect is to subject those who act in public affairs to severe difficulties. These are perhaps even more pronounced in 'foreign' than 'domestic' affairs.

In power politics, the mingling of what is and is of necessity so, with what should and ought in right be, and with effort can (perhaps) be brought about, presents complexities all of its own. In the diplomatic system the external relations of states that make foreign affairs neither accidentally nor temporarily but inherently opaque add to the moral uncertainties associated with all public actions. Foreign ministers and their envoys have to 'act and react' to the 'agitations' of their numerous counterparts, denied the advantages of demonstrably reliable knowledge. They cannot be certain of what other states intend, how far they are prepared and willing to press forward their actions, or what will be be the response of others to one's own decisions. Where might and right are connected but not the same, judging events is not a matter of 'correlating forces'. All states contribute to unchess-like but all-too-human confusions where 'national interests' are asserted by power, conveyed by means of diplomacy and coercion, and justified in right. All in turn are exposed to the resulting repercussions that keep the train of events in ceaseless and unforseeable motion. For as long as states belong to the diplomatic system, they cannot escape from being unable to plan their external actions with the same foresight as well-ordered governments are able to proceed internally via legislation, executive decision and administration. The reason for this is as commonplace as it is insurmountable. Whereas governments that enjoy the consent of the governed can direct domestic affairs and hence bring a measure of predictability to their policies, in foreign affairs other states make the genesis of trust based on reliably fulfilled promises unusually difficult. Since self-governing states are not answerable to each other's laws, none can rightfully demand of others that they make known their powers and adjust them to comply with one's own. Because this would encroach upon the authority that states exist to uphold, it was accordingly ruled out at the inception of the diplomatic system.

The contingencies that are inseperable from foreign affairs thus derive from the mutually agreed separateness of states. The guesswork and frustrations of diplomacy reflect the lengths to which states go in order to protect their own affairs from the unwanted pryings of foreigners. The system of diplomatic representation that was originally treated as no better than espionage is usuallly agreed to because it is understood as necessary to the interests of states. Contrived around the authority of states, the diplomatic system is thus a system of *arbitrary* power. What cannot be rightfully, lawfully or authoritiavely demanded by states of each other is sought by means of power.'Law and arbitrary power', Burke thundered during his impeachment of Warren Hastings, 'are at eternal enmity'. Yet in foreign affairs, the arbitrariness of states stands starkly out. The international law agreed upon by states goes hand in glove with their power politics. Sometimes the exercise of power is confined to persuasion. But the full meaning of diplomacy is that because states do not have political authority over one another, persuasion is often effective only when accompanied by threats of force, or by other inducements. Among the latter, economic benefits and penalties are as familiar as they are varied. States are responsive to the power exerted on them because they are not otherwise responsible to each other.

The mutual unaccountability of states, which sets limits to how systematic or adminstered foreign affairs can be, goes some way to explain the persistence of power politics. The vagaries of the diplomatic system that make it impossible to know in advance which way events are about to turn is not therefore the outcome of poor planning or defective organization. Improved means of communication and the more systematic acquisition of ever larger quantities of 'information' may equip states with more knowledge of foreign affairs – though it may also submerge them – but these are not solutions to power politics. They rather highlight the essential dilemmas of states that derive from their plurality and juxtaposition. The flows of 'information' that enable one state to achieve a detailed picture of another also provide opportunities and motives that may induce governments to alter course. 'Perfect knowledge' of all 200 members of the diplomatic system, from their schoolrooms to the heartbeats of every politician, businessman, judge, soldier and diplomat, would not resolve the enigmas of power politics. The effect would be to shift them to a different level. The space technology that allows the USA to survey the earth with worm-length accuracy, and keeps Saddam Hussein hidden indoors, derives from science that cannot for long be monopolized by one country, or divested of political and diplomatic use. The actions of those who are presently a step ahead agitate others to invest in research and development. Power politics is not a set of conundrums amenable to computation by technical wizardry.

Reservations of a similar kind also apply to the remarkable diversity of means now available to the practice of diplomacy. The stilted movements of resident envoys have been repeatedly enlivened since the invention of the telegraph, but air travel, grandiose buildings, hot-lines and cyberspace have not led to the 'arts of diplomacy' being taken out of the hands of impressionists and placed in the care of systems analysts. As the world in which foreign affairs take place has been transformed by science and technology, diplomacy has adapted its creations to tasks that continue to depart from and return to the interests of states. Means that have made it possible to negotiate in novel ways have at the same time maintained the centrality of states.

The measureless uncertainties of the diplomatic system are the outcome of the determination of states, and particularly great powers, to subject themselves only to restraints compatible with their interests, or which they lack the power to ignore. The rules and conventions of diplomatic life may therefore be adhered to and vigorously defended just because they leave largely intact the arbitrary 'freedom of action' valued by states. The international laws of peace and war do not adjudicate matters of substance affecting 'vital national interests'. They revolve around the independence of states who remain arbiters or judges in their own causes and who therefore rely more on their own powers than the Permanent Court of International Justice. How-ever much some protest to the contrary, states are unaccountable to the laws created by them. Only with their consent can they be taken to law. Even when states make appearances in The Hague, international law has no 'sword' to enforce compliance with its decisions. It is only a slight exaggeration to say that the entire diplomatic system is the stage-management of foreign affairs by powers who gain most from ensuring that their actions are coralled only by what is too weak to bind them. Rousseau concluded that under a system whose members held each other in check by means of countervailing power, and not by means of law, its 'continued agitations' would remain unpredictable.

Not in 1919, at San Franciso in 1945, or at the break-up of the USSR in 1991, were the great powers willing to subordinate them-selves to the rule that all states are equal and equally bound by their treaty undertakings. Small states might be provided with an assembly, encouraged to deliberate and vote on 'resolutions', but the great powers had meanwhile institutionalized their arbitrary powers and had them sanctioned by treaty. Although the retention of the veto by permanent members of the Security Council does not give them immunity from the influence of other states, or imply refusal to co-operate, it surely marks the threshold beyond which the most mighty are unaccountable. The USA was naturally keen to summon diplomatic support in the UN for military action against Iraq in 1991 and for its sabre-rattling in 1998. The mobilization of force did not, however, depend on a 'mandate' from the UN. The USA used its advantaged position to warn others of what it had in mind and seek their endorsement. This was easier to achieve in the immediate aftermath of the Cold War when US influence was irresistible, than seven years later when its power appeared less supremely awesome. The change was not the result of the UN having gained in authority, but in the sensitivity of the USA to its altered diplomatic position in the Middle East, and the need to minimize conflict with China, Russia and France.

## VII

The defects of the diplomatic system have been unsparingly noted. The record of its inability to civilize power politics along with proposals to reform and replace their follies, form a parallel counter-story to the diplomatic history of Europe. In the 'century of total war' this has come to include comment on the defects of a regime of foreign affairs that now embraces the world.

The perennial stumbling block to remedying disorder in foreign affairs has been the desire of states to retain their powers and the regular discovery of fortifying means. In matters of defence and security some of the methods of violence have become so potently indiscriminate that they are barely usable as instruments of war or as the stiffening force of diplomacy. The powers of men to generate power have outdistanced even power politics. Yet unless states also had reason to co-exist and co-operate, the diplomatic system would be a misnomer. The order that collaborative voluntary action sustains, is none the less limited by insistence that the peace states together uphold leaves unimpaired their authority to act and react independently. Despite the mayhem of the first half of the twentieth century and the nuclear armed peace of the Cold War, there is scant evidence that states are about to forgo their powers. The impresssive numbers of states that have signed the renewed Non-Proliferation Treaty (NPT), which includes more invasive inspection procedures, has not diminished the attractions of weapons of mass destruction to the ambitious, the aggrieved and the fearful. These now include India and Pakistan. Even though the EU testifies to the ability of like-minded peoples to share government, it contains two countries that possess nucelar weapons and who show no signs of relinquishing them or sumbitting control of them to shared government.

The fact that many of the world's states are weak and riven with internal convulsions has not led to the abandonment of national self-determination and self-government as the aim of nations. It has resulted in the creation of more states and to experiments with regional international organizations. At times the corsetting bipolarities of the Cold War and its rhetorical flamboyance gave the impression that the diplomatic system had been reduced to antiquated decor against which the superpowers conducted their rivalry. Yet although the collapse of the USSR has left the USA uniquely powerful, the diplomatic system has shown renewed elasticity. It is far from clear that even if the USA has the means, it is willing to constrict the effervescence of world-wide power politics where its own interests are not at stake. Although the nuclear arsenals of the USA and Russia have been pared down, the termination of the Cold War has not issued in the generalized disarmament that proponents of the League of Nations and the UN always attached to schemes for reforming the diplomatic system. The peace of the world remains armed as well as vulnerable to forms of disturbance linked to localized arms races, rickety and impoverished states, ethnic and religious hatreds, terrorism, drugs, crime and fears aroused by the prospect of largescale population movements. Even if states continue to dispose of the principal means of war and peace, it does not follow that even in co-operation they are sufficiently equipped to police a much disturbed world.

Between the Congress of Westphalia in 1648 and the Paris Peace Conference of 1919 the diplomatic system remained the creature of its authors. Attempts to overthrow it by force and replace a multiplicity of states with universal rule failed. So did subsequent proposals to reform power politics and constitute a world order on postulates that downgraded states. After two world wars and half a century of superpower rivalry, the expanded diplomatic system shows signs of renwed vigor that the EU will ignore at is peril.

Among the changes to the diplomatic system that have accompanied its distension, one in particular presents especial difficulities unusually difficult to compute. However arbitrary and volatile were the power politics of Europe's states, until the twentith century their mutual relations were constrained by the sense that a Europe of some sort existed. How far the 'similitudes' and 'resemblances' that familiarized relations among Europe's rulers restricted war and prolonged peace is hard to say, and in view of the manic self-destruction of 1914–45 shamingly painful even to contemplate. Yet the present-day world brings together the diplomatic envoys of states representing more acute differences of thought and feeling than anything faced by the provincial diplomatic system of Europe. States with distinct and perhaps incomensurable inheritiances rub shoulders in a diplomatic system that carries the powerful imprint of European countries and the USA. It is not yet clear whether China, for example, or parts of the Islamic world are reconciled to an ordering of affairs they are not as yet powerful enough to contest openly. The ability of the diplomatic system to secure the interests of peoples whose histories do not dovetail, and who regard the present distribution of might and right as morally unfounded, will affect the stability of foreign affairs. If this implies amendment of the present diplomatic system, Europe's chances of securing its own interests may impose on its states the necessity of acting in unison. Having bequeathed the world a diplomatic system it no longer dominates, it remains to be seen how a reformed Europe will adapt not only to shifts in the balance of power, but to demands by newly powerful moral denominations to tailor the workings of might and right more to their own wants.

## Notes

1. Edmund Burke, *Burke's Writings and Speeches* (London: The World's Classics, 1907), vol. VI, p. 252.
2. Ibid, pp.155–7.
3. M.G. Forsyth, H.M.A. Keens-Soper and P. Savigear, *The Theory of International Relations* ( London: Allen & Unwin, 1980), p. 140.
4. Ibid, p. 140.
5. Ibid, p. 171.
6. Thomas Hobbes, *The Leviathan*, introduction by Michael Oakeshott, (Oxford: Basil Blackwell, 1946) p. 109.
7. Ibid, p. 112.
8. Edmund Burke, *Reflections on the Revolution in France* (London: Dent, 1964), p. 59.
9. Ibid, p. 60.

# Part II

# Systematic Disorders

# 3 Globalization

I

The consolidation of world-wide markets within a progressively compacted globe is permeating states. The effect is to undermine and perhaps relocate the powers of government and the expectations of the governed. If it is not possible to foretell with accuracy the new 'shapes of life' globalization is busily bringing into being, it is confidently asserted that the familiar composition of the world as a manifold of states will not escape its transforming influences. Some have already concluded that the EU is an early expression of how impersonal forces beyond the control of individual states has led to their combination, and that this development is a foretaste of how globalization is forming similar groupings elsewhere. At the same time others have depicted the EU as a regional body inspired by localized concerns that threaten to disrupt the homogenizing powers of globalization.

Arguments kindled by the extent and effects of globalization agree on at least two propositions. The anvil on which it is being forged is market capitalism. It is this that accounts for the energizing compulsiveness with which trade and finance, investment and manufacturing, transport and communications, are establishing unbroken connections throughout the world. In the vanguard are to be found businesses and corporations driven by hopes of gain. While none of these 'private' but often 'publicly' supported activities is entirely novel, each has recently undergone and produced such impressive changes that increasing numbers of people are gaining their livings, spending its rewards and envisaging the world in radically altered ways. Globalization is not, however, caused by the existence of markets or the ingenuity of entrepreneurs, neither of which is of recent origin, but by the pervasive effects of the second influence. The erosion of time and space that so dramatically conveys a sense of a world foreshortened and conjoined is principally due to the economic exploitation of science and technology. Above all it is the breathtaking speed, ease and falling costs with which people, goods, services, images and information move about the world, that explains both the productive aspects of globalization and other, variously connected, examples of the same phenomenon. The products of market capitalism that span the world are accompanied by news and entertainment, crime and religion, military force and satellite surveillance, art and sport, science itself, wanted and feared migration of people, tourism and terrorism, and by environmental and other anxieties prompted by human activism.

In keeping with the opportunism that makes entrepreneurs inventive, the lately acquired ability of businesses to site their productive activities in whatever country offers competitive advantage, and the adoption of English as the language of the market place, now allows market capitalism to view the world in the round. Thanks to modern communications a single field of diverse possibilities makes entrepreneurs worldly in more than one sense. Whatever therefore hinders businesses from making the most of their assets is more than wasteful; those, like protectionist or interventionist governments, who raise barriers to the creation of wealth, are said to be marooned on the wrong side of history. Whereas states stand, so to speak, on their delimited and nervously armed frontiers, trapped in localized passions, rooted in territory and bounded by its extent, multinational companies see before them seamless markets, and a populous humanity eager to consume their wares. Like the industrial revolution of which it is a more knowledge-laden continuation, globalization comes readily to be seen as the benign, if often unruly, crucible of an irresistible and inclusively better future. The multinational companies that are portrayed as the visible presence of tomorrow's working world may retain close links with their countries of origin, but the unpoliceable contours of their economic calculations lead them to regard all governments as but one consideration or hindrance among many others. What excites those who view the globe as an appetizing oyster is not the geologized dogmas of national interest or the balance of diplomatic power between states, but the common and peaceable coinage of competitive economic performance.

This line of optimistic reasoning in connection with globalization soon awakens a sense of *déjà vu*. It evokes memories of eighteenth-century arguments over the wealth of nations and the role of governments, and beyond that to yet more venerable and expansive speculation. If, as is sometimes claimed, globalization is indeed replacing war (and perhaps even foreign affairs in their entirety) as the great generative force of the times, it is not surprising that thinking about world affairs is forced back to fundamentals.

Nor are issues raised by the rush of globalization likely to be quietened by the reminder that for all the vigour of earlier disputations we appear no nearer to systematic knowledge of how economics and politics are related, or of how both activities are circumscribed by foreign affairs. Europe has imposing reasons for not shying away from the exacting business of reordering its mental grasp of a world made daily less familiar by globalization. Large as its internal markets are, the EU is not as economically self-sufficient as the USA or immune to the turbulence recently visited upon the Asian 'tiger' economies. To the extent that they can be given shape and direction, no other part of the world has a greater economic interest than Europe in the progress of globalization. The governments and institutions of Europe will need to decide how far it lies within their separate or unified powers to harness the advent of global markets to their purposes, and how far adjustment is in any case made unavoidable by whorls of apparently unbounded change.

Although one may ruminate on how far globalization has proceeded, and labour the difficulties of exact exposition, where the love of knowledge has been harnessed to the love of gain in order to satisfy the bottomless desires of six billion mortals, the result is likely to be of greater importance than solving a riddle. The well-being of the world and Europe's place in it may turn on which arguments carry the day and what decisions are based upon them. Globalization may appear melodramatically overdrawn or overwhelmingly powerful, but its inevitablility makes public if not private reactions to its spread imperative.

'The great changes and variations, beyond human imagining, which we have experienced and experience every day' drove Machiavelli to bouts of fatalism and passivity. But however inexorable *fortuna* appeared, he nevertheless considered it probable 'that fortune is the arbiter of half the things we do, leaving the other half or so to be controlled by ourselves.'[1] He described *fortuna* in terms similar to those used by enthusiasts of globalization, as well as by those who fear it. 'I compare fortune' Machiavelli argued, 'to one of those violent rivers which, when they are enraged, flood the plains... Everyone flees before them, everybody yields to their impetus, there is no possibility of resistance.'[2] Provided one knows how and when to act, he did not believe, however, that men lacked countervailing resources or that nothing could be done. By constructing 'dykes and embankments' beforehand, he went on to suggest, 'the force of the river can be channelled into less harmful ways'.[3] 'So it is with fortune', he wrote. 'She knows her power when there is no force to hold her in check; and her impetus is felt where she knows there are no embankments and dykes built to restrain her'.[4] In this view, the irruption of disorderly change is not a signal to abdicate from politics and diplomacy in faint-hearted submission, or console oneself with the hope that tried measures will once more suffice, but a summons to exhibit the resourcefulness that makes bold action worthwhile and which Machiavelli called *virtú*. The EU already exemplifies the *virtú* or prowess of its makers and the impetus of globalization will evoke the need for more of the same.

## II

The financial markets of the world are now so attuned to each other that they seem like clusters of indefatigable relay runners, passing batons of information between New York, Tokyo, London and Frankfurt in ever wakeful cyberspace. The price of gain is world-wide information, as well as athletic vigilance. Although one cannot say exactly what new 'shapes of life' globalization is fertilizing, or measure how rapidly and how far the continents of the world are being recomposed in its image, the general direction is confidently proclaimed. Of especial interest is the assertion that globalization is breaking down political barriers to market-centred activities and thereby knitting the world together as never before. It is often assumed that globalization will therefore gather the world together in lasting peace. In the 1920s Ortega Y Gasset was similarly impressed by the impact of rapid transport and instant telephonic communication. 'The nearness of the far-off' he wrote, 'this presence of the absent has extended in fabulous proportions the horizons of each individual existence'.[5] Yet less than two decades later, long range strategic bombing and mobile warfare had brought home to millions the mixed blessings of living in rapid and vulnerable reach of other people. Perhaps because of the scars left by warfare that breached national frontiers as never before, some Europeans greet with relish the disruptions of globalization. The spread of global markets can plausibly appear as a peace-bearing solvent of power politics and the needed complement to Europe's attempts at political reformation. Global economic interests that cover the earth are made to tally with the idea that economic competition is preparing the way for ever more inclusive harmony. As a powerful trading bloc, the EU is well positioned to back its own market-based example of peace and prosperity with influence derived through exporting its products to global markets. By this means, it is urged, the force of Europe's redemptive example can be multiplied externally by the weighty effects of the EU's overseas trade and investments. Although rivalry for markets is often cut-throat, the crucial difference is that multinational companies do not wage war. Although European states may not welcome the pressures exerted by globalization on their welfare provisions, or on reducing the role of governments in economic management, these painful political adjustments have to be set against the prospect that competitive and integrative global capitalism will wipe power politics between states from the face of the earth. In seeking their own 'private' fortunes, individuals and companies will entwine the world so closely that the beneficent though unplanned outcome will accomplish more lasting good than all the covenants, charters and 'public' international organizations established to promote cosmopolitan solidarity among states. The promise of globalization is that it may dispense with the need for a diplomatic system while serving the interests of peoples who have hitherto been the victims of power politics.

The reasoning on which this selective view of globalization relies is not always explicit, consistent or persuasive. Although it shares with much other comment on human affairs a weakness for allowing wishes to father thoughts, it can hardly be singled out for failure to distinguish what is from what ought to be. Discussion of globalization is, however, plagued with elisions of another kind to which economic thinking has for long been exposed. It is one thing to contrast the productive energies of markets with the wealth-consuming functions of states, and quite another to pretend that because economic power is considered generative rather than destructive, its coinage does not confer power. The opposite viewpoint, which recognizes that economic activity 'empowers', easily produces an equally wayward assertion. The manifest powerfulness of successful companies and financial markets is elaborated into an argument where wealth becomes the sole substance of all effective influence, whether or not this appears overtly or behind the cloaks of politics and diplomacy. Economic muscle is presented as the only sort of power that really flexes.

It does not however, follow that because wealth is created most efficiently through the activities of individuals and companies, states play no essential part in economic life or are unable to harness the results of productive effort to their own quite distinct purposes. The history of government is inseparable from taxation. Nor does the fecundity of markets demonstrate their ability to work better or even at all without laws and the 'salus populi, or people's safety' that states exist to maintain. A global economy left to the devices of markets might be favoured by anarchists who for moral reasons see no good in government, but captains of industry are more interested in laws that validate contracts and protect property than whether Godwin was right to see government, like dress, as 'the badge of lost innocence'. As the peoples and businesses of central Europe have discovered since the end of party states, escaping from the tyranny of overbearing government does not ensure that its ineffectual replacement automatically supports the development of markets. For over a decade civil war in the Lebanon condemned a country that was once the entrepôt of the Middle East to lawless penury. The post-war economic resurgence of western Europe that helped solidify public order was first made possible by the re-establishment of lawful government and the confidence this inspired in the safety and value of productive activity. The continuity of settled expectations that investment and high levels of consumption crave is not within the powers of markets to create or maintain. The economic life of Europe in this century has not been plotted by markets and the interchanges of supply and demand. During the first half it was contingent on war and rumours of wars, and in the second half it was hostage to the brittle and nuclear armed stability of the Cold War. The thirty years of unmatched prosperity from which western Europe benefited after the Second World War, rested on a strategic balance of power in which the crucial element was less the wealth of the West than the diplomatic foundations upon which its prosperity rested. Even during periods when economic life seemed to move in accordance with its own internal rhythms, market forces turned out to be subject to their own species of disorderly and contagious crash, recession, boom, bust and stagflation. Although peace may promote their efficiency, markets have no special overriding or hidden powers that enable them either to keep their own affairs in good order without the interference of governments, or to ignore or purge the world of power politics.

This glum reasoning was of course disputed even before the first industrialization set in motion developments that globalization now furthers with alarming speed and penetration. 'What is toleration?' Voltaire mused. He replied that it was the 'endowment of humanity'.[6] In contrast to the religious passions whose bigotry tore at Europe's innards and spread economic misery, Voltaire considered the money markets and traders of the world as models of enlightened forbearance by whose example men should learn to live. Drawn together by the lure of gain, traders from every corner of the globe disregarded differences of creed and colour the better to concentrate on the business at hand. Markets, Voltaire concluded, make unequal fortunes, but by overcoming prejudices they make the world a more tolerant as well as a more productive place. He did not, however, dwell on how it was the Bank of England and the wealth it represented that funded the alliance of powers which battled to preserve the 'liberties of Europe' against the ambitions of Louis XIV. At the conclusion of this conflict England had been transformed into a great power. A century after Voltaire contrasted the worldly camaraderie of markets and traders with the spendthrift and vicious vanities of royal courts, Richard Cobden voiced sentiments of a similar kind that encapsulate many of the hopes now invested in globalization. 'Free trade', he wrote, 'is God's diplomacy, and there is no other certain way of uniting people in the bonds of peace'.

Although globalization is more than free trade, both encourage the belief, or prejudice, which in addition to economic arguments that favour leaving markets unmolested by governments, views the exchange of goods and services as a mighty purveyor of humanizing sentiments. Globalization is thus said to carry within its bosom a civilizing mission of all embracing proportions. It is in this spirit that it is welcomed as a liberating as well as a combining force. As economic activity is untangled from regulations made by states, it weaves the more generous sentiments of private, or at least corporate, life into the affairs of the world. The effect, so it is claimed, is to privatize or civilianize foreign affairs and demonstrate the hampering irrelevance of a diplomatic system of states. The speed and reach of modern communications are credited with the additional effect of endowing globalization with powers never claimed by free traders. Whereas dismantling trade barriers erected by states requires diplomatic action in organizations like the WTO, satellites and cyberspace disarm the outward carapace of states by ignoring the existence of national boundaries. Faced with the innovations of science, and their ever more lively exploitation, governments are portrayed as floundering like beached whales. Cobden's liberal minded descendants, who see weak states and ineffectual governments as evidence of freedom, thus join company with pessimists allergic to the notion that any good can come from scientific progress. Whereas liberals rejoice in globalization as the meatiest evidence of 'internationalism', Cassandras harp on the dangers that arise when human beings play with the fire of knowledge. Science and technology unleash globalizing forces intended to increase man's powers of self-direction, but they all too often set in motion forces they subsequently have little hope of controlling and whose effects they are unable even to glimpse.

If globalization truly is the latest and most potent engine for creating wealth, the scientific knowledge of nature on which it thrives may indeed be drawing a fragmented world closer together. That, however, is no more than a preface. Likening the energies and scope of global markets to a force of nature does not lead to the conclusion that an untroubled journey is in store, or that the end will be more desirable than its beginnings. Proximity is no guarantee of harmony. The Internet that is said to ignore political frontiers and put the whole world in instant touch also transmits products that sharpen existing divisions and advertises new ones. Governments are as well equipped as companies to take advantage of new means of power and exploit them for reasons of state. Satellites that distribute financial information without giving a thought to the existence of states, share the heavens with other machines put there by governments. Satellites put in space by states, and whose purposes include monitoring the civil, economic but also the military affairs of the entire earth, can also be destroyed by means unavailable to markets. The appetite of globalized markets for economic information has not replaced or neutered the diplomatic interests of states in political intelligence and military preparedness. Globalization carries no promise that its precocious development will marry with our wishes or fulfil our worst fears.

### III

The desire to interpret an economically unbounded world as evidence that humankind has discovered a common purpose is not easy to resist. Able to view the earth as a whole and peer at the uncomforting spaces about it, the spectacle of a world of disorderly states readily appears outmoded. After a century disfigured by war, the nuclear stand-off of the Cold War, and the vandalism of party-state central planning, the cry of *enrichissez-vous* rings out as a raucous chord of universal fraternity. Energetically chased by the ambitious economic development of Asia and Latin America, the prosperity of Europe and the USA can be seen as a path all can follow. As globalization invigorates the world, a boundless division of labour can be expected to bring opportunity to the poor as well as further benefits to the prosperous. This exposition of the future may lead even the cautious minded to believe that not only have the peoples of the world discovered a common interest in betterment, but also to the more ambitious claim that economic interests, and the markets that serve them, have finally acquired ascendancy over the obsolete public affairs of states.

Even if it is true that the desire for rising standards of living increases as they come within reach, this does not demonstrate that the economy of the world is already a single entity, [7] and neither does a widespread wish to earn more indicate that the internationalization of markets and ease of communications presage unhindered movement towards that end. Seamless markets are manifestly foreshortening the world, but that does not enable one to predict what global order, if any, will result. The 'international' economy of Europe in the nineteenth century, which in many ways was more integrated than its global successor, did not curtail power politics. Largely frontier-free markets, governed by the gold standard and comparatively untouched by the interferences of states, were casualties of the war of 1914–18 they were unable to prevent. This reminder is not intended to dampen the zeal of prophets and prognosticators, but to avoid conflating the apparent direction of globalization with claims to have visited the land promised as its outcome. To pretend they are one and the same is to rely on determinism as a substitute for observation. From there it is but a bird's hop to being carried forward on wings of historical inevitability from whose vantage point the present is illuminated, and simplified, by the light of the future. Although this may not be the tattered dialectical materialism of Marxism, the version of liberalism that informs much thinking about the powers and direction of market capitalism also relies upon a progressive and hence tyrannical view of history.

One of the favoured propositions concerning a fully globalized world economy is that it will run best under its own volition. Where mechanisms of management are needed, markets will provide them. States and international organizations that presently seek to administer economic affairs on behalf of citizens, will wither in significance or be re-jigged to play subordinate roles. Reasoning of this kind overlooks the fact that there is no such thing as 'the international economy' divorced from the political and diplomatic conditions that sustain, shape and also frequently queer its workings. None has ever existed or is conceivable. The omission of the word *political* – more accurately *diplomatic* – from mention of 'the international economy', saves more than a troublesome word or two. It is economical with the evidence of one's worldly senses. The international economy is always and everywhere the international political (or diplomatic) economy. The idea of an economy floating freely and supported only by the oxygen of its own energies is historically incoherent and fosters illusions that have practical implications. It surrounds economic activity with an aura of indefeasible right enjoyed by few other public or private concerns. Even when it is reluctantly admitted that markets of any substantial kind depend on foundations they cannot themselves supply or function without, globalization encourages the dubious belief that because unbounded markets are said to be leading to a new kind of world order, their organizational and even moral self-sufficiency is already in evidence. A shorthand version of this sleight of hand leaves the impression that a world made safe for global markets by their own autochthonous functioning will secure and satisfy the entire plenum of human desires. What is good for McDonald's nourishes the whole man and fulfils the good of the world. Consequently the existing apparatus of state-centred life, along with its diplomatic corollaries, are no longer needed. Nothing of consequence is to be feared by the disappearance of public orders maintained by states, and much is to be gained. Foreign and defence ministries, courts, parliaments and parties may live on as reliquaries, but under globalization the privatized and corporatized affairs of the world will be in the hands not of states but of financial markets. According to this picture, it is not only the states of Europe and their publicly accountable governments that are surplus to economic requirements, but the EU as well. It too is a hidebound impediment to a globally integrated world economy.

The impression given by globalization of a force of nature even less governable than Machiavelli's *fortuna* suggests the futility of states trying to erect 'dykes and embankments' in its path. Yet the international economy that presently exists depends umbilically on underpinnings and organization provided by states. Many of these are commonplaces that escape attention. The frameworks that surround the world-wide exchanges of goods and services and go some way to monitor and supervise the 'international economy' compose an assortment of multilateral organizations and less formal gatherings. The repertoire includes the IMF, the World Bank, the WTO and the Organization for Economic Co-operation and Development (OECD), as well regular meetings between small numbers of states notable for their wealth. There are in addition growing links between regional bodies like the EU, the Association of South-East Asian Nations (ASEAN) and Asia Pacific Economic Co-operation (APEC). Diverse as these acronymous agencies are, their most instructive feature extends beyond involvement in the world's increasingly connected economic affairs. They share that interest with stock markets, foreign exchanges, banks, companies, investors, and anyone at all affected by what money will do. The most significant aspect of the cluster of organizations mentioned is also their most obvious. Without exception they are composed of states and are answerable to these bodies, who collectively make up the diplomatic system. Those like the IMF and the World Bank that have influential bureaucracies and exercise powers of decision without direct reference to the wills of member states, nevertheless operate under their auspices and depend on states for the bulk of their funds. Although neither is entirely in the pocket of the USA, both form part of America's post-war scheme designed to spread its own economic practices as far abroad as its powers extend. If organizations created to regulate the workings of foreign trade and support market capitalism exercise only modest powers, and have limited influence on economic events, the lack of overall system reveals how circumspect states are in yielding authority. The long hauls of the General Agreement on Tariffs and Trade (GATT) rounds that are associated with a prodigious growth in world trade were diplomatic events conducted on behalf of states who laboriously negotiated in traditional fashion. National interests had to be brought into alignment, and although the WTO (established at the conclusion of the Uruguay round of GATT) has unprecedented powers of obligatory arbitration, its existence highlights the role of states in the world's economic affairs. The objective of less inhibited trade that brought states to the negotiating table did not imply that power politics were in abeyance. Globalization may similarly illustrate the increasing dependence of world-wide markets on rules and regulations that depend for their formulation and application on the diplomatic system. The effect of a more integrated world is to make the good ordering of market capitalism too important to be left to chance, or to providentially reliable hidden hands. Nor does increasing attention to one area of concern mean that states are about to ignore or sacrifice their other national interests. Globalization represents a new field for foreign affairs, not their disappearance into markets.

Where it exists, the 'international peace and security' necessary to the confidence of markets is the achievement of diplomacy not markets. The laws that protect property, persons and contracts, without which buying and selling would be quirkishly risky, are among the most irreplaceable contributions of states to economic life. For all the ability of financial markets to punish government mismanagement and ill-conceived policies, they in turn depend on regulations administered by the central banks of countries. Where national laws and international agreements prove defective or are themselves wrongheaded, it does not follow that the money markets of the world are capable of operating in a political and diplomatic vacuum. Although a multiplicity of states each with its own laws and economic policies may be a cumbrous way of developing a global economy, a world without the means of laying down rules for the conduct of wealth creation would be unlikely to provide a surer foundation. The remarkable thing is how far international law, backed by the interests of powerful states, has succeeded in establishing conditions that for the most part states find it in their interests to uphold. A world where freer trade is espoused in conjunction with the denationalization of state-directed economies makes deregulated business and multinational companies even more reliant on a reliable regime of law that only states can enforce. Companies that are co-operating with the riparian states of the Caspian Sea, and competing with each other to exploit oil and gas resources, are unlikely to invest large sums in the area until they are persuaded that contracts entered into are worth more than the paper they are written on. The essential legal conditions upon which economic undertakings rely are not only the product of trustworthy government; they are as precariously fragile as the stability of states. Laws, economies and governments are only as durable as the actions of rulers and ruled that maintain them.

While impinging on the powers of states to manage national economies in isolation, globalization furthers the need for secure diplomatic conditions favourable to the activities of markets. The interest of states in the diplomacy of market capitalism does not, however, lead to the conclusion that foreign affairs are about to become identified with a single preoccupation. The wealth of nations is one of the spurs to ambition. Like all power it is a means as well as an end. Although economic prosperity cannot divorce itself from the diplomatic system, the essential purpose of the latter is national interests in the broadest sense. Countries that exercise most influence in formulating rules of foreign trade have interests that extend beyond the cultivation of wealth. The USA, which played so important a part in designing the WTO, is first and foremost a superpower whose abiding interest lies in the global balance of power. The clutch of states that compose the G7 grouping and who dominate the IMF and the World Bank are not 'economic powers' with horizons fixed exclusively on enrichment. Japan's coyness in asserting its national interest in the Asian balance of power is unlikely to reflect indifference to all but market considerations. Its economic prowess is the means by which it proceeds diplomatically in a region still alarmed by Japan's earlier approach to power politics.

With a geographically truncated world in view, no economist or businessman would have designed a diplomatic system of the present historically derived makeshift kind. Adapting economic life to the oddities of political demarcations and human passions has, however, been the rule rather than the exception. Like philosophers, market capitalists have never been in a position to lay down conditions of their choosing. The coal and iron deposits of north-west Europe that suggested they should be exploited in common, were developed in defiance of geological and economic logic by Germany, France and Belgium. The apparent oecumenical triumph of market capitalism in the wake of the Cold War does not imply that a multitude of states that often frustrates 'the markets' is about to be refashioned to fit in with globalization. Although diplomatic and military muscle is not the most obviously systematic foundation on which to decide what medicine is necessary for the economic health of the world, great powers are unlikely to commit hara-kiri merely because the primal nature of their power politics disturbs economic calculations. The effect of globalization is more likely to be the determination of great powers to ensure that wherever decisions affecting their interests are at stake, they will place themselves to act on their own behalf. If for the moment the effect of unwarlike power politics among the great powers is to fix attention more on the WTO than the NPT, it is not a matter of surprise that China and Russia want admission to the former. Even more important than the desire to benefit from participation in a world-wide trading regime is the need to gain a say in the WTO's powers of decision. The rules by which a global economy is run will be determined less by economic reasoning than by power politics.

## IV

Prominent as it is in matters of war and peace, and in providing the setting in which states seek to profit from the boundless energies of a world economy, the diplomatic system is unable to underwrite stability with anything approaching certainty. It is an 'aggregation' of states not the sovereign master of its components. Conflicts having little to do with productive economic activity disrupt the peace and bedevil markets. Civil wars like that in Afghanistan and the wars of secession that destroyed Yugoslavia frequently find outside powers at odds. Investors and markets take fright at the spectacle of political disorder. Even where the great powers collaborate to maintain peace, circumscribe conflicts, and co-operate in the G7, combined efforts are no guarantee that actions will be adequate to dyke and embank the flow of events. Although the USA acted to prevent the Yom Kippur war of 1972 from spreading, its undoubted might was unable to control the economic dislocations that involved a fourfold increase in the price of oil. As one of Machiavelli's fellow diplomats wrote to him in the course of negotiations, 'I arrange my affairs hour by hour, because the times are more powerful than our brains'.[8] Our powers of setting events in motion repeatedly outstrip the ability to control their consequences. Scientific inventiveness and economic demands for its products compound this dilemma.

Nor does the absence of war and civil upheaval, leave markets to their otherwise untroubled ways. Capitalism which like nothing before it generates wealth, thrives on competition, innovation and risks, all of which excite passions, court uncertainty and make a virtue, or at least a profit, from unpredictable behaviour. Even where growth is not disturbed by cyclical distempers, economic rivalry provides a disorderly torrent of material for power politics. The desire of states to control resources like energy and water and to secure commercially important trade routes on land and sea, is set to be intensified by the effects of globalization.

The willingness of states to support agreed macroeconomic policies, and promote bodies like the IMF and the WTO, may thus be to the good without being good enough. Even the closest diplomatic co-operation within the G7 may fall short of what is needed to persuade rulers and ruled in some Asian countries to adjust their economic, political or military habits. If globalization is proceeding at the rate believed, agreement, that financial markets need more vigilant policing by governments may, even if feasible, amount to plugging one hole while computerized technology makes breaches elsewhere. Global markets that multiply opportunities in parts of the world mired for centuries in poverty cannot be relied upon to sift from their activities unwanted and dangerous consequences. Tourism which is now the largest industry in the world, and would seem to confirm the humanizing hopes voiced by Voltaire and Cobden, may turn into as much of a cursed source of pollution and friction as of wealth, pleasure and cross-cultural amity. Although the resolution of this kind of issue may yet illustrate the wisdom of leaving solutions to self-interested markets, the same argument can hardly be applied to something like global warming. Along with deforestation, overfishing, species extinction and profligate consumption of finite resources like water, the emission of greenhouse gases confronts the entire world – or so we are currently instructed – with public issues that only a global standpoint can resolve. Terrorism and crime, along with other topics alluded to earlier, should perhaps be added to the litany.

It is possible that in connection with global warming, which derives directly but only cumulatively from the desire for betterment, Hegel's 'cunning of reason' has devised diabolical means of bringing humanity to its common senses. Plenty of NGOs with memberships that disregard states and nations have organized to persuade publics throughout the world that unless 'sustainable development' is adopted as the credo of a globalizing world, the earth will cease to be a place where human beings can be at home. Is not this the occasion to drop power politics and bypass states who are notoriously equipped to act only in the interests of sliced-up portions of humanity? While one of the aims of pressure groups is to galvanize citizens, their principal target is states. This is itself enough to indicate the incorporation of global warming into the business of the diplomatic system.

At Rio de Janeiro in 1992 the stage was held by the 108 heads of state and government who agreed that they must act to 'save the earth'. Naturally enough the agreed way to do this was to proceed by means of diplomacy. The failure of most states to fulfil their Rio promises did not hinder the assumption that the next conference at Kyoto would again assemble a large portion of the diplomatic system, whose members would once more represent their national interests while seeking to accommodate the demands of others. Rather than rising to an occasion said to affect the whole globe, and the well-being of future generations, negotiations displayed no such levitational impulse. They demonstrated instead the persistence of power politics. And since the assembled diplomats and specialists were largely the envoys of states, one should not perhaps be taken aback that national interests rather than the fate of the earth were the centre of attention. For reasons of its own, the EU sought to establish binding targets to reduce emissions, whereas the USA, with its own interests to safeguard, chose a more flexible measure based on market principles and traded quotas. Because rich countries account for 75 per cent of carbon emissions, poorer ones resented the argument that they too should make cuts. Calculations were then presented indicating that by 2020 'have-not' states would produce half of the expected pollution. In reply, developing countries charged rich parts of the world with seeking to arrest their industrial progress, reminding Europeans and Americans of past industrial malfeasance, and how the greatest of all pollutants is poverty. Criticism was heard from the US Senate that if poor countries were allowed to proceed free of constraints, cost-conscious companies would decamp to areas unaffected by restrictions on emissions. Employment in the USA would thereby suffer. Western countries were then diplomatically invited to bribe 'emerging economies' not to follow in their own polluting footsteps.

The moral of this episode in the affairs of a rapidly globalizing world whose diplomatic organization is the reverse of a polity, is revealing. Despite the unprecedented nature of the topic, which only scientists can fathom, in almost all other respects the bargaining had an entirely familiar ring to it. Although armies were not sent on manoeuvres, proposals and counter-proposals were submitted with national interests in mind. As with most other operations of the diplomatic system this was the criterion of acceptability. A tolerable outcome needed to be agreeable to all the principal participants. It also follows that where states nevertheless fail to cut back on the emissions agreed to at Kyoto, few penalties will follow. The domestic laws passed by states in order to implement their foreign undertakings, will be applied by national governments with their own business, employment and other interests in mind. Since the USA is a superpower, little can be done by other members of the diplomatic system about its unmatched squandering of the earth's resources. And because it cannot be held accountable to other states for its economic habits, trying to restrain global warming against the wishes of the USA (by, threatening it with sanctions, for example) would be futile. Letting off diplomatic hot air is unlikely to improve the earth's atmosphere because, as with other aspects of globalization, global warming is hostage to global power politics. Should, for its part, the EU wish to implement more severe reductions of greenhouse gases, this too will expose the limitations of even virtuously self-interested example. If global warming cannot be halted at Europe's borders, the only effective means of protecting its interests is to muster and exert what powers of persuasion it can. Here as elsewhere the solution lies not beyond or in defiance of power politics, but by means of them. In order to influence Washington, Tokyo, Moscow, Beijing, Delhi, Brasilia and Jakarta, the EU will be have to be more cogently influential than is likely to result from merely harmonizing fifteen supplicant voices.

The diplomacy of greenhouse gases illustrates how solutions to the unwanted effects of industrialism, market capitalism and their universal extension, are bounded by the diplomatic system. Fears aroused by the side-effects of globalization do indeed ignore the territorial jurisdiction of states, but remedies designed to allay them reinforce the centrality of states. Problems that cry out for decisive action, and which defy the powers of individual states, do not lead to the conclusion that the species is dispensable. The need for co-operation between states exemplifies their position in world affairs. The powers of decision available to states may be no match for the 'violent rivers' of industrialized global markets, but as matters stand they remain the only bodies equipped to construct 'embankments and dykes' to channel them.

## V

An integrated global economy requiring only the expertise of 'technical' management would leave undisturbed quite separately compelling reasons for the existence of states. These have little to with the argument that a global version of the US Federal Bank would constitute a centre of power which would need to be appointed, replenished and held accountable. States with no part in supervising a body of experts, but who were none the less subject to its edicts, would retain other, perhaps more important, reasons for preserving themselves. Instrumental as they are in safeguarding markets by making and maintaining law and by sustaining the conventions of the diplomatic system, states value themselves for reasons unconnected with their utility. The primary purpose and justification of the state does not lie in its functional relation to the international economy or to its diplomatic undergirding, or indeed to anything beyond itself. Although the desire of rulers for self-governing states long predates modern collective demands for national self-determination, there is little doubt that nationalism is largely responsible for the size and global dispersal of the diplomatic system. Most twentieth-century states assert their existence in shocking defiance of anything that could be described as 'economic viability'. Even if the freer trade and reduced costs associated with globalization now tend to favour small states, that is not the explanation for the existence of 87 countries with populations of under five million.[9] The Irish Republic was not created in obedience to the postulates of an economic drawing-board. States derived from the collective make-believe of nations do indeed care about their prosperity, but although their rulers and ruled are not indifferent to the logic of markets, that does not persuade them to become vehicles of only productive gain. Europe's empires were cast off because they represented alien rule.

It is difficult therefore to see why globalization should undermine the rationale of political bodies whose ultimate justification is unconnected with economic computations. Were economic sense and good government conditions of self-government, nearly all the states of the world would fail the test. What is the functional or instrumental point of being a small state in a diplomatic system dominated by large powers? Or even of straining to be a great power, only to find that one is compelled to share the field with bodies of comparable and often rival capacities?

Only if it can be persuasively argued that global capitalism is generating a universal 'shape of life', to which national and religious attachments are becoming subordinate, can one conclude that a state-centred world is being reformulated. There is nothing implausible in claiming that in times when change straddles the world, its means of government is likely to figure among the alternations. The power of financial markets is sometimes cited as evidence that governments and economies are now the playthings of forces greater than they, but to emphasize the ability of markets to detect and punish weaknesses, side-steps an important consideration. The financial hubs of the world whose daily turnovers dwarf even the largest economies, are situated in states whose governments and central banks regulate stock markets and foreign exchanges. They thus maintain legal orders without which risk-taking would be improvident. The debt deflation suffered by Thailand, Indonesia and other Asian countries followed the exposure by ever wakeful financial markets of defects associated with government connivance in unsustainable banking practices. Demands by the IMF, the USA and Germany for greater distance between governments, banks and their industrial clients imply not that banks and financial markets should be left entirely unregulated, but that they should be made subject to stringent laws that prevents governments and their favourites from interfering in decisions affecting which companies get loans. Requirements of this kind, for more robustly independent regimes of law, can only be made good by states with enough constitutional authority to place both governments and markets under their rule. The need to police the operations of globalized markets thus appears to necessitate less government involvement in the direction of economies, but vigorous action by constitutional states to ensure that judiciaries and banks are independent of rulers. This in turn requires more robust, not weaker, states.

The claim to detect a politically unified world sprouting in the compost of globalization is also inclined to favour the argument that free and deregulated markets turn out free and independent men. Conveniently passing over differences between liberalism and democracy, it is then intimated that world democracy is implicit in world-wide markets. One impediment to this line of advocacy is that in a century that has seen the multiplication of self-governing states there is little sign of an incipient global *demos*. The most secure democracies are rooted in the discriminating and bounded fellow-feelings of nations. The mutual recognitions that bind some people together and urge them towards political self-determination cannot avoid fragmenting or at least diversifying, the world. Nor is it evident that, even where global markets are universally popular, this is producing corresponding 'resemblances' and 'similitudes' transcending all other attachments. The widespread availability of Coca-Cola, Big Macs and Hollywood films has not weaned peoples away from their own desires. Just as law is valued not only because it protects property and secures markets, but also because it upholds dignity and makes justice realizable, so states are both useful and their own sufficient ends.

Powerful states may be better able to provide for both aspects of Aristotle's distinction between the preservation of life and the promotion of the good life, but if the *authority* of states rested wholly on their *powers,* small states would presumably all be impotent tyrannies. As it is, all states, whatever their size and powers, are obliged to adapt to circumstances beyond their control. Not even the USA with a defence budget of $250 billion can secure itself against terrorism, the traffic in drugs, illegal immigration, or impose a peace settlement on the small and fractious states of the Middle East. The far from limitless powers of states, which globalization is said to encroach upon yet further, is not, however, evidence that the species is about to succumb to global markets. Where it is sought, the authority to govern is not derived from claims to omnipotence any more than the touted sovereignty of states is impaired by the fact that small and weak countries are no match for great powers, or for the financial markets of the world. The juridical and constitutional sovereignty that indicates where the authority to make laws is located is no defence against the powers of equally sovereign bodies, some of whom will be stronger than they. A state lacking all powers of decision would doubtless forfeit its authority in foreign affairs, though even here exceptions can be found. During the Second World War, several countries occupied by Germany maintained governments-in-exile in London that retained the allegiance of far-off citizens. It has taken a generation of systematic Chinese persecution in Tibet to undermine the theocratic authority of the exiled Dala Lama.

The grounding of states in men's passions as well as in their mundane needs and worldly ambitions, suggests that governments and governed share powerful reasons for exerting their political separateness. The incentive to perpetuate themselves, which amounts to the first axiom of states, does not of course imply they are immutable or providentially destined to survive. Reasons for their persistence do, however, caution against ideas that globalization is about to sweep all before it, and that the development of globally deregulated markets will be followed by the dismantlement of states.

## VI

If large numbers of states seem set to endure, representing diverse forms of authority and magnitudes of power, this is all that is required to perpetuate the treadmill of power politics. It is the unremitting activity of states to preserve themselves and uphold their interests, to acquire powers and constitute them as authority, that keeps the diplomatic system in being and in agitated motion. In addition to the abilities of states to spread law and order, and satisfy demands for self-government, they enjoy other advantages denied to even the largest multinational companies and the most extensive markets. Not all the rewards go to flexibility and nimbleness of foot. The ability to transfer money and capital instantly throughout the world, and site businesses wherever conditions are propitious, has to be set against the benefits of fixity of place. Legal authority over a parcel of territory is an important source of control over the conduct and mobility of persons and organizations. By the beginning of this century most of the earth's surface had been politicised, and since then vast tracts of sea and airspace have been claimed by states. The gas and oil deposits that excite multinational companies lie within the jurisdiction of states. Countries fortunate to own valuable mineral, energy, timber and water resources are not in a weak position because they need foreign companies to extract, transport and market them. Saudi Arabia, which is one of the more fictive states and no advertisement for constitutional government, is nevertheless able to lay down the law to oil companies and secure its position in the favours of the USA. Territorially mapped resources which make the fortunes of global companies, also sustain the diplomatic position of more than one constitutionally dubious regime.

While the control of territory, resources and persons by states can hardly be denied, it is possible to interpret these powers as fading assets. In a world technologically dismissive of political boundaries, raising the aura of government over slabs of real estate can be portrayed as being as comically futile as tilting at windmills. However much they brandish their laws and armaments, neither large nor small states can stem the circumambulation of news, opinion and information in words, figures, images and sounds. Cyberspace is boundless. Yet because not every liberation is evidence of freedom, the unfettered dispersal of 'information' is not universally applauded as the sundering of Leviathan. Nor are states helpless in the face of science and technology. What now passes under the umbrella heading of information has been of close and systematic interest to governments since long before satellites were placed in orbit.

The intimate links between the government of opinion and the government of people has been well understood since rulers first commanded subjects. Rulers habitually wish to school the thoughts and feelings of the ruled because subjects and citizens who are of one mind with those who govern them are likely to be pliable. Although totalitarian regimes of the twentieth century developed this aspect of rule with novel administrative brutishness, democracies are far from indifferent to the opinions held by their citizens, producers and consumers. As electorates were being expanded throughout Europe, Disraeli noted that 'whenever is found what is called a paternal government, there is found state education. It has been discovered that the best way to ensure implicit obedience is to commence tyranny in the nursery.' A century later it is difficult to name any state whose government is not paternal in this sense, or any democracy whose political parties do not vie with each other to promote a national, if not secular, education. Businessmen implore governments to produce a disciplined and educated citizenry able to be of use to them in markets in need of cerebral know-how. As de Tocqueville predicted however, the expression of educated opinion is hedged about by more than government fears of unruly citizens and the needs of businesses for employable workforces. Freedom of speech is attuned to what pleases and repels the will of the majority, to whose alternating feelings no elected government can afford to be unresponsive.

There is nothing inherently liberal about democracies, and the desire of rulers and ruled to shepherd opinion is a powerful inducement to states to equip themselves with technically apposite means. The present reputation of the increasingly global media as beyond the control of governments may be no more than a temporary shift of advantage in a protracted tug-of-war that states are by no means bound to lose. In rich countries, governments promote science and improve technology partly in order to keep up with entrepreneurial efforts to stay ahead of, and beyond, regulation. As the Internet perhaps suggests, the race between the hare and the tortoise is an unconcluded contest. The Manhattan project, missiles, satellites, space and surveillance technology, as well as Chemical Bacteriological and Radiological (CBR) weapons, all demonstrate the ability of states to extend and apply universal knowledge for purposes of enhancing the powers of government. In Britain, residential areas as well as markets are inceasingly subject to Closed Circuit Television surveillance (CCTV) which uses policing techniques based on technologies similar to those employed to transmit news and business information. Collusion between rulers and ruled in the use of CCTV, in order to improve security, supplies the state with Orwellian powers sanctified by public opinion.

For every innovation that astounds the world with its frontier-defying feats, there are equally resourceful developments engineered by states for civilian as well as military purposes. The USA is in the forefront of both market-led technologies reputedly binding the world together, and the advancement of science for reasons of state. Where one state leads, competitors and rivals are soon likely to follow. While research and development promoted by businesses is transforming the world into an economic whole, the same bodies of knowledge used to further global markets are being pursued by elected governments to substantiate their powers.

## VII

There is one line of reasoning that steadfastly believes globalization offers a unique opportunity to understand and direct events without resort to politics and power politics. If the driving force of globalization is science and technology, does it not become feasible to seize upon their characteristics to plan the future. Since science makes the world measurably explicit, and as economic change becomes increasingly the creature of exact knowledge, surely it is at last possible to rescue public affairs from the fumblings of politics and the disorderly agitations of foreign affairs.

This is of course to refurbish the dream, or nightmare, of a science of human affairs in which *fortuna* has submitted to systematic knowledge and foolproof administration. Musings of this kind are misconceived because the prominence of science and technology in the elaboration of a global economy does nothing to transform politics and diplomacy into tributaries of the natural sciences. Whereas nature is governed by cause and effect, the poles of human action are set by passion as well as reason, calculation but also imagination, principle along with prejudice. To obscure the differences that mark the inexactitudes of human affairs is to make it more difficult to bring conduct within civilized bounds at the very time when globalization is making it necessary to do so. Neither genetic engineering nor climate control is a scientific or economic problem. The desire to unload on to science and economics the unwanted burdens of deliberated action is to limit the powers of decision that the diversity of human abilities make possible. Harbouring the pretence that a safe and reliable route exists that avoids the need to decide politically and diplomatically upon the alternatives raised by globalization, is to indulge a yet more dangerous misunderstanding for which Europeans already have a noted weakness. The temptation is to believe that quantifiable information offers the technical means of extracting power from politics and diplomacy. Were this will-o'-the wisp credible, Europeans would, with wondrous simplicity, be saved from the ambiguities resulting from their post-war internal reformation and from the need to adapt themselves to a globalized diplomatic system.

No promise, or threat, of this kind is, however, to be found in the offerings of globalization. The prospect is more mundane. Rather than divest human affairs of their prickly inconclusiveness, science and technology have already invested the public affairs of the world with their own demons. As the advent of nuclear weapons illustrates, this has led not to the replacement of power politics by the kind of detached scientific management imagined by Saint-Simon at the onset of the industrial revolution, but to nuclear deterrence and a diplomatic system suffused with the disorderly effects of systematic knowledge.

The effect of changes associated with globalization is that Europe cannot prepare itself for only a single future because it is impossible to draw up even a trustworthy short-list of what the world's tomorrows will be like. Unable to *know* what action to take in times of acute change, the prudent, (if wearisome) response is to remain politically alert to as many eventualities as lie within one's powers. For the EU and its peoples to trust in the course of events, or rely on others to protect their interests, is to forgo the chance to shape the world.

## Notes

1.  Niccolo Machiavelli, *The Prince* translated by George Bull (Harmondsworth: Penguin, 1961), Ch. XXV, *How far human affairs are governed by fortune, and how fortune can be opposed,* p.130.
2.  Ibid.
3.  Ibid.
4.  Ibid.
5   Ortega Y Gasset, *The Revolt of the Masses* (London: Allen & Unwin, 1932), p.29.
6.  Voltaire, *Philosophical Dictionary* translated with an Introduction by Peter Gay (New York: Harvester 1962), p.482.
7.  The discussion by Paul Hirst and Grahame Thompson in *Globalization in Question* (Polity Press 1996) is to the point.
8.  Quoted in Quentin Skinner, *Machiavelli* (Oxford: Oxford University Press, 1981), p.16.
9.  *The Economist*, 3 January 1998.

# 4 Powers of Decision

I

The forces busy binding the world together are not thereby binding up its divisions. The wealth that market capitalism creates and spreads generates much else besides, and the sociability implicit in globalization is no guarantor of solidarity. Rousseau's cardinal observation was that mutual dependence in confined circumstances stimulates conflict. Proximity is a recipe for friction and it is to put paid to the wretchedness this occasions that government of almost any kind comes as a relief. Although he wrote before industrialism and improved communications produced the great concentrations of modern urban life, the dense policing that is now a commonplace of large cities suggests he was right to urge that living huddled together in large numbers results in living under powerful government. Perhaps because cities are fulcrums of wealth and imaginative activity, they need most ruling. Abrasiveness and creativity are disorderly.

Rousseau was also unusual in casting beyond the powers of decision necessary to domestic order to consider the external consequences of government. It is here that his clear sightedness remains of value to a world dominated by the rule of powerful states but increasingly subject to proximities produced by globalization. 'The independence which is removed from man' Rousseau wrote, 'takes refuge in societies; and those great bodies, left to their own impulses, produce collisions which grow more terrible the more their weight takes precedence over that of individuals'.[1] To quell internal disorder, governments accumulate powers of decision, and are gratefully elected for doing so by citizens and markets whose principal fear is lawlessness. The consequence of domestic pacification is to magnify conflicts between states. The powers acquired to suppress internal disorder find expression in foreign affairs. As increasing numbers of states co-exist in ever more densely peopled diplomatic space, so their mutual relations become infected with antipathy. Closeness kindles wariness which in turn necessitates, or at least justifies, measures of precautionary insurance. Once set in motion, mistrust feeds upon itself and becomes contagious. Once armies settled down within arms' length of each other, the alliance that fought its way to victory in the centre of Europe in 1945 became unhinged. Living head to toe rubs in the relativities of power.

77

What is true of family life is more lethally evident in the family of nations. NATO's impending eastwards expansion brings home to Russia its diminished sphere of influence and reduced powers of decision. American high-handedness rankles among some Europeans because it is so closely associated with their own truckling powers.

In telescoping the world, globalization can thus be seen to be mixing the ingredients of unsociability more solidly together. In turn, this has the effect of concentrating power in the hands of states best equipped and most eager to harness science and technology to their powers of decision. Globalized mutual dependence extends the powers of states on whom the rest of the world most heavily depends. As this becomes apparent, the privileges acquired by the most powerful arouse resentment. The links of power that bind the world together, and on which the international economy rests, are felt as chains of servitude by the weak and aggrieved. Because the inter-dependencies of globalized markets cannot be relied upon to gestate fraternity, the dominant position of powerful states confirms the arbitrary basis of foreign affairs. Goaded by the spectacle of superpower, the ambitions of aspirant countries go far to ensure the 'continued agitations' of power politics.

II

If the habits of power politics ingrained in a diplomatic system of states seem unlikely to be dispersed by globalization, the powers whose decisions carry most weight invite closer attention. Ungoverned as the great powers are, and disposed therefore to treat one another as rivals, mutual distrust does not preclude peace or rule out co-operation. Conflict may be endemic to the systematized disorder under which states choose to live, but for that very reason they respond to powerful impulses urging them to mitigate the most dangerous consequences of independence. Were states continuously at war, diplomacy would be no more than a verbal prologue to battle and the register of its outcome. Few rulers welcome such dire circumstances or expect to benefit from them. The element of system in the diplomatic system of Europe was the determination to limit and regularize, if not rule out, the occurrence of war. While on occasion Europe's great powers colluded to make war, formed rival alliances for the same purpose and, in the case of Poland, combined to dismember a state, their actions were equally notable for the way they co-operated to maintain a minimum of common order. Although the 'public law' of Europe presided over by the great powers did not ensure balance or equilibrium, the balance of power was neither illusory nor always ineffectual. What Metternich called *une pentarchie morale* maintained the peace of Europe for a generation after the Congress of Vienna. If Bismarck's diplomacy bequeathed to his successors a statecraft too nicely poised to endure, the breakdown of the balance of power in 1914–18 came after a century during which unprecedented change occurred without generalized war. The most vicious and prolonged fighting of the nineteenth century took place in the American civil war. The failure of the European balance of power in 1914 was unexpected and probably sought by none of its closely related principals.

For all their railings against the malpractices of Europe's power politics, Woodrow Wilson's successors have been willing to embrace alternative sounding possibilities like the League of Nations and the UN only under conditions that left the USA's powers of decision uncircumscribed. Despite possessing overwhelming advantages and visceral dislike of the idea, once the USSR deployed Inter Continental Ballistic Missiles (ICBMs) that exposed the civil population of America to nuclear bombardment, the government of the USA engaged in the necessary co-operation directly with its *frère ennemi*. The diplomacy of superpower arms control was an exercise between what Aron called 'enemy partners' in the arts of manipulating the despised balance of power, which demonstrated that conflict among states is capable of generating enough co-operation to make the world safe for power politics. The collaborative restraints that preserved the Cold War as a military misnomer were of course akin to the survival stratagems of scorpions bottled-up together; since neither could resist the other's weaponry, both had reason for self-control. The shared predicament of the USA and the USSR which induced mutual forbearance did not prevent both countries from searching with all their technological might for means that would give them the upper hand. Although nuclear deterrence is based on vulnerability, and therefore adds to the pronounced riskiness of power politics, it also exemplifies that being forearmed, fearful and threatening does not pose insuperable obstacles to diplomacy. Under some circumstances all are powerful inducements to negotiate. The difficulty lies in correctly judging the circumstances in which willingness to bargain is sound policy. Munich leaves a bad taste. The diplomatic clumsiness of the Cuban Missile crisis is unnerving. Yet the stuttering motives that persuade states to keep their conflicts within bounds are of less importance than the resourcefulness of *virtù* that is repeatedly thrust to the fore by the bald needs of survival. These hold even the mighty in their grip. The most powerful are not immune to fear.

However compulsive, the need of states to co-operate in order to save their skins cannot be relied upon to set in motion enduring diplomatic accommodations. Where the impulse to conciliate derives from necessity rather than choice, one foot forward does not make the advance irreversible. The marriages of convenience that litter diplomatic history are seldom long-lasting because alliances rarely proceed to the creation of political unions. Diplomatic agreement between great powers does not imply trust or prevent a temporary coalescence of interests from timely disavowal. Because diplomatic co-operation rests on the shifting ground of nationally assessed *raison d'état*, the unstable predicament of states is re-enacted and reinforced with every realignment within the diplomatic system.

The end of the Cold War was nevertheless greeted with more than temporary relief that a particular great power rivalry had been diplomatically concluded. Both the USA and the USSR had for a generation trumpeted their conflict as a tussle of might in the service of right. The failure of one of the protagonists to keep up with the other was therefore greeted by the victor as evidence of moral rather than Machiavellian virtue. Vindicated by its proven mettle, the USA inaugurated a 'new world order' wherein, for the third time this century, its heartfelt belief that co-operation among states could be made durable once again found expression. The inlaid distrusts of a diplomatic system of states were finally to be dispelled and with them the treadmill of power politics arrested and despatched to the past.

When however, the USA sought to enact reform of power politics, it found itself the prisoner of a dilemma made acute by the ascendancy of its own unrivalled power. When it tried to revitalize the UN as the instrument of world order, its own powers of decision crowded the stage. The more the USA encouraged the putative 'world authority' to promote active 'peacekeeping' operations, the more risks it ran that its own national powers of decision would be bounded by the wishes of other states. Having given the UN its head, the USA was carried along in directions that soon failed to square with its own national interests. As long as the UN did Washington's bidding this did not arise, but conflicts of interests soon occured. Investing other member states of the UN with some of its home grown authority confined the USA's own powers of decision. When the blue berets became embroiled in Somalia's civil wars, USA soldiers placed in the firing line were exposed to the consequences of disorderly lines of command and control reaching back to both the UN and Washington. As seen on American television, the body bags that mattered to mothers and fathers were those of USA citizens. The idea that they had been 'peace keepers' representing 'the international community' rang hollow. The operation was rapidly called off. Somalia exposed the fallacy of supposing that a diplomatic organization like the UN could act as a government representing the governed of the world. It registered the folly of believing that co-operation of the kind mustered at the UN is a transcendence of the power politics the organization exists to institutionalize. Once the USA called a halt to UN interventions, the Security Council was obliged to revert to its more credible and useful function as a standing diplomatic conference. In that capacity it allows and encourages the great powers to examine their mutual interests and, where they converge, authorize UN action in their names. The UN's powers of decision are those of its great powers.

Although the rhetoric surrounding of the UN dwells on the existence of a 'global neighbourhood', a 'common future' and an 'international community', the falsity of attempts to reconstitute the world merely by spraying graffiti on its torso is that the principal rhetors are the representatives not of universal humankind but the delegated envoys of states. When therefore the great powers signal willingness to co-operate within or beyond the UN, it is because they have concluded it serves their national interests. They are expressing a readiness to engage in diplomacy, not to set it aside or submit their countries to external government. Even if the UN's existence contains a summons to states to think and act beyond the confines of their self-serving interests, it possesses scant powers of decision able to bring that about.

The habits of power politics installed in the UN have migrated with similar ease to regional groupings of states, whose titulars form a lengthy appendix to the diplomatic system. Some, like the Arab League, the Organization of African States (OAS), ASEAN and the Council of Europe, are seasoned associations of states with the independence of their members as the reiterated basis of co-operation. They exist to encourage diplomacy among like-minded states without infringing upon their equal standing or impairing individual freedom of action. Several more recently created gatherings, such as the North American Free Trade Area (NAFTA), MERCOSUR and APEC, are principally concerned with the promotion of trade, and it is this particular spawning that has suggested that something of unusual importance is happening in foreign affairs. After the furious growth in the numbers of states that accompanied the end of colonial empires, and the more recent disbandment of the USSR, the diplomatic system is seen as undergoing a phase of consolidation. Like a concertina expanded to its limits, it is now drawing in upon itself. It has even been suggested that the EU is the model and stimulus for this region-alized inhalation. A more wide-ranging conjecture sees in geograph-ically concise groupings a crucial missing link between the general proliferation of states of all sizes and descriptions, and the coming together of a global 'international community'.

As soon as the picture of a shorter chain composed of larger links is outlined, a contrary, more cautious interpretation of the same devel-opment is forthcoming. The partial consolidation of a fragmented world into fewer though more cogently organized regional bodies of states will, it is said, 'produce collisions which grow more terrible' as the weight of their aggregated powers is added to foreign affairs. The spectre perhaps is that of Orwell's *1984* where three constellations of compacted power, Oceana, Eurasia, and Eastasia are locked in con-flict reminiscent of Hobbes' interminable 'war of all against all'. It would, however, be wrong to describe the plethora of loose-knit groupings of states as if for the most part they were like NATO. Their hallmark is not military alliance under a dominant power, but diplomatic and economic advantage compatible with the full authority of states. If that is so, very little can be said with exactness about the future of regional bodies. Advocates of global free trade fret that the EU, NAFTA and so on will undermine the WTO, questioning thereby whether regional free trade is not a misdescription of protectionist partiality. Combinations of states can hardly avoid discriminating against outsiders since closer alignments among some cannot at the same time include all. Were the most formidable of regional groupings open to all states, including Russia, it would be difficult to see why NATO is needed at all. Why safeguard a house against burglars when all the possible felons are members of the family?

Although the mere existence of numbers of regional bodies does not imply enmity, they cannot escape becoming subject to the same cate-chism of diplomatic anxieties suffered by individual states. Like limb-less jelly fish, regional bodies trawl the same inhospitable waters as sharks. The more organized such organizations become, the more exposed they are to the vagaries of power politics. Where a regional body of states acts as one, other states and organizations will treat it accordingly. So long as the EU flounders in the shallows of foreign affairs, its shapeless exterior allows it to scuttle away when challenged too boldly. Faced with Croatia and Serbia, the EU revealed itself bonelessly inept and with no sting in its diplomatic antennae.

Without means of action, aggregates of states cause few ripples in the diplomatic system. They may help to keep the local peace among members and promote joint economic interests, without reordering the wider conduct of foreign affairs. Once the internal affairs of a regional body are constituted to exercise powers of decision, however, as with the EU, and these are thenceforward deployed externally, which thus far has been the sticking point for the EU, then the body in question becomes party to power politics. It ceases to be a mere forum for diplomatic co-operation between consenting members of the group, and becomes an actor. It becomes so by virtue of its powers of decision *vis-à-vis* other bodies. Once actively involved in foreign affairs, a regional body with powers of effective decision falls victim to the conditions under which a diplomatic system operates. With the tantalizing exception of the EU, which straddles the threshold, the diplomatic and free-trade groupings of states which have recently swum into view are not therefore political bodies. Russia hoped that the CIS would retain powers of decision but, like the British Commonwealth, it has lapsed into being a forum for anodyne discussion where national differences are diplomatically shunned. The Conference of Islamic States seems to operate in a similar way. When, however, the EU holds meetings with ASEAN and other regional gatherings, a significant difference is observable. The fifteen states form a single delegation, which also includes the Commission. In this respect, and for purposes usually limited to trade, on these occasions the EU becomes more than the sum of its parts, even though the parts are decisively present. In the eyes of ASEAN members, they are dealing with the single entity of Europe.

To those schooled in 'spheres of interest', regional groupings are recognizable as the means by which great powers extend their influence without subjecting neighbouring states to government. Although NAFTA stands to benefit Canada and Mexico, as the hub of the enterprise the USA draws its partners ever more closely into its orbit. The same is true of NATO. The effect of a Free Trade Area of the Americas that included both south and north would substantiate USA power by consolidating its sphere of interest along roughly the same lines as the ones contained in the Monroe Doctrine. Once begun, it becomes tempting to examine every regional grouping for signs that a great power is busy harnessing other states to its ambitions. APEC appears of interest to the USA because it does not wish to be excluded from a gathering that otherwise might gravitate towards the ambit of China. The absence of client states stationed around Japan similarly suggests that its powers of decision are thereby limited. What to make of India's disinclination or failure to skirt itself with allies, associates, partners, co-operators? When the magnifying glass is placed over the misshapen anatomy of the EU, some detect first a French attempt to extend its sphere of interest, and then a more recent ploy of united Germany to clothe its extended powers in the garb of Europe. Bismarck found 'the word "Europe" on the tongue of those politicians who demanded something from other powers, which they did not dare ask for in their own name'.

The argument that restricted groupings feed, disguise, institutional- ize and justify the ambitions of large states can also be turned on its head. Instead of capaciously swallowing down adjacent states, strong regional powers can be portrayed as pivotal to the well-being of smaller fry. Shorn of USA protection, Europe would, it is said, be like a lobster without its carapace. Africa is said to lack an activating power able to impose a continental order conducive to economic development. Arab disunion is subject to similar comment. To the chagrin of brother countries and rival aspirants, Saddam Hussein proposes Iraq for the role of unifier. Brazil seems to meander in and out of contention as a great power in the making. Were it to exert itself and bring others, including Argentina, to accept its leadership, Latin America might be a power to be reckoned with.


III


As the diplomatic system of Europe was tailor made to suit the interests of its principal states, no mystery surrounds the privileged position enjoyed by great powers. In this respect the Cold War perpet- uated the most seasoned feature of power politics. Although, like its predecessor, the UN spelled out the equal independence and sover- eign equality of states, the five permanent members of the Security Council represent an all-important qualification of this principle. Great Powers proclaimed themselves more equal than others. Only those who wished to be hoodwinked by the UN Charter, or who were successfully deceived by governments, could mistake the continued hierarchy of the diplomatic system. A bi-polar world cleaved and paralysed the UN. Disavowals of immodest power soon gave way to a world commanded by a new class of continental superpowers, armed with weapons of mass destruction.

Although powers of nuclear decision were more starkly persuasive than the lofty terms of the Cold War, the 'ideological' conflict between the USA and the USSR was not uniquely given to misrepresentation. In public affairs hypocrisy – in the sense of feigning – is not the same as lying. The affairs of states cannot be subject to the same order of judgements that colour private and individual life. At whatever level it is found, power cries out for re-presentation. The 'private power' of parents over children is no exception. Love seeks to reconcile parental power with the naturalistic fact that children have negligible means of fending for themselves. In order to be justifiable the 'public' power of states has to be convincingly raised and re-presented as authority. The mannered aspects of war and diplomacy cultivated with such opulence by the states of Europe's *ancien régime* was made humanly necessary by the military rawness of power politics. To be morally and emotion-ally acceptable, power has to be imaginatively recreated. This can seldom be achieved merely through the persuasive devices of propa-ganda and public relations. It requires more than a stunt. Few can exercise or submit to power devoid of what Burke called 'the pleasing illusions, which (make) power gentle and obedience liberal'.[2] The 'decent drapery of life' is humanly essential to the civilization of power. 'Superadded ideas' Burke argued, 'furnished from the ward-robe of a moral imagination, which the heart owns, and the under-standing ratifies', were falsely condemned by those who saw in them only deceit. Although open to repeated abuse, the moral imagination that unites heart and head, is nevertheless necessary 'to cover the defects of our naked nature, and to raise it to dignity in our own estimation'.[3] The duplicity this encourages, which Machiavelli became infamous for suggesting should be exploited by rulers, does not mean that states, any more than individuals, can use their powers, or defer to the actions of others, divorced from a satisfying sense of their own 'estimation'. In a passage that rings true of Europe's heartless and unratifiable power politics after 1914, Burke adds that 'power of some kind, will survive the shock in which manners and opinion perish; and will find other and worse means for its support'.[4]

While unadorned power lacks civility, the 'pleasing illusions' needed to humanize it can hardly fail to pamper the powerful. The Cold War, which wore thin the beliefs used to superadd moral sentiments to superpower, is unlikely therefore to be the last occasion when the urge to lay bare power politics and reveal them for what they are stumbles into the requirement to acknowledge, rather than dismiss as worthless, the wardrobes of moral imagination. To represent foreign affairs as if the re-presentations of its activities are best ignored is to misrepresent power politics. When pressed too hard, the desire to puncture the suspect and frequently shoddy exterior of public actions in order to reach the hard core of their inner cores finishes up re-emerging from the opposite side having altogether missed their in-between reality. Once 'power' is severed from the actions which compose and direct it, its 'realism' becomes irreproachably unintelligible.

The human near impossibility of being clothed with powers of decision without 'affecting' the part, itself forces actors and audiences alike into dependence upon ploys of the moral imagination that often wilt under scrutiny. When Churchill, Stalin and Roosevelt met at Yalta in February 1945, it was not a 'private' gathering of personal acquaintances but a 'public' event of the utmost importance to the fate of Europe and Asia. It was nevertheless held in wartime secrecy behind closed doors. Without being seen by publics or questioned by their representatives, the powers of decision of the 'big three' were starkly indisputable. The same became true of the superpowers during the Cold War. Draped in the nuclear apparel that was mostly hidden from public sight in silos and beneath the oceans, the USA and the USSR towered 'visibly' above less fearsome Leviathans. At their heads stood two mortals representing countries responsible, though unaccountable, for the peace of the world.

When Khrushchev and Kennedy held a 'summit' in 1961 it was a gathering of only two. Britain had been relegated, though by what rigmarole of criteria and into what less august category was not made plain. What nevertheless stood out beyond any need of imaginative elaboration was the level to which USA and USSR had raised themselves by virtue of their novel powers of destruction. Since then China has undergone a contrary experience to that of Britain. It has crossed a threshold from being a power with much history, plenty of people and extensive territory, to a country, or civilization, whose potential is now concretized. No one, however, knows exactly (or can say with authority) what marks the threshold or what it takes to pass over it. At the same time as Russia was 'declining' and China 'rising', the position of the USA seemed to call for fresh superlatives to describe its unmatched powers. Perhaps it is because states are simultaneously manifestations of power and human entities shrouded in moral imagination that the exposition of power politics is often the plaything of resourceful nomenclators.

The bedrock like quality of states is not therefore all it seems. Their imputed 'concreteness' is no more unequivocally substantial than the assorted antics that weave them together as 'moral denominations'. Population, territory, resources, wealth, government, law, administration, military equipment, sentiments, interests, education, knowledge and ambitions may be itemized and collated as the 'raw materials' of states; but ingredients no more constitute a body politic than discrete portions of sand, cement, gravel and water demonstrate the existence of concrete. Until the raw materials have been puddled together a state has no identity or durable body, and hence no powers of decision. The 'elements' of the USSR did not decompose when it broke up. Until humanly activated, US superpower is an inert conglomerate. Although Europe lacks concretion because its component parts are already coalesced bodies, the difference between fully formed entities like effective states, and a creation like the EU, is not therefore as distinct or unbridgeable as may at first be supposed. What marks a state from a political union of states is only incidentally a matter of organization. The combining substance of political bodies is affective and imaginative. Their 'concrete' powers of decision are suspended in human attachments.

## IV

Great powers confer distinction upon themselves. Because this is so, the explanation of why certain countries belong to the most exclusive category of states becomes an exposition of power politics. No supervening authority or electorate composed of individuals exists before which states parade their claims. The qualifications that result in permanent membership of the Security Council, inclusion in the G7, or attendance at summit meetings, are not derived from reason, revelation, agreed rules, historical or economic deserts, but are the outcome of power politics. Entitlement is a matter of self-assertion vindicated by diplomacy. It leads to acceptance by a group of states whose existing members have already recognized each other's great power status. In the century of the common man, the method of oligarchic incorporation that establishes great powers and endows them with the privileges of power has more in keeping with the diplomatic system of the *ancien régime* than with the conventions of representative government.

In the European diplomatic system, decisions governing which countries counted as 'powers' was settled by the turn of events.

Success in war against an existing great power raised the victor to its level. The great powers of the nineteenth century all won their diplomatic spurs in battle: France at Rocroi (1643), Britain during the War of the Spanish Succession(1702–13), Austria at Zenta (1697), Russia at Poltava (1709) and Germany in 1866 and 1871. Much to its irritation, a question mark hung over whether Italy belonged within the fold of what Bismarck called the *europaischen Senioren concert*. After victory over Russia in 1904, Japan was inducted and classified upwards. Entry into the First World War clinched the USA's standing in the councils of the world. During the Second World War Churchill and Roosevelt clashed over whether France should still be included among the elite. The American verdict still rankles. Since Suez, Britain has found itself in the position earlier undergone by Venice, the United Provinces, Spain, Portugal, Poland, Sweden, Austro-Hungary, and the Ottoman Empire. With the passage of time all slipped in the rankings, or were driven from eminence, to have their august standing in 'the college of the states of Europe' prized from beneath them by the upwardly mobile exertions of ambitious rivals.

By playing down their military potential and playing up the generosity of their economic achievements, constitutionally reformed Germany and Japan have worked their passages back into the company of decisive powers. They are not, however, examples of some fanciful category of 'economic powers' whose prowess in the world's market places has replaced and outdated military power. Although it is in large measure because of their economic performance that both countries are able to court permanent membership of the UN Security Council, their aim is to achieve a recognized position at the centre of foreign affairs. Too much is at risk for the direction of world affairs to be left to the decisions of others. Despite a relative lack of economic success India claims that a country of its size and importance deserves a position in the diplomatic system comparable to China's. Once party to a superpower duopoly so manifestly exclusive it needed no further embellishment, Russia covers its present nakedness with whatever drapery can shield its plight. The diplomatic scurrying for place in the pecking order of states thus illustrates the rest of power politics. As long as states vie for position and covet the privileges of power, so the diplomatic system will remain a hierarchy of states.

Although countries of all capacities engage in them, foreign affairs register the actions and reactions that most agitate events. The diplomatic system of Europe which made room for a manifold of states of unequal size relied for its coherence on a handful of great powers of roughly equal strength. A familiar recitation of the balance of power pronounced that so long as no one power or combination was allowed to dominate the rest, the plurality (if not the peace), of the diplomatic system was preservable. At times this formula sounded like the operation of a system of diplomatics, with laws akin to those of mechanics. 'As long as the world is governed by the uncertain balance of power among five great powers' Bismarck wrote, 'all there is to policy may be summed up in the formula; try to be one of three'.[5] The twentieth century which covered the baldness of this equation with a variety of superadded international organizations and sought to discover fresh foundations for foreign affairs, did not banish great powers or diminish their importance. At Yalta, the alliance of the 'big three' represented what Bismarck had earlier called 'the only real protection against the rival combination of two'. The UN Security Council was designed to perpetuate, while clothing in 'decent drapery', the imbalance of power resulting from victory over the axis powers. When this alliance was rent in bi-polar rivalry, the far reaching effects of the Cold War stamped the balance of power between the USA and the USSR on close to half a century. The demise of one superpower has left the other in a class of its own. Its powers of decision are unbalanced.

Whether this eventuality is to be welcomed, endured, feared or countered is of great consequence to Europe. From Charles V and Louis XIV onwards, via Napoleon, Wilhelmine and Nazi Germany, and the USSR, the diplomatic system of Europe was bedevilled by efforts from within to dominate and overthrow it. At a time when globalization is said to make the rivalries of states dangerously dysfunctional, the incomparable power of the USA has been greeted as finally arresting the treadmill of power politics. Does not prudence suggest, especially to Europeans, that a *pax Americana* that spreads the virtues of the USA as well as its power, offer the best of a good bargain? A global *political* order raised in the image of the USA, and under its stabilizing direction, is surely, so it is urged, preferable to the haphazard disorders associated with a multitude of wilfully self-governing states. Governed by the USA, the world's affairs would beneficially cease to be power politics. Although the imposition of a *pax Americana* might be initially resisted, bit by bit it would, (so this line of reasoning proceeds) weather into authority and eventually find expression in law and other suitably magnanimous institutions. By way of illustration, the Roman Empire might be rescued from the mischievous historiography of a fragmented world. It would be suitably recalled that although achieved by conquest, the Roman Empire bequeathed the world an extensive juridical order. It transformed might into right. With no evident need for coercion or imperial rule, and with the entire world at its feet, has not the USA the chance to go three better?

There is no shortage of dissenting views to this image of the future. For those attached to their own states, to their own habits of thought and feeling, and willing to risk safeguarding them, the global hegemony of a single power, however benignly intentioned, represents too draconian a price to pay for order. Subordination to the will of Washington's *imperium* would place other rulers and ruled in vassalage. Without a balance of power, all but the USA would fear for their liberties.

Anxieties aroused by the exorbitance of US power are countered by the argument that they are misplaced by at least half a century. The USA's best chance of refashioning the world to please itself occurred in the decades immediately following victory over Germany and Japan, when the USSR was incapable of counter-balancing its industrial and military might. At the peak of its power, America declined to push home advantages that since the 1970s it no longer enjoys in anything like the same measure. Other powers have arisen to erode its once unchallengeable position. Despite the disappearance of its Cold War adversary, its own renewed economic vigour and enhanced military superiority, these developments have not, it is observed, established American omnipotence. Even though its superpower may for the time being be unbalanced by powers of comparable standing, numbers of other states exist and flourish, several of whom are, or could become, great and perhaps global powers. With plentiful reasons to prevent the government of their interests by Washington, China, Russia, India and perhaps the EU and Japan, represent weighty counter-influences to a single power's overmighty mastery of foreign affairs.

Europeans are reluctant to consider whether US power is to be feared as well as welcomed. Because of the Cold War, there remains aversion to the idea that what under one set of circumstances was desirable to the point of necessity might be made less so because the outcome of that conflict saw the emergence of a single superpower. Throughout the Cold War western Europe's governments beseeched the protection of US power and sensed that questioning their dependence might encourage American withdrawal. At greater historical distance than the events that gave rise to NATO lie memories that resurrect unresolved dilemmas about great powers and the need, or futility, of seeking to establish balance or equilibrium among them. The spectre of unbalanced power evokes the whole cast of modern European history. In that experience the ascendancy of a single power led to attempts to confine it. This often meant war and was not always successful. Even so it represents one thematic impulse in modern European history. William III's coalitions against Louis XIV were organized in defence of the 'liberties of Europe'. These liberties were attached not to individuals but to the states of Europe whose independencies were threatened by a 'universal monarchy' of the Bourbon kings of France. The same continued attachment to a diplomatic system representing a diversity of self-governing states is seemingly the fundamental explanation of Britain's and France's refusal to concede the dominance of Europe to Germany in 1914–18. The justification for the stalemated horror of the trenches was negative; to prevent one power overwhelming the rest. As it turned out, Britain and France were not strong enough, even in alliance, to quell Germany, and in the Second World War it was the Red Army of the USSR that repulsed Hitler's mastery of Europe. The USA moved to thwart the extension of Germany's grip only when it threatened, along with Japan, to produce a new global balance of power. The 'liberties' of western Europe, both individual and collective, were eventually salvaged by US power, at the cost of conceding their loss in eastern Europe.

In Europe's experience therefore, a diplomatic system has seldom for long been secure from designs to overturn it and replace plurality with enforced uniformity. From this angle, the EU can be viewed as a stratagem by the instigators and victims of Europe's power politics to negotiate themselves out of a centuries-old dilemma by creating a voluntary political union. This remedy to the 'internal' affairs of Europe's systematic disorders, at whose centre lay bloody contests for primacy, has had the unwanted but unavoidable effect of bringing its governments up against a global and luridly reminiscent replication of the essentials of their own historic predicament. Since the EU lacks the means to transform hundreds of states into a universal copy of its reformed self, it is implicated in the persistence of power politics, to whose enigmas its own more restricted and closely bound diplomatic system notoriously failed to find any lastingly peaceful conclusion.

If even in the shape of a *pax Americana* the idea of a 'universal monarchy' sticks in the historical throat of Europe, so equally do the self-destructive methods used to resist its imposition. Both impulses drum for attention, with neither able to win the argument or attract unequivocal support. What consummate good fortune, it might therefore be argued, that Europe's crucial external affairs are shouldered by a country to which it is related by so many affective resemblances and political similitudes that serious, let alone armed, conflict with it is unthinkable. Could any European, not bereft of his or her senses, contemplate opposition to the USA merely because its power appears so universally abundant?

Perhaps the good fortune extends further, and there is no conundrum to resolve. The USA is said to be a state unlike any other, a unique political body. The exceptional virtues incarnated in its constitutional and economic development are all the warranty other states need, or should prudently demand. The accomplishments that account for the rise of the USA to global power are, in this view, unlikely to become vices now that it has achieved unparalleled power. More instructive than its tutelary position is the democratic composition and generous disposition of America. American political virtue, not European nostrums of the balance of power, is the most reliable safeguard against the abuse of superpower. Never mind that, from before the time of Athens, the ambitions of great powers have swelled with success and encroached upon neighbours; the past that matters most to the present is the twentieth century. And in this century the USA's constitutionally bounded powers of decision have championed the rights of other nations and a world order designed to secure them. It has been the most redoubtable bulwark against the efforts of European and Asian states to impose their wills on other peoples by force. If this has inadvertently led to the position where it is now the indispensable bastion of the world, the lack of a so-called balance of power is more aptly described as the merciful absence of anarchy. Rare as it is in foreign affairs, where might and right seldom stand harnessed together, the appropriate response to US superpower is not to belabour the need for what Gentz called a 'system of equipoise', but to institutionalize and thereby anchor a fortunate scheme of world affairs.

America is its own most trenchant critic. It supplies cogent reasons for distrusting accumulated power, even where this appears married to principle. Suspicion of concentrated power, no matter how democratically derived, vitiates the Constitution of the USA. The separation of the various powers of government is safeguarded by the highest law of the land. In foreign affairs, the tussle between the White House and Senate that often hampers executive powers of decision is not an oversight. Between them, the Presidency and Congress jealously guard the external interests of the USA. There is, however, no evidence that either is ready to see their country's actions subordinated to a global equivalent of the American Constitution and its workings. The electorate of the USA is not about to settle for being a modest numerical portion of a world-wide *demos,* producing from within its sovereign body a universal executive. Were it needed, this would be sufficient reminder that the government and people of the USA remain attached to their own national powers of self-government and vigorously use them on behalf of American interests.

Like all great powers, and for reasons already touched upon, the USA is naturally driven to esteem itself as the purveyor of something of more lasting worth than power. Perhaps American exceptionalism lies in its constant need to furbish its actions with the products of its moral imagination. Its rulers and ruled continuously urge themselves to see their own interests enveloping rather than impairing those of others. Somewhere in Arthur Miller's *Death of a Salesman* Willie Lomax says of his brother Biff, 'he's liked but he's not well-liked'. The American desire for both self-approval and approval by others, is not, however, a prologue to disinterested action. Nor does the progress of the USA as a great power establish it in a uniquely virtuous category or free it from judgements that apply to other states. Despite rooted public distaste for the rawness of power politics, to which Protestant countries appear most susceptible, the longer the USA has figured at the centre of foreign affairs, the more its conduct has become recognizably similar to that of other great powers. Since its own national interest is the unvarying focus of interest, this is cause for neither surprise nor criticism. As a consequence however, power politics have cumulatively rubbed off on the country that has sought more than any other to transform them. The urge to reform and better while simultaneously exerting power on its own behalf, may explain the trajectory of US relations with the UN, whose moulding spirit America originally was. The present distemper of the USA with the organization reflects a determination, made explicit in Congress, to make the UN more amenable to US power, on pain of relegating the organization to the margins of events. The USA is not willing to defer to UN resolutions unless they reflect its interests. Yet like other 'universal' powers before it, the USA desires approbation for actions it is persuaded are also disinterested. In the clash with Iraq over inspection of its armaments, Clinton sought confirmation that USA actions embodied 'the will of the international community', intentionally or guilessly associating that expression with its own national interests.

In a way that sometimes causes alarm in Europe, the superpower of the USA is oudoubtedly exceptional. Many Americans appear unconvinced that their country must exercise it world-wide and without respite. The idea of a *pax Americana* is far from universally popular in the USA. Perhaps thanks to the deliberations of representative government, Americans may refuse to maintain order in the world. That the world's superpower may be too inactive in foreign affairs is thus as worrying to some as fears that the USA interferes too much in other people's business. The belief that the USA is somehow fated to hold the balance of power or make its weight felt in the scales wherever they tilt, is regularly contested in Congress. Instead of dominating power politics, and being thanked for its pains with accusations of self-aggrandizement, the USA is powerful enough to decide neither to act nor react to the continued agitations of world affairs – or so the impulse of isolationism fervently asserts. History and geography have favoured the people of America with 'dykes and embankments' that, exceptionally, allow it a choice that no continental European state can contemplate. With little need to fear the consequences, the USA is at liberty to withdraw into the continental or hemispheric expanse of its own affairs. Should it tire of the frustrations of foreign affairs, the USA's exceptional grasp of technology enables it to disregard them. In this view globalization is something of an advantage to business that imposes no need on the USA to be drawn into remote conflicts. In short, at the heart of America's indisputable might are powerful home-grown doubts about the prudence and worthwhileness of external exertion. Perhaps because it is a democracy notably less dependent on foreign trade than European countries, US superpower is supersensitive. When shifts occur in the gusts of public opinion, the weathervane of foreign policy registers the change of direction. Beckoned to Somalia by television coverage of suffering, the USA reacted with petulance when its good intentions were rebuffed as interference. Presented with body bags, as seen on television, American opinion concluded that the conflicts of far away African warlords were not worth the bones of its servicemen. US interests suffered no discernible damage from its fitful actions.

Examples of America's volatile *demos* sit awkwardly with the foregoing claim that the USA has been increasingly forced by the circumstances of power politics, to adapt itself to their demands. It has no monopoly on this dilemma. The difference however is that how America resolves its degree and form of engagement in foreign affairs directly affects the rest of the world. From the hangover of Cold

War habits, if no longer from necessity, Europe's security and collective peace of mind swing on the hinges of US foreign policy. How many American fatalities would it take in Bosnia, or elsewhere in the Balkans or Mediterranean, before Congress decided that Europe should clear up the mess in its own backyard? Because it is not possible to know with comforting certainty what the answers to these questions are, the effect is to rivet attention on the pivotal position of the USA. Whether the USA is, to adapt Kissinger's aphorism of German history, presently too weak or too strong for Europe and the rest of the world, is perhaps of less immediate importance than the realization that no permanent clear and precise answer to this question is ever likely to be available. With the Cold War no more, Europe has to face the prospect of a USA that at one moment is too powerful and at the next indifferent to EU concerns. The uncertainties of a superpower veering between action and inaction, for reasons that are an amalgam of national interest, principle, fitful public opinion, economic special pleading and government pique, is bound to compound the systematized disorder of the diplomatic system.

Even the extent of USA power is difficult to judge. Its tutelary power that appears so decisive in Bosnia, the Gulf and the straits of Taiwan, so persuasive in the IMF and the WTO and so central at the Kyoto Earth Summit, falls well short of omnipotence. If one could gauge precisely by how much the USA lacked the means and will to impose a *pax Americana*, the entire exposition of power politics, and perhaps their substance as well, would instantly and forever be altered. The exuberance and reach of US power is not for that reason proof that it is now absolute or even excessive. Universal as American influence is, the world has not been reduced to monarchical rule. Even were that to come about, no one can do more than conjecture whether the government and people of the USA would for long sustain the effort of rule.

The closest example of a country credited with sustaining a long period of widespread peace is the *Pax Britannica*. In the nineteenth century Britain's industrial and commercial power enabled its navy to patrol the sea lanes of the world. One sixth of the earth's inhabited surface for a time came under imperial sway. At the height of its influence, Britain's margin of power over other states was persuasive enough not to require repeated or protracted use of force. Commanding though it was, Britain's position in world affairs did not for long deter or contain challenges, and neither did the foreign office treat every shift in the balance of power as of equal importance. Although

Russian advances towards Constantinople were countered, the unification of Germany left London apparently unmoved by the rise of a continental power with means and desire to assert dominion. Only when Germany embarked on naval power and *weltpolitik* did Britain edge closer to alliance with France and Russia. When it did so, the principal concern of policy was not with the overall diplomatics of equilibrium, but with the circumstances best suited to preserve British power. Until the lights were already dimmed, the British cabinet remained undecided as to whether Belgium's neutrality needed fighting for, or indeed whether that was the central issue. During the Cuban Missile crisis of 1962 no one then alive could predict how Moscow and Washington would interpret their interests and gauge the risks. As superpowers, the USA and the USSR were transfixed by each other, not by any wider requirements of 'international peace and security'.

Whether in the aftermath of the Cold War the USA enjoys a more favourable position than Britain's at the close of the last century is more than intriguing. As with Britain's global empire, America's superpower is a goad to some and reassurance to others. China cannot be relied upon to resign itself to permanent inferiority to the USA in the Pacific any more than the USA is likely to remain indifferent to Beijing's actions. Although diplomatically gnomic, the suggestion that a 'large and proud country' like China will seek 'equality in strength with the strongest'[6] rings true and suggests an extended future for power politics. Should Russia recover from its present tribulations, this too will have the effect of generating new questions about its external ambitions, to which no bankable answers will be available. Were US power in the Pacific to waver, Japan would be compelled to decide where its exposed position left it in relation to China, Russia and Indonesia. If US interests in NATO faltered, the effect would be to place all the states of Europe on the spot. It is a matter for later argument whether this would be the making or the breaking of the EU.

It is those states or political bodies that are big enough and organized to 'act and react' in response to eventualities they can neither predict nor expect to control that have the best chance of turning the unforeseeable to their advantage.

## V

As rivalry among states is grounded in the arbitrary conditions of their enforced co-existence, there is little reason to believe that weapons of

mass destruction, globalization, or the science and technology implicated in both, are capable of suppressing power politics. Along with
fears for the earth as a place fit and just enough to be at home in,
considerations of this kind may nevertheless induce the great powers
to co-operate as never before. It is not inconceivable that China,
Russia, Japan, India, and perhaps the EU, would be ready to accept
the pre-eminent position of the USA and collaborate under its aegis.
Were that to occur it would remain necessary to call their co-operation
by its proper name. A concert of powers would represent an exercise
in power politics. If successful, it would be thanks to effective diplomacy. An achievement of this order would not support the supposition
that greets every act of co-operation among the great powers as
evidence that power politics are being attenuated into global politics.
The institutionalization of a cartel of powers in places like the UN
Security Council denotes neither the existence of a world polity, nor
moves to create one.

A concert of tutelary powers would require unblinkered attention to
the operations of power politics whose agitations are unlikely to be
calmed so long as large numbers of states value their separateness and
assert it. Nor can an oligarchy capable of bringing greater order to the
diplomatic system be counted on to survive or consolidate, merely
because its disunion is too scary to contemplate. The fears aroused
by the nuclear rivalry of the Cold War were not responsible for its
conclusion. Gorbachev wished to sustain a bi-polar world of nuclear
superpowers, albeit at lower levels of cost and risk. Faced in the future
with too forthright rivalry, the USA might be provoked into coercive
action or, if denied the support of allies, choose withdrawal into
hemispheric isolation. Contrariwise, a world too willing to accommodate the USA, might find itself forced to accept a definition of its
diverse interests refracted through the prism of a single national state.

Whatever its exact composition, a lopsided oligarchy of five or so
self-appointed powers could not be counted on to act as a government.
Their concerted actions would perpetuate the unconstitutional basis of
power politics. At any time, co-operation might give way to conflict.
Aware of this, great powers would insure themselves against the
eventualities of discord, feeding thereby the mistrust that set limits
to co-operation. A cartel of states, each retaining its great powers of
decision, would not readily be answerable to 'the international community' even were it possible to discover its identity and whereabouts.
Nor is it clear that proposals to make great powers accountable to a
diplomatic conference of all states would not mimic the disfiguring

illusions of the general assembly of the UN. The effect of the latter body is not to hold great powers responsible for their actions, but to humour with cruel cynicism the limitations of small states. It is to register without appeasing their Caliban-like frustrations.

## VI

The supposition that states have identifiable and fairly constant interests is one reason for believing they are able to co-operate. Awkward as they are to compute and bring into acceptable alignment, the existence of discernible interests at least provides diplomacy with promising scope. In the seventeenth century Puffendorf wrote a *History of Europe* classified around the view that its component states had 'real' interests. These consisted of permanent and temporary interests. Schemes to achieve 'the monarchy of Europe', or 'the universal monarchy', were discounted as imaginary interests because designs by one power to impose its will on the rest would inevitably provide the 'fuel with which the whole world may be put into a flame'.[7] Puffendorf was worldly enough to know that ignorance, vanity and malice led rulers and their advisors to mistake their true interests, but what intrigues a twentieth-century eye is the thinking that makes statecraft appear a rational pursuit of calculable interests. How far the notion of 'interest' was coined in order to divest diplomatic thought of its preceding religious passions is of less concern than Puffendorf's determination to establish foreign affairs on solidly reasoned foundations. For much of its existence between the Congress of Westphalia and the First World War, the diplomatic system of Europe operated as if the interests of states were separable from the passions of men.

We are now less certain that a distinction of this kind can or should hold good. With the advent of nationalism and the spread of other movements appealing to the sentiments of enfranchised or enraged populations, the interests of states became heady with collectivized feelings. Once territory is sanctified with a sense of birthright, no toehold of a motherland is negotiable. Severing a sliver of a nation's organic whole is treacherous immolation. At the close of the twentieth century, both Europe and the world have more states than ever before largely because the entire surface of the earth is saturated in the fellow-feelings and make-beliefs of nations. The authority of states is vested not in republican ideas of civility and their modern majoritarian mathematics, but in the passions of sovereign peoples extolling their national identities. Had a Bosnian electorate been able to decide matters of state, its composition as one nation rather than three would have been confirmed. Palestine and Kashmir have proved diplomatically unyielding because the interests of states are copious with national and religious attachments. China says Taiwan 'belongs' to it in the same way that Irish nationalists pine for Ulster, Armenians cling to Ngorno-Karabakh and Chechens were willing to disfigure their country in order to be rid of Russian rule.

Although the nationalization of the interests of states led to the wholesale recomposition of the diplomatic system, for the duration of the Cold War it was sentiments of a more doctrinaire kind that inflamed events. It is now difficult to fathom what American interests were served by 'containing communism' in Vietnam, or by the Soviet Union's embroilment in Angola. The conflicts that have succeeded the Cold War may no longer sound like the catechism of a historicist confessional, but foreign affairs have not reverted to the more diplomatically manageable idioms of 'real' interests. It is true that in Europe many of the fires of nationalism have been doused in shame and exhaustion, realized within recognized frontiers, or accommodated within the politics of the EU. The enfranchisement and legal protection of national minorities form part of Europe's post-war reformation. Even so, Europe still gets the jitters when nationalist parties win electoral support. In Ulster, the Basque country and Corsica, unconciliated passions threaten civil order. The regional reorganization of unitary states to accommodate Catalans, Scots, Flemings and so on testifies to the continued power of fellow-feelings. Passions as well as interests constitute powers of decision.

Beyond Europe nationalism has not spent its force, with the result that large tracts of the world's surface remain the subject of rival claims. It is not even clear how appropriate it is to rely on idioms derived from eighteenth-century Europe to describe the various passions associated with a sense of place and demands for self-government. Nations are only one expression of fellow-feeling. Nor are localized attachments likely to be quickly and conveniently swept under the carpet by the blanket effects of globalization. It is misplaced to suppose that because markets are conducive to wealth, globalization will impose cultural forbearance on peoples it juxtaposes as neighbours. Because the upheavals of the so-called third world can be quarantined by agreement between developed countries, and therefore appear of limited danger to foreign affairs, it is easy to overlook that the most insensate conflicts of the twentieth century have occurred in the richest and most highly educated parts of the world. The rational administration of men and resources in modern bureaucratic states has included instilling and exploiting feelings of patriotic love and hatred of foreigners.

In *The Tribune's Visitation* David Jones speaks of how 'the 'known-site' that fixes fellow-feelings to particular places, when dislocated becomes 'bitter fruit for world-floor'.

> As wine of the country
> > sweet if drawn from wood
> near to the living wood
> > that bore the grape
> > sours if taken far
> so can all virtue curdle in transit
> so vice may be virtue uprooted
> so is the honey-root of known-site
> > bitter fruit for world-floor[8]

Even if it is appropriate to follow Ernest Gellener in interpreting nationalism as the compulsory entrance ticket to the modern world,[9] the wholesale reorganization of once familiar ways of life propels the feelings of nations into the maelstrom of foreign affairs. The same industrialization and adherence to a world economy that offers escape from poverty, also invests power politics with collectivized passions. The argument that adaptation to a closely-knit 'world-floor' of global markets is one thing, and the preservation of 'known-sites' another, does nothing to lessen the possibilities of conflict unless it is explained how the former does not disembowel the latter of content. Whether governments succeed in tethering dislocated feelings to their interests or sail before their tempests, the overall effect is to charge and recharge the interests of states with emotional gusto. The 'bitter fruit' of politicized sentiments that season after season produced bumper harvests in Europe, shows no sign as yet of mellowing into a 'world-floor'.

The need to adapt the particularisms of nations to the effects of global change can be stated in robust terms. If modernization means Westernization, and the latter signals Americanization, this may have to be accepted as the judgement of historical fate. Where the 'known-sites' littered about the world fail to accommodate themselves to the coming of a superpowered 'world-floor', the disappearance of antique attachments, along with the diversity they represent, may not even justify resentment or regret. The USA, it can be argued, can no more

avoid depositing its 'shape of life' in the wake of its powerful achievements than did previous exemplars of historical change. Nor perhaps
is the USA uniquely vain in believing in the universal applicability of
its own ebullient experience.

None of these arguments, however, provides reasons why peoples
who worship other gods should submit without protest to American
influence. Even in Europe, the American face of globalization evokes
criticism that the benefits of proximity are paid for with losses to
Europe's sense of its own diverse particularity. It is the weight as
much as the content of a superpower's 'known-site' that makes the
idea that nations of all sizes and descriptions can live amicably side by
side so difficult to realize. If the USA is indeed creating a global
'world-floor' in its own likeness, none should be surprised if the
embittered reactions reach into the human centres of power politics.

Even if local attachments on a small scale have little chance of
withstanding superpowered cyberspace, the existence of more than
one set of powerfully backed universal claims is perhaps a more potent
source of dissension. The presence, in ever closer proximity, of differing conceptions of right, reason, revelation and worth, to which millions are both unthinkingly and consciously attached, cannot fail to be
diplomatically combustible. As between contending religious and pro-
fane accounts of the origins and ends of life, there exists, as Isaiah
Berlin urged throughout his life, no arbitrator above the mêlée to
whose transcendent gaze rival yearnings can be submitted for passion-
less adjudication. Even within each vast category of explanations,
differences agitate and divide. The disputations of believers within
and between religions are as doggedly interminable as are controver-
sies between liberal and collectivist descendants of the European
Enlightenment. Although controversy that embraces just about everything of value may invest populist power politics with venomous disorder, disputation may also be necessary to keep life enlivened.

Although the dispersion of new knowledge stimulates venerable
passions, it also arouses new areas of feeling. The tolerance of disparate opinions, which Voltaire considered essential to human well-
being, sane government and the increase of knowledge, was in part the
by-product of indifference to the inexhaustible claims of religion.
There is little evidence that a world newly confused by its compression
and the scientific innovations that have brought it about is about to
lose interest in the upheavals of inequitable change. The 'West', or at
least the USA, is every bit as convinced of the rightness of its opinions
– over 'human rights' for example – as are critics who find Christianity

and the legacies of the Enlightenment unpersuasive, and the incessant admonitions of their supporters intolerable. Although the need for adherents of incommensurable beliefs to learn to live together may therefore make its way into diplomacy, this is likely to make the rapprochement of interests yet more difficult to manage. The admixture of might and right on a globally transmitted scale, and under circumstances where a plurality of competing 'superadded ideas' will excite billions, will surely perpetuate and exacerbate the arbitrary elements of power in a world that lacks politics.

## VII

An intriguing variant of how fellow-feelings have invaded the interests of states is suggested by the recent rediscovery of civilizations.[10] In response to dislocations occasioned by the removal of the Cold War and by globalization, civilizations have apparently surfaced to shoulder the burden of existential disarray. As with drunks lurching homewards, disorientation is accompanied by a grappling desire for the steadying hand of enduring familiarities. Only groupings attracting men's widest and most rooted sympathies are said to offer the requisite moral support. The 'known-site' of nations has become magnified to the scale of a 'world-floor' of several juxtaposed civilizations.

The unexceptional idea that civilizations constitute the broadest level of mutual recognitions is one that Burke took for granted. It supplied the idea of Europe with precise and pervasive substance. Despite its fragmentation into umpteen bellicose states and religious factions, Europe encompassed all its varied peoples in a persuasive whole. Huntington, however, now wishes to attribute to civilizations a more urgently cogent function. With the passing of the Cold War, civilizations have affectively become the most binding of fellow-feelings and are consequently of prime political importance.

'Spurred by modernization', we learn, 'global politics [*sic*] is being reconfigured along cultural lines.'[11] As peoples press against one another and overlap, they are forced into recognition of what they are unlike. This in turn arouses a sense of who they are. This speculative dialectic of collective identity draws attention to a category of fellow-feeling hitherto ignored because attention has usually concentrated on societies, economies, classes, nations, religions and states. Although none of these is said to have faded, each has become revivified by a quickened sense of intimate association with and ultimate dependence on a handful of civilizations. 'Nation states', we are informed, 'remain the principal actors in world affairs. Their behaviour is shaped as in the past by the pursuit of power and wealth, but it is also shaped by cultural preferences, commonalities and differences.'[12] If this amounts to the observation that relations between states from different civilizations exist on especially ambiguous footings, this is true and germane, but hardly novel. The centuries-long record of Europe's dealings with the Ottoman Empire comes immediately to mind. Indeed the entire diplomatic system of Europe is steeped in habits and precepts of conduct peculiar to one civilization. But although this body of mutual recognitions enabled the *corps diplomatique* of Europe to function as a figurine of aristocratic manners, it neither prevented European states from treating one another as enemies, nor inhibited the formation of alliances with political bodies from beyond the boundaries of their civilization.

The argument about civilizations extends beyond the commonplace that people exposed to the weight of experience are forever marked by it. 'In this new world', Huntingdon says, 'local politics is the politics of ethnicity, global politics is the politics of civilizations. The rivalry of the superpowers is being *replaced* [emphasis supplied] by the clash of civilizations.'[13] It is this latter claim that raises an eyebrow. The world according to this author is composed of some nine civilizations whose incommensurable sentiments but geographical propinquity issue in antipathies. Each of the five most powerful civilizations also has a great power at its hub. For 'the West' it is the USA, although Europe may act as its helpmate. China lies at the centre of Sinic civilization, Russia of Christian Orthodoxy, India of Hindu civilization, while Japan is a world unto itself. Were Islam to combine, it would form a further element in a 'multipolar and multicivilizational world'[14]. As western dominance is challenged by cultures with the size, populations and resources, and above all the will to contest, clashes between civilizations are said to be the future of world affairs. The place to look for conflict is fault lines between civilizations. Bosnia illustrates the ferocity of fighting between combatants representing hostile civilizations and the ominous readiness of core powers to identify with cultural kith and kin. Hence the idea that the world is converging on 'western values' is as misplaced as the belief that it should. Opposition to western power is part and parcel of the self-assertion of other parts of the world. The desire for economic improvement does not slake ambition: it whets the appetite for things that prosperity helps to bring within reach. Among these are powers of decision; the power to command attention, to be listened to and to have a say in what is done. Rather than being made over in the likeness of the USA, the world is becoming fraught with new rivalries as other centres of power, representing the superadded ideas of several civilizations, emerge.

Where Huntingdon appears wrong-footed is in the belief that rivalries between states are upstaged and replaced by clashes of civilizations. In the passage just quoted, he writes that 'people use politics not just to advance their interests but also to define their identity'.[15] Matters of identity are however grist to the mill of states. As the US well demonstrates, the powers of decision of nationalized states includes the production of patriots. The great powers Huntingdon sees as the animating centres of civilizations are not their handmaidens. The reverse is nearer the truth. If sentiments of civilization and religion now appear more potent rallying cries than nationalism, or are used to invest its passions with fresh vigour, what it enhances is the powers of states. Where belonging to the same civilization helps to draw states into regional groupings, the decisive effect is to uphold the powers of governments. Civilizations may tell us who we are, but they lack the means of doing much about it. As Kissinger once complained of Europe, they lack telephone numbers. Their powers of attraction and revulsion are not powers of decision. It is states that are equipped with governments, administrations, armed forces, schools and so on. Although civilizations may inspire love and loathing, they are ill-equipped to act and react. The Ayatollahs of Iran who carried everything before them in 1979 on waves of religious feelings, swept Iranians into a theocratic state. Hindu nationalism in India and Mao's triumph in China were similarly realized in states. Movements that captured the hearts of millions produced states whose governments soon set about ruling the passions of their sovereign masters. As members of a global diplomatic system, these countries now have their sights set on more than safeguarding the past. Their independence implicates them in power politics, where the appetites of states are fed by the passions of men.

**Notes**

1.     M.G. Forsyth, H.M.A. Keens-Soper and P. Savigear, *The Theory of International Relations* ( London: Allen & Unwin, 1980), p. 169

2.   Edmund Burke, *Reflections on the Revolution in France* (London: Dent, 1964), p. 74
3.   Ibid.
4.   Ibid, p.75.
5.   Quoted in Carsten Holbrad, *The Concert of Europe* (London: Longman, 1970), p. 98
6.   The continuation of this quotation is worth giving.

>    This extended meaning of independence is not necessary for most countries. Smaller countries have to be content with independence as defined in international law and as guaranteed by bigger nations or by alliances. The Chinese would recognize that this is perhaps all that small nations can hope for, but would not accept such a limited form of independence for China. The reasons are rooted in China's history. They stem from traditional perecptions of China's place in the world, that is, the parts of the world directly relevant to China. Wang Gungwa, *China and the World since 1949* (London: Macmillan, 1977), p.2. I am grateful to Murray Forsyth for this reference.

7.   Samuel Puffendorf, *An Introduction to the History of Europe* (London, 1712), Preface.
8.   John Matthias (ed.) *Introducing David Jones* (London: Faber &Faber 1980), The Tribune's Visitation, p.197.
9.   Ernest Gellener, *Nations and Nationalism* (Oxford: Basil Blackwell, 1983).
10.  Samuel P. Huntingdon, *The Clash of Civilizations and the remaking of World Order* (New York: Simon & Schuster, 1996).
11.  Ibid, p.125.
12.  Ibid, p.21.
13.  Ibid, p.28.
14.  Ibid, p.21.
15.  Ibid.

# Part III

# Ever Closer Agitations

# 5 Ineffectual Europa

The EU is first of all interested in itself. Far from being aberrant, the self-interestedness of political bodies is evidence of their will to endure. The desire of the EU to promote itself into the future and to clad itself with powers of self-perpetuation is therefore evidence that it is more than a timely diplomatic and economic convenience among a plurality of co-operatively inclined states. The singleness of mind hesitantly produced out of fearsome diversity has brought about more than the semblance of an 'it'. The single market, EMU and enlargement are undertakings as organizationally awkward as they are politically ambitious. Those involved in the furtherance of the EU are at work on a construction site where it is necessary to make a virtue of the fact that the ground is already occupied by the 'known-sites' of established political bodies on whose support the new edifice principally rests. The master builders have no architect's assured contours to guide their actions, no guarantee that the footings will hold, and therefore no foreknowledge of what will result from their labours.

For these reasons alone, Europe is more than a building site. The politics and economics of the EU are forcing it and its member states to raise their sights to consider what their concerted actions are producing. What form and substance is appearing from the tumble and thump of inward directed effort? What 'body' equipped with what powers of decision is emerging from the politics of union?

With questions of this order to be determined it is unsurprising that the place of the EU in the foreign affairs of the world has been of subordinate interest. It might also be argued that opening itself to further members demonstrates the opposite of self-absorption. The countries of central and eastern Europe, Cyprus, Turkey and the Baltic, represent sizeable slices of the diplomatic system. The diplomacy of enlargement is, however, of a singular kind. It is designed to bring states, with whom at present the EU has foreign relations, to a position where once ensconced in Brussels, this will cease to be so. On accession, Poland and the others will thereafter belong to the internal domestic politics of the EU. Although the diplomacy of enlargement is likely to take as many years as did the admission of Spain and

Portugal, like those negotiations it has a terminal point. At the end of no doubt lengthy periods of transition, the intention is that new members will thereafter be on the same footing as existing ones. This prospect has already concentrated minds on how enlargement will affect the constitutional and budgetary workings of the EU. Although at Amsterdam in 1997 decisions on re-organization were postponed, a bout of continuous enlargement that may last for a decade and more will have the general effect of once again focusing the attention of the EU resolutely on itself.

If the prolonged indeterminacy of the EU is one reason why foreign affairs figure mainly in the margins of interest, there are plenty of others. 'Europe' has no unequivocal form, and therefore no forthright standing in diplomacy, because in addition to the EU there are other Europes. The OSCE, WEU and the Council of Europe represent only some of the Taxonomically and Acronymously Stupefying complexities of Europe (TASTIE). TASTIE  may well testify to Europe's diversity and constitute an impressive reservoir of vitality, but it can hardly be claimed as a source of diplomatic strength. NATO in particular reflects how few powers of decision Europe possesses. The effort of forming Europe into a body able to act and react towards other countries in persuasive unison will be so tirelessly problematical that it has led many to conclude that the consequences of any such attempt would not only be unresolvable disagreement, but produce an additional bias towards introspection.

Narcissistic self-attention at least holds out the possibility that, long as it may take, once the chimney is on, 'the house of Europe' will eventually be fitted to take its place in the great estate of the world. A different view of Europe's worldly fate disclaims any such suburban rendezvous with global affairs. It makes a virtue of parochialism and seeks to build on the advantages of minding one's own business. This is Candide's Europe (CE). At the end of their peregrinations, Candide and his troupe find refuge in the countryside of Asia Minor as subjects of the Sublime Porte. Exhausted by venturing they agree to abjure the world and its spur to philosophical speculation, and busy themselves instead with cultivating land and living from its proceeds. Quizzed by the incurable Pangloss to comment on the turbulent events of Constantinople, a neighbourly Turk sets a lesson they agree to follow: 'I suppose it's true that those who enter politics sometimes come to a miserable end... but I never bother myself about what happens in Constantinople. I send my garden stuff to be sold there, and that's enough for me.'[1] Candide does not dispute that a chain of events links all men and places but, after so many dire escapades, he takes the point and decides that 'we must go and work in the garden'.[2] After centuries bedevilled by the bloodied paths of power politics, the existence of a single market garden is likewise seen as best suited to keeping Europeans gainfully employed and out of harm's way. By attending to their own affairs, and resisting temptations to meddle elsewhere, Europeans (and perhaps the world) will be better off. For their security and protection they must follow Candide's example, and resign themselves to the forces that be. For the moment these represent a transatlantic equivalent of the Ottoman Sultan's benign despotism.

A more optimistic variant of this somnambulism worthy of Dr Pangloss, is to cast about the world and find it heartening. Even if not everything in the garden is rosy, the bordering edges of the twentieth century are seen to be full of productive growth. Since mid-century there has been no general war. Whatever their role in the Cold War, nuclear weapons remained sheathed. Though disturbing, their proliferation has been less speedy than feared and the topic is now a source of agreement (at least between those states with declared arsenals). Among signatories of the NPT, inspection procedures are more interventionist than was once thought acceptable to states. The numerous trouble spots of the world, within and between states, have not ramified into universal chaos. The disorders of an expanding diplomatic system, a developing world economy and the surgings of scientific innovation, have all been kept within bounds. Above all, the peaceful end of the superpower rivalry of the Cold War encourages a well-placed sense that the arbitrariness of foreign affairs can be diplomatically confined. If there remains plenty to worry about, to safeguard, prevent and quell, there is not much in the 'bitter fruit' of power politics that Europeans cannot safely leave to others while they advantageously concentrate on tilling their fertile patches. There are plenty of politically rich pickings in a consumer's Europe.

Should this complacent outlook suffer from the suggestion that like the weather, times do not always change for the better, this still does not imply that 'Europe' must, in some shape or other, raise a united umbrella above its many headedness. If the turn of foreign events is less to the ease of a provincially absorbed EU, there is always Mighty America in Europe (MAMEE) to hold on to. For half a century MAMEE has safeguarded western Europe as well as suckling its internal calm. Europe should thus thank its lucky stars and stripes and continue to do whatever is necessary to ensure that it continues to be undisturbed by the need to protect its stakes in the international economy. As Europe's pacifier and protector, the superpower at the centre of NATO supplies enough order in foreign affairs to enable CE to cultivate its garden. If reliance on so much power perpetuates dependence on the internal decisions of a foreign country, one tested answer is to be grateful for powerful mercies. Europe may be a strategic passenger in NATO, but that is as maybe. When Candide suggested to the greatest philosopher in Turkey that a great deal of evil remained active throughout the world, the dervish's reply was tersely unPanglossian. 'And what if there is? When His Highness sends a ship to Egypt, do you suppose he worries whether the ship's mice are comfortable or not?'[3] So far as Europe's foreign affairs are concerned, MAMEE knows best.

An apparently different view is taken by those who foresee plenty of turbulence but who take a less angular view of NATO. It is recognized that 'Europe' cannot risk behaving as if it were too busy nourishing its own welfare to have time for the distractions of foreign affairs, or take refuge in the virginal idea that its own inward striving for self-development provided protection from external hazard. Nor, it is claimed, is such a picture faithful to the present situation. Separately as well as co-operatively within NATO, Europe's states are strenuously engaged in external affairs. They have matchless experience of the diplomatic system and need no persuading that, unless upheld, their interests may go by default. If Europe's individual states suffer nowadays from a lack of influence compared to the world's mightiest powers, this is a verdict of history, not evidence of passivity. In their reduced circumstances, and because of the Cold War, European states need no reminding of the benefits of co-operating to maximize their powers of influence. Although NATO is the most vivid setting of allied activity, it is false to depict MAMEE as a harridan. Within and beyond NATO, the US goes out of its way to respect and support Europe's Feisty National Unities (FNUs). These FNUs are said to embody the true strength of Europe because it is the loyalties of national fellow-feeling that makes its states authoritative and still formidable. The real mainstay of European unity is thus claimed to be found in its unities of nation and state. And it is these which make a CFSP beside the point and indeed a threat to their effectiveness in foreign affairs. While the Brussels of the EU slices away at its members' powers of decision, the Brussels of NATO is an alliance of consenting equals long familiar to diplomacy. The tested readiness of the FNUs to co-operate gives the lie to the charge that the states of Europe are so jealous of their individual standings on the world stage that they cannot bring themselves to act together.

When it is suggested that times have changed, and that the states of Europe have become outclassed by more sizeable powers alongside which mere co-operation among smaller states is unconvincing, the FNUs are driven to defend themselves by reference not to their powers of action but as bastions of collective identity. It is from within the unsharable feelings of nations that last-ditch roars of defiance resound; even if unable to go it alone – as both the EU and NATO imply – Europe's FNUs are at least able to bar the creation of an effective European foreign policy. Europe's FNUs thus represent a preference for diplomatic independence (in deference to national identities) over effectiveness in power politics which might better serve national interests, but which would necessitate the erosion of their separate powers of action. Even where the consequence is the forfeited opportunities of greater influence, small and medium are still sacrosanct. Although a CFSP might bring added effectiveness in the diplomatic system, Europe's FNUs, or at least their governments, ensure that in foreign affairs the EU has nothing to compare with the cogency of its states or the sentiments they continue to excite. On neither score is Brussels permitted to offer anything alongside or in their place. How far the fellow-feelings vested in Europe's doughty nations preclude sharing a single foreign policy, or inhibit the advancement of a parallel sense of a Europe-wide sense of patriotism, has not of course been put to the electoral test of the EU's citizens. Although the doctrine of nationalism upholds self-government it is by no means clear that Europe's nations are hostile to the extension of the shared government they have come to accept in many domestic matters, to the domain of foreign affairs.

Two further images of Europe's place in the world are discernible. Both acknowledge the persistence of power politics and accept that neither Europe's FNUs, co-operation among them, nor even MAMEE, can insulate governments and peoples from exposure to foreign affairs. Each however draws contrary conclusions.

As its acronym implies, Exemplary and Radiant Europe (ERE) aims to behave well at home and set an example to the rest of the world in keeping with its reformed political habits. The hope is to deal actively and widely with other parts of the world without participating in the sorry side of foreign affairs. Although less self-possessed than CE, ERE has no greater desire to be caught up in the kind of power politics it has come to regret. Its fondest desire is to let the healing accomplishments represented in the EU resonate as a penitential model of peace, civility and prosperity. By keeping itself decently detached from power politics, bountiful with aid and developmental assistance to others, the entire world may gradually adopt variants of Europe's reformed self. The view of foreign affairs favoured by ERE is accordingly centred on Fantasizing the United Nations (FUN) as well as on non-governmental agencies that strive to privatize and denationalize global affairs. Quite how this version of Europe's future squares with the powers being generated by political union and economic integration, and how ERE is to fare in a world that in large measure prefers its own counsel or rival examples, is less important than the determination of ERE to be a force for good free from the entrapments of power politics.

The meliorism of ERE is absent from Houdini's Europe (HE). From this angle it is plain that while Europe cannot hope to be left alone to nourish its fortunes unaffected by power politics, it is also wasteful of resources and effort to rely on diplomatic and military previsions. Europe's peoples have tasted the bitter fruit of such costly and self-defeating illusions. Nor is it worth placing confidence in the equally empty but opposite belief that international organizations and FUN can rid the world of power politics. Although risky it is better to stick with CE for as long as the sun shines, shunning attempts to construct institutions and alliances designed to buttress security. MAMEE may or may not be at hand but Europe's FNUs will rise to whatever self-preserving feats are called for. If nonchalance of this kind leaves Europe in the position of mice in the hold of a rickety vessel, the inventive agilities of its great civilization can be depended upon to rescue it from the tempests of ill fortune. Since in any case there is little to be gained from preparing for unpredictable eventualities or in believing that precautionary measures will work, gambling on Houdini's escapological talents makes even diplomatic sense.

## II
## HOME TRUTHS AND FOREIGN AFFAIRS

These various standpoints are so insouciantly jumbled together as to suggest indifference to fortune's 'cold and steady malice'. One way or another each ignores or misrepresents the diplomatic system and the power politics it encapsulates. A recapitulation of the exposition offered in an earlier chapter may bring home the extent to which the EU and its states are exposed to greater hazards than is presently believed.

The diplomatic system put together for the mutual convenience of its principal members places states fully and four square at its centre. This is as true in the aftermath of the Cold War as it was at the time of Westphalia, the Congress of Vienna, the Peace Conference of Paris and Yalta. In so far as a more widespread system is also culturally less homogeneous than its European forebear, the stable juxtaposition of large numbers of states at differing stages of development is more difficult to sustain. International organizations, the interests of multi-national companies, pressure groups indifferent to nationality, as well as the tried habits of continuous diplomacy may help to mediate conflicts, but their point of reference remains the self-regarding inclinations of separate states. These are the bodies whose relations determine what measure of peace the world enjoys and what chances their peoples have of realizing their hopes.

The multiplying of states entwined together around the fragile pergolas of the diplomatic system form an indivisible field of diplomatic forces. The 'actions and reactions' of states keep them in a condition of 'continuous agitation'. This does not imply that all states are alike or that they enjoy comparable powers of decision. Many of the world's states are so tiny, poor, or pre-occupied with holding themselves together, that their impact on events is slight. Their fate is to be ignored or exploited. The aim of states currently disabled by civil divisions is, however, to become more state-like and to claim an active say in foreign affairs. To the extent that they succeed, the diplomatic system will have exchanged difficulties arising from weak states for difficulties connected with states better able to assert their interests. Algeria is as anxious to regain its unity of action as China guards its refound ability to speak and act as one. Neither weak nor powerful states can ignore the turn of events on their borders or elsewhere, and there is nothing about Europe to suggest it is an exception. The imperative of vigilance holds good as much in times of peace as of war. Globalization, the fits and starts of financial markets, pollution, the vagaries of food and energy supplies and the vulnerability of their routes – in short the general conditions of the international economy and the ambitions that ride with it -- ensure that 'market forces' provide no reprieve from change or from power politics.

The mutual exposure of states to one another and the events they generate heightens the sensitivity of governments to encroachments on their authority. Since states deny that others have authority over their 'sovereignty', the power exercised by one state over another dramatizes the arbitrary basis of foreign affairs. If states had a political right to interfere in each other's affairs they would scarcely have to treat one another diplomatically. When the USA shows its might towards China over Taiwan, brandishes it to keep Greece and Turkey from one another's throats, or uses it against Iraq, it is made all the more striking just because Washington can claim no authority over these, or any other, independent and sovereign countries. The acquisition of a 'mandate' from the UN Security Council is a convenient diplomatic ploy, signifying the agreement of other great powers not to hamper its actions. The UN is vested with the authority of states, not vice versa. International Law derived from treaties does not subject states to its provisions without their consent because they are its authors and the only means by which it can be upheld. In the case of the essential rules of diplomatic intercourse, these are largely observed because in their absence states would be hard put to conduct foreign policies. Hence the general respect for the inviolability of embassies and the immunities of envoys. These oases of exterritoriality, granted in reciprocal fashion by states, do not indicate the forfeiture of sovereignty because it is the condition essential for its exercise. This is far removed from states agreeing to place themselves under government by higher authority, or subjecting themselves without demur to the findings of international tribunals.

The EU may itch to intervene in Algeria's civil war, but the state of Algeria was created after a bloody war waged against France in order to assert a nation's right not to be governed by foreigners. In consequence the EU is obliged to proceed diplomatically. It has no authority to do more, and its powers of economic and other influence, though considerable, do not extend to the threat or use of force. This in turn confines the scope of its diplomacy.

The conditions of power politics reveal the unpredictabilities of human actions with unusual force. Lack of foreknowledge about the turn of events and how states, including one's own, will respond to them, means that foreign affairs lie outside certainty. They are resistant to exact computation. No one in Europe knows what will happen in Russia in the next few years, or what would follow were the USA to succumb to internal disorders or isolationism that hamstrung NATO. If the best that can be hoped for is foresight without foreknowledge, the consequent insights, on the basis of which decisions have to be taken, cast another dark shadow on the arbitrary operations of the diplomatic system. It might be argued that the handicap of imperfect knowledge is equally true of party politics in constitutional states, but the comparison only underlines poignant differences. Under law-governed politics, the procedures and time-tabling of events, and even more their advance acceptance, are rails of continuity which narrow down uncertainties. By comparison a country's foreign affairs are always threatening to escape its control because the outcome of policies lies in the hands of numerous other states. One of the advantages of power is that with enough of it to nudge or resist events, one is less their helpless victim. At the Kyoto Earth Conference the EU's powers of decision were unequal to those of the USA.

In Europe as elsewhere, diplomacy has thus to be prepared for both the foreseeable and the foreclosed. Under such conditions it is scarcely a sign of aggressive intent that bodies, entrusted with the safeguard of national interests, forearm themselves. Force is a form of self-insurance when other forms of security are absent. National armaments are justified as insurance against the occurrence of events that cannot be ruled out and cannot be predicted. Even though it is seldom clear what precisely they are forearmed against, few states forego national defence. The spiral of armaments that frequently produces unwanted results, consumes resources, and often fuels the insecurities they are designed to appease, cannot therefore be dismissed with a tut aimed at men's unreasoning follies. The military provisions of national security have their origins in the clear-sighted observation that where distrust is made endemic by the mêlée of unequal powers in pursuit of their own interests, it is foolhardy and perhaps irresponsible not to be prepared to defend one's vital interests. Many a well-insured citizen of law-governed and reliably policed states lies abed fretting over his personal security and pondering whether his property is adequately safeguarded.

Supporters of CE, ERE and HE tend to treat these commonplaces of power politics as unpersuasive. Their precautionary counsel has not, however, been made obsolete either by the Cold War or its conclusion. The reinvigoration of a diplomatic system no longer trussed-up by the twin alliances of superpower rivalry is bringing to the surface anxieties that have little to do with the strategic balance of nuclear power. Even a single superpower surrounded by handfuls of unequal states chafing over their interests suggests a reversion to power politics reminiscent of great tracts of European history. The imbalance of power, that on occasion makes for compliance and co-operation among those wary of offending great powers, also advertises the advantages of great power and spurs its emulation. Hence the superpower of the USA, which at present supervises the diplomatic system, also ensures the continuation of power politics.

Since the EU and the states of Europe are party to this diplomatic setting and have, like others, interests to shield and advance, the conclusions that follow are, or should be, chastening. The absence of war does not demonstrate the durability of peace. Europe is not fenced off from the sound of thunder and civil strife to its south and east. Although Bosnia was remote enough to induce indifference in some European capitals, and fears of involvement in others, an upsurge of violence in the Mediterranean, the Gulf, the Indian sub-continent, around the Caspian Sea or over the Molucca Straits would implicate Europe sooner or later. No matter how much CE wished to concentrate on horticulture or ERE advertised its probity as a guide to others, neither would distance Europe from conflict.

Just as the absence of war carries no promise of perpetual peace, so it is false to equate order with the suspension of conflict. Almost by design a diplomatic system is inherently disorderly and although the resources of diplomacy are able to settle disputes, their aim is usually the temporary one of aligning the interests of states. The vast enterprise of seeking to dismantle a system of states in favour of other more globally encompassing loci of authority is quite a different matter. A successful resolution of the dispute over Kashmir would still leave heavily and nuclear armed India and Pakistan eyeing each others' ambitions with distrust. The co-operation of states, which is the redeeming feature of power politics, cannot therefore be relied upon to father trust. Shifts in the balance of power unhinge one set of alliances only to lead to the formation of others. At Yalta the 'big three' were bound together by Hitler; four years later the Berlin airlift was underway. With the demise of the Warsaw Pact, NATO has reinvented itself in preparation for eventualities that can be seen in outline but are hard to specify.

The dictums of power politics suggest that in none of its present embodiments is Europe adequately adapted to foreign affairs. In one way or another each of the TASTIE labels gives the impression that the world holds few dangers, or that Europe is providentially secure from them. How far this is a hangover from the influence once exercised by Europe's states, or the result of Cold War prophylaxis, is not yet apparent, but the suggestion that the world still takes its cues from Europe is the reverse of the truth. Whether Europe's FNUs act independently or co-operate in foreign affairs, contrive an EU foreign policy, or continue to rely on MAMEE, 'Europe' is fated to power politics. It is forced by the circumstances of its own diverse interests and by the consequences of the diplomatic system, to act responsibly in the most rooted sense of the word. It must *respond* to the world.

This imprecation implies no grounds for deploring the present calm in power politics or reason to disregard well tried alliances. The drawback of undisrupted times, however, is their siren like seductiveness that flatters belief in the adequacy of Candide's Europe (CE), the propriety of Exemplary and Radiant Europe (ERE), the sufficiency of Europe's Feisty National Unities (FNUs), and unthinking reliance on Mighty America in Europe (MAMEE). In so far as these attitudes represent confidence in the continued utility of yesterday's stratagems, they rest on dubious foundations. They wrongly suggest that the diplomatic profile of power politics is unchanging, or imply that come what may Europeans have decided to place their trust in the dexterities of Houdini's Europe (HE).

## III
## NEAR AT HAND AND FARTHER AFIELD

Since it is impossible to consult a catalogue of future events, foreign affairs are conducted piecemeal. While the far-reaching contingencies of power politics oblige states to keep themselves informed about their entire diplomatic surroundings, governments also preserve a sense that what lies closest is of more compelling importance than distant events. Though lightly pencilled, a sketch of Europe's circumstances confirms both of these truisms.

Of the two main axes of modern European history, the one linking St Petersburg (and thereafter Moscow) to Vienna (and then Berlin) remains in the forefront of its foreign affairs. The other one, between Paris and Berlin (and more recently Bonn), has been reformulated within the EU. Europe's relations with Russia may none the less cement or sunder the post-war reconciliation of France and Germany on which the future of the EU principally rests. Although Russia has been a European great power since 1709, its European credentials have been continuously disputed within Russia as well as by its neighbours. Because Russia extends to the Pacific this is partly a matter of Burke's 'similitudes' and 'resemblances'. Even after the dissolution of the USSR, Russia remains a central Asian power with vast oil, gas and corresponding strategic interests abutting the Caspian Sea and its Turkic republics. From Europe's point of view, Russia's 'transition' to capitalism and representative government is more than a temporary phase that once concluded, will see its peoples settle down to the consuming pleasures of bourgeois life. Were Russia to break up or be consumed in civil disorder, Europe would feel the effects, but if it surmounts present difficulties Russia is likely to reassert its status as a great power. Although central and eastern European countries that have recently emerged from Russian control want membership of NATO and the EU for numbers of reasons, uppermost in their calculations are fears that a reinvigorated neighbour to their east would again tower over them.

Without making clear what policies to pursue Russia therefore puts all of Europe on the spot. The eastwards extension of NATO manifestly shifts the balance of power, though the tempered diplomacy undertaken by the USA in order to humour Russia's acceptance of its altered position is equally noteworthy. In exchange for conceding NATO's enlargement, Russia's status and importance to European security has been fullsomely acknowledged. It has a foot in NATO's door. Only the USA has the power to make a diplomacy of this kind successful; to appease Russian fears and wounded pride, while simultaneously reassuring countries like Poland, the Czech Republic and Hungary that their security is thereby enhanced. While many Europeans quaked at the risks of stimulating Russian nationalism, the USA was able to reorder the affairs of the continent because it was powerful enough to offer concessions and promises without weakening itself or devaluing its word. If a western-looking Russia relieved of its fears about 'Western' intentions is vital to Europe's interests, it is surely salutary that, despite the EU's wealth and stability, the attempt to seek diplomatic accommodation with Russia is something well beyond the present powers of the EU and its states. It is NATO and MAMEE that are crucial to relations with Moscow. Important as the EU is to Russia's economic prospects, the riches of the single market do not confer organized powers of decision-making necessary to dealing with a country of Russia's size and military standing. Although the inauguration of regular diplomatic get-togethers between France, Germany and Russia may signal awareness of the need to identify distinctively European interests, unless this becomes a motive to equip the EU to negotiate with Russia on equal terms, it will reveal and perhaps widen Europe's confusions in foreign affairs. This is in turn will reinforce Europe's dependence on MAMEE and the subordination of the former's interests to those of the latter. There is also the danger that in so far as Russia responds to the power and diplomacy of the USA, the governments and governed of Europe will falsely conclude that the resources of ERE are all that is needed when dealing with Russia. Why cannot the 'community methods' of the EU be applied with equal political effect to Russia? By this sleight of wishful reasoning, ineradicable problems posed by a great and unassimilable power to the east are painlessly shuffled off. Were the assumptions on which this confusion rests true or safe, the need for foreign policy in the direction of Russia would at a stroke be transformed. Russia would stand in relation to the EU on much the same footing as Poland and other central European countries once they are members of the EU. Even though Russia has shown no interest in applying to join the EU, were the political methods of the EU applicable to relations with an independent power like Russia, the effect would be to dispense with power politics to Europe's east. In the case of Russia no such substitute for diplomacy exists.

Stable and peaceful relations with Russia require a Europe sufficiently united so that its differences of outlook are not a source of diplomatic weakness. They also imply acceptance that a democratic and market-based Russia will be a formidable power, more able and more likely to champion its interests than a country bruised by incapacity. Similarities in the form of government cannot be relied upon to nullify the self-interestedness of states. Like the USA, a law-governed Russia voicing the will of its *demos* would have its own interests in mind. Whether Russia finds itself embroiled with China over sparsely settled Siberia, or at odds over energy supplies from central Asia, Europe cannot expect to be unaffected. Nor is the predicament posed by Russia to a Europe with as yet no settled eastern frontiers a thing of the moment. Although diplomacy is synonymous with the need for patient and continuous activity of the kind described by Richelieu, in an age of quick-fix technologies neither of these qualities is now fashionable. Europe's relations with Russia press the need for treating Moscow as more than an incidental problem to which organizational solutions must be hurriedly found.

The Bolshevik revolution was the most fertile outcome of the First World War, and when Hitler's Germany overturned the Versailles settlement and for a time divided central Europe with Stalin, it was the military victories of the Red Army in 1943–5 that swept Soviet power back into the heart of Europe. It remained there throughout the Cold War. There is no reason to believe that the future of Europe will not be comparably affected by relations with Russia. A reunited Germany has shifted the diplomatic focus from Europe's western shorelines to the centre of the continent. Germany's position *vis-à-vis* Russia will therefore be pivotal, a fact unlikely to have gone unnoticed in France or among its post-Versailles allies in eastern

Europe. Whether the EU manages to conduct a CFSP may therefore affect its internal harmony. The disturbing possibility that an indecisive Europe, wracked by disunion, may lead to an independent German foreign policy directed towards, and perhaps with, Russia, cannot be ruled out. Tender as the topic understandably is, its mention resurrects the ghosts of another supposedly bygone Europe. This is Recidivous Europe (or RDE) where, broken on the wheel of foreign affairs, or mangled by the failure of EMU, Europe retracts its mid-century reformation and reverts to the power politics of its previous incarnation. Not even Europe's FNUs warm to the idea of reverting to that past.

As with Russia, so Europe's relations with Turkey will affect its internal composition as well as its external interests. Both countries baffle Europe. Like Peter the Great's westernizing, Ataturk set out to 'modernize' his country by modelling it on Europe. In both cases the efforts have left unresolved the measure of success. Who can say whether Russia and Turkey are European countries? This long standing enigma has, however, been given a much less speculative urgency by Turkey's desire to join the EEC. Its first application dates from the 1970s when Turkey was already a member of NATO but when 'Europe' was even more inchoate than now. The formation of the EU has not, however, resolved Turkey's candidacy because, in addition to the imponderables of Attaturk's legacy and of European interpretations of it, the application raises equally unsettled and unsettling questions about Europe's own identity. Since 'Europe' is still in the making, neither party to this mutual interrogation has cause to feel embarrassed. But as the EU presently includes only fifteen of Europe's sixty-two states, and is therefore only a partial embodiment of what it claims to represent, its inability to declare where its frontiers run (or should extend to) carries dire diplomatic costs. It constitutes a further element of uncertainty in the diplomatic system. For its part, Turkey is no trivial country, and its future importance to the affairs of the Middle East and central Asia, as well to Europe and the Mediterranean, appears assured.

The hurdle to Turkey's membership of the EU is raised by the political nature of Europe's incomplete union. No obstacles have arisen over Turkey's membership of NATO, or its full participation in other organizations such as the OSCE or the Council of Europe, because, like most alliances and international organizations, these depart from and return to the independence of their members states. Because it promotes shared political authority, specifies democratic

government as a condition of membership and heralds the achievement of 'ever closer union', the EU is categorically different from
other co-operative associations composed of states. Hence Turkey's
membership has little to do with readiness to fulfil economic and
administrative conditions, arduous as these may be. Although the
stumbling block is 'political', even this description fails to convey the
distinctive essence of the matter. Only part of the difficulty lies with
Turkey's suspect democratic and liberal credentials. Were Turkey able
to absorb the entire *acquis communautaire* and put its own house in
order, doubts about its aptitude to share government and form a
political union would persist. Issues of this imprecise though fundamental kind are made yet more difficult to resolve by the geographical
extent of Anatolia, the size of Turkey's population, the religious disposition of its citizens, and the whereabouts of its eastern frontiers.
None of these factors is an obstacle to alliance or close diplomatic co-
operation, or indeed to the Customs Union now agreed with the EU.
Turkey's importance *vis-à-vis* the Middle East and the oil and gas
deposits of central Asia are powerful and well recognized reasons
for cultivating harmonious relations. If, however, the principal obstacle to membership is the EU's political character, it becomes clearer
why long running and now acrimonious hesitations cannot be resolved
by diplomacy. Even if it is just about possible to envisage Turkey
assimilated into the governmental institutions of the EU, it strains
belief that Turkey's borders close to the Tigris and Euphrates can be
inwardly digested and recognized by all other countries of the EU as
the frontiers of Europe. Although Russia has lodged no application to
join the EU, it is perhaps easier to contemplate, as de Gaulle once did,
a Europe bordering the Urals.

Incredulity is, however, only part of the story. The timorous eva-
sions over Turkey's assimilability within a political union, also reveal
how ill-prepared the EU is to conduct foreign affairs. Once again the
defects extend beyond institutional shortcomings remediable by
changes of the kind made in the Treaty of Amsterdam. A CFSP
would only improve relations with an independent Turkey, or help to
remove impediments to EU membership, once questions of another
kind had been resolved.

EU countries are confined in discussing Turkey by the very political
principles purposely established at the centre of their reformative
enterprise. The essential purpose of liberal democracy in the aftermath of 1939–45 was to draw the teeth of nationalism. Based on its
principles, good government would tame collective passions while at

the same time maintaining the value of nations, or what the Maastricht treaty later referred to as 'their history, their culture and their traditions'. The guiding idea however, is to pass lightly over the importance of nationality to the coherence of states in order to emphasize that the most trustworthy schooling in liberal democracy comes from its practice. Without disowning collective identities derived from history and manifest in their cultures, Spain, Portugal and Greece would distance themselves from tyrannical rule by virtue of being party to the EU, all of whose members were now wholesomely governed and keen to spread their example. The flavour, if not all the practices, of EU institutions is likewise redolent with the merits of civil liberties, the rule of law and representative government. One of the attractions to the countries of central and eastern Europe of EU membership lies in helping them live down their pasts as party-states while reuniting them with their pasts as nations belonging to the 'family' of Europe. Tucked within the liberal belief that practice alone prepares for perfection is however, an even more sweeping belief, whose airing in connection with Turkey's application causes paralysis of a kind not experienced in connection with previous entrants to the EU. Important as national cultures are recognized as being within the 'common cultural heritage' of Europeans, neither nationality nor the similitudes of 'Europeaness' is anywhere mentioned as among the stated and necessary conditions of EU membership. The collective identities of nations, along with the materials of thought and feeling that compose them, were pronounced valuable but politically taboo. The post-war reason why the derived inheritances of nations were politically unmentionable in connection with EU membership was that in the revised repertoire of liberal democratic thinking designed to purge Europe of nationalism, collective sentiments were deemed dangerously divisive and hostile to civil orders whose purported focus of interest is individuals.

From this principled standpoint it followed that no pasts of whatever kind can form part of the conditions for EU membership. The tests that count are political not historical. Fitness for good government, which could be acquired only by practising it, was fervently divorced from all mention of nationality. The philosophical blindness of liberal democracy to history, geography and religion means that the only consideration that is openly admissible is the form and practice of government. No other feature of the governed is of account. Neither Turkey nor any other country can therefore be turned down for reasons that contemplate the palate of its particular historical inheritance. The fact that no voluntarily formed political body in Europe has successfully survived the attempt to practise this feat of principled myopia is evidently of less importance than ERE's need to guard itself from accusations of illiberal and undemocratic prejudice. That even John Locke's individualism took for granted that *people* willing to be governed together needed to recognize each other as composing *a people* bound together in common likenesses is overlooked. The predicament of the EU is that, for principled reasons to do with Europe's past, the historical link between nations and states is suppressed or passed over in embarrassed silence. So too is the post-war effort of western Europe's liberal democracies to cultivate a sense of national fellow-feeling as the necessary basis of government based on the consent of the governed.

Since a country's accumulated experience is only citable as a storehouse of value, the only grounds left for rejecting Turkey's application are political, and the EU's political principles make this impossible. The most that can be said is that for the present time Turkey's record of civil liberties, shaky rule of law and treatment of the Kurds precludes admission. Were these political defects, which NATO has seldom been troubled by, to be removed, no other obstacles to membership would exist because none, including nationality, religion and 'common cultural heritage' can be morally recognized as politically significant. The hiatus over Turkey is therefore of Europe's making and reveals that its attachment to liberal democracy has the unwanted consequence of leaving it with no cogent or defensible means by which to recognize itself and determine its own composition.[4]

The diplomatic repercussions of this incoherence are considerable. Relations with Turkey are left hostage to subterfuge. In the meantime Greece and Turkey glower at each other in the Aegean, and Cyprus festers. If the truth is that no matter what Turkey does to demonstrate attachment to liberal democracy, this would not gain it entry to a political union of European countries, then it is prudent as well a diplomatically courteous to say so. A draught of forthrightness would be less insulting to an important neighbour, and therefore less damaging to Europe's interests, than a diplomacy burdened with prolonged mendacity. The diplomatic use of prevarication is one thing. A diplomacy tied to it and designed to perpetuate indecision is another.

Whereas Russia and Turkey are powers to be reckoned with, the Mediterranean has no single focus of attention. Largely under the control of Europeans since the battle of Lepanto (1571) it has been an American lake since Suez (1956). Opposite the countries of southern Europe are Arab states, no longer subject to colonial tutelage but mostly poor, badly governed, weak, aggrieved and with expanding and underemployed young populations. Portions of them are thus drawn magnet-like across what for centuries was a divide between Islam and Christendom, to the job markets of a rich Europe undergoing political consolidation. For their part the Mediterranean countries of Europe fear the instabilities of North Africa, migration and the religious passions associated with them. Secured throughout the Cold War by NATO, the USA is the only military power able to prevent the external spread of violent disorder in the Mediterranean. Under its own national control, American forces keep the peace between its NATO allies in the Aegean, stand guard over Israel, bomb Bosnian Serbs into compliance, deploy roving envoys hither and thus in the Balkans, and patrol the sea from end to end. After Israel, Egypt and Turkey are the largest recipients of US aid.

Although Europe is not threatened by any Mediterranean country, unlike the USA it is directly exposed to the effects of civil turmoil in the region. It is the weakness and disorder of North Africa's states that disconcerts. The USA may marshal the peace, but it has neither the means nor the inclination to promote internal order in the Maghreb. In contrast, and despite their interests in preventing overseas distempers from reaching their own shores, EU countries fight shy of organizing effective policies in North Africa. They are deterred by the past. Disjointed as they are, Europe's neighbouring states of North Africa fought against Europeans to acquire governments of their own. Europeans do not therefore relish being accused of drawing them back within their sphere of influence because they do not know how to justify the exercise of power or how to combine it. They are also dissuaded by the difficulties of discovering an appropriate diplomacy. If the states of North Africa are ramshackle, Arabs possess in Islam at least one thing of unquestionable value to them that is not derived from Europe or dependent on the wealth and capacities of the USA.

Even as the EU envisages widespread economic co-operation with all the countries of the Mediterranean, its own gathering consolidation is likely to sharpen differences with the Arab countries of North Africa. These external consequences of its own development easily go unremarked. As the EU draws into itself with increased definition, so the single market, and the Shengen accords now incorporated in the Treaty of Amsterdam, are turning Europe's southern coastlines and islands into an extended political frontier. As Europe becomes delimited and policed at the borders of Greece, Italy, France and Spain, so this development will proclaim existing cultural and economic divides with novel abruptness. Although illegal migrants and asylum seekers entering Italy arouse friction elsewhere within the EU, the effects on Europe's foreign relations with Mediterranean and African countries may be even more acute. Should, as seems probable, Europeans come to recognize themselves as mobile members of a widespread union using a single currency, new common external frontiers pinpointing where foreigners begin will emphasize with unmistakable clarity that the EU is more than a single market and an experimental political theatre. Differences will become more remarked upon on both sides of Europe's passport, customs, immigration, asylum and refugee checkpoints. This is not so much a new story as one of the oldest fables concerning the constitution and policing of political bodies. Determining who has right of entry, residence, work and citizenship is an inseparable part of formulating a state.

Although Europe's relations with Russia and Turkey are also likely to chafe at their human frontiers, in the Mediterranean the interplay of political bodies which eventually establishes their respective identities is accompanied by passions that are especially difficult to mediate. ERE balks at the idea that Europe cannot determine its own character without simultaneously distinguishing between those who rightfully belong and those for whom entry to the EU is conditional. All such distinctions are suspect as means of unfair discrimination. Yet establishing political frontiers while declining to police them as ramparts is to demand a distinction whose effect is to negate the purpose in question. A preference for just laws of entry to the EU does not dispense with the need for regulations whose enforcement will give expression to the EU's 'body' even as it creates friction with other political bodies. Europe's reformation makes the issue of its openness to outsiders particularly delicate, because access to the EU and decisions affecting its human composition once more sets liberal principles at jangling odds with collective anxieties and their democratic espousal. With Europe's twentieth-century bigotry in mind, fears persist that the issue of immigration will deprive democrats of their liberal consciences. The universalism of liberalism that identifies only individuals clad in transparent rights, pulls in the direction of indifference to the cultural and religious make-up of individuals, whereas, in the form of *ethnos*, the *demos* asserts the collective rights of the people to determine its own composition. Relations with Mediterranean countries will thus put to the test how far the EU is able to form a union that cannot be indiscriminately open to all, without enraging liberal and collectivist passions liable to divide it yet further from neighbouring states.

Ingress to Europe is the one area of foreign affairs of direct concern to public opinion, and in democracies as elsewhere populism is no bar to electoral power. Although trade and access to the EU's markets may help both sides of the Mediterranean to live and let live, co-existence is the occasion for persistent diplomacy, rather than reason for believing it is no longer necessary. The conciliatory uses of diplomacy in dealing with the interests of states and the passions of men are weakened by the Cold War habit of treating foreign affairs as the pretext to ram home a single view of government and virtuous civil life. In dealing with Arab states, using power to induce them to become politically and economically more like oneself is a clumsy practice that Europe's envoys should renounce. The liberalism of forbearance that matters to Europe in the conduct of its external affairs should have little to do with the hectoring universalisms of a bi-polarized world.

In one other respect the EU should also set aside habits formed as a consequence of its past failings. The division of labour in the Mediterranean between the USA that brandishes the stick, while its EU and NATO allies furnish carrots, is a lopsided dualism that hampers European interests. MAMEE freezes, perpetuates and justifies the EU's indecisiveness in foreign affairs. Indispensable for the duration of the Cold War, NATO's preoccupation with stigmatizing rivals is currently of less relevance in the Mediterranean where what matters more than the military alignment of states is the arduous diplomacy of co-operating with ineffectual regimes.

The near-at-hand that includes Russia, Turkey and the Mediterranean is distinguishable from Europe's more distant connections largely by the play of spatially convenient words, and the mental inertia they justify. Israel's relations with its Arab neighbours and the world of Islam, bears no less importantly on Europe than civil strife in Algeria. Europe is more dependent on the oil and gas of the Gulf area than the USA, and the tussle for influence further north in the surrounds of the Caspian Sea already attracts Russia, the USA, Iran and Turkey, as well as China and Japan. Some three-quarters of the world's oil reserves and half of its natural gas deposits are said to lie within this area. They are the fuel of industrial life. Central Asia is also a region of unstable states and would-be states, prey to ethnic and religious passions. As businessmen and financial markets lick their lips, a new fulcrum of power politics is being prepared in which globalization is unpicking the distinction between regional and world powers. Most of the principal contestants are armed with intercontinental missiles and increasingly with the means of airlifting whole armies. Advantage lies with political bodies equipped with unified powers of decision. The EU's world-wide economic interests are not the only things likely to be at risk should a disorderly scramble for central Asia revive memories of previous imperial carve-ups. The apportioning of influence among great powers, local states, multinational companies and indigenous peoples will test whether Europe can afford to remain detachedly ineffectual. The ability of the EU to foster prosperity and remain competitive may turn on its willingness to hold its nose, ignore ERE and engage in power politics. The governed of Europe may not in retrospect thank their rulers for overlooking important interests merely because the effort of combining to exert maximum influence obliged the EU to equip itself with powers of credible decision.

Like pegging out washing, additional items can be attached to the congested storyline of prospective disorders. They include the Indian sub-continent, dislocations in the aftermath of south-east Asia's economic setbacks and, perhaps most vividly apparent, the Pacific area. Here China observes the rewards of US superpower, Japan registers the antics of both countries, and Russia casts an eye of perhaps only temporarily suspended interest. Hanging a tubfull of conjectured trouble-spots alongside each other does not imply that violence is inevitable or that conflicts are untreatable. It suggests only that Europe is vulnerable to the disturbances of ungoverned change. The diplomatic system will not become less anarchic unless those who have the power to make it so exert their influence. To assume that Europe's conservative interests in orderly and peaceful development will be secured without laborious efforts of its own, is to confuse well founded trust with an optimistic version of fatalism. Even were co-operative relations among the great powers to produce a cartel of tutelary powers, unless party to its decisions Europe's interests will go unrepresented.

## IV
## THE GIVEN WORLD

A world whose fortunes are tied to a clutch of great powers ungoverned by higher authority will be kept guessing. At times great powers may act to maintain a balance among themselves. They may co-operate to police a global peace, repress challenges to their own positions, accept new members to their oligarchy and surround themselves with institutions tailored to reconcile other members of the diplomatic system to their unequal status. Under different circumstances, and with as much plausibility, the rivalries of great powers may dominate events, with the rest of the world looking on. Between the extremities of these positions, and affecting every point of possibility between them, are the vagaries of economic life that tug power politics now this way and now that. The inventiveness of science and its ever more widespread and rapid applications furrow the earth in disorderly patterns. Aroused by the churning of events, men's passions cannot be expected to plod meekly in the wake of change.

Captivated by the spectacle of 'the great game' of power politics played out on the roof of the world, a hundred years ago Kipling relished the contest of empires straining and plotting for pride of strategic place. A century on and with a keenly felt sense of intervening events, Europeans tend to be dismayed or repelled by great powers lording it over the world.

The spectacle of power politics conducted in their names before the citizen audiences of the world is not, however, the only show in town. Though unlikely, some have confidently predicted that it is rapidly ceasing to be the main attraction. As marketization wraps the world in its skeins, the political and diplomatic effects of globalization may sooner rather than later make the fragmentation of the world into a kaleidoscope of states appear quaint. The posturings of great powers may turn out to be the last gasps of impotence. The powers of economic management thought vital to the functioning of states since Colbert's times, are now said to be confined by the activities of global markets which are shaping a new world. In the financial institutions that ignore political boundaries and operate consecutively in three time zones, one is always busily awake. The place to observe the formation of new coagulates of authority is therefore said to be in regional and international organizations which, though composed of states, are developing independent bureaucracies better attuned to world-wide markets. The scale of markets, and their purported indifference to states, is bringing to the fore agencies of equivalent range whose main purpose is to establish the ground rules essential to economic life. In line with this, the EU is often cited as a regional economic grouping whose single market is its main purpose as well as its principal achievement.

The argument adopted here is, however, that the EU does not so much register the obsolescence of states as represent a particular, and perhaps unique, formation of a political body that, should it progress, will be forced into the company of states. Through a combination of internal developments and external abrasions, it will become more like the diplomatic company it keeps, and will hence be obliged to find a place for itself within a diplomatic system dominated by great powers. If it does not make the choice for itself, the EU will find itself allocated a position designed to suit the interests of those with the organized capacities to decide the matter.

International organizations like the UN, and more especially agencies such as the IMF, World Bank, WTO and IAEA, are indeed noteworthy for their increased prominence, but the EU is unlike them and mistakenly numbered as one of their kind. At the decision-making centres of international organizations are usually to be found great powers whose positions are thereby yet more securely embedded. As stages on which the great powers have the most say, inter-governmental bodies are thus forums of many sided diplomacy rather than nuclei of 'international government'. If so, they are not free of power politics and lack the powers and authorization to rise above them. The effect of power politics, globalization, science and technology, and the myriad public, private and commercial bodies of no fixed national addresses that scud the world, is thus to widen the distances between two long established classes of states. One grouping consists of states large, rich, populous, educated and politically organized enough to hold their own even under the most stringent circumstances, while the other is made up of states that lack these attributes. Diplomatic bargaining power favours not the 58 countries with populations under $2^1/_2$ million.[5] but a superpower, three, four or five great powers, and several ambitious tyros. Even though small states may be beautiful, affluent, well-governed, competitive, contented and enviably – though conditionally – tangential to the main axes of power politics, in foreign affairs they lack the crucial ingredient. Whatever the attractions of powerlessness, they are not an advantage in a diplomatic system dominated by great powers.

For all their eminence, great powers may nevertheless not be individually powerful enough to withstand the much advertised 'disappearance of space' that currently appears beyond all powers of public control. Not all agree that globalization needs regulation, but the effort of bringing disorderly change under rule, which may be too much for individual great powers, may in consequence push them in the direction of far reaching co-operation. Their motives would be to make themselves the beneficiaries of change, while safeguarding their interests from the unwanted effects of scientific inventiveness and their commercial and military applications. Small states may set the pace and urge on the need for action, just as international organizations may prod and provide the oecumenical setting, but it is the largest powers who will govern what decisions are reached. If, for example, financial markets need to be better and more widely regulated, who else but those with most stake in their stability is able to provide an appropriate legal order and enforce its rules? It is the duty of governments not companies, banks, foreign exchange dealers or NGOs, to order the workings of the global economy, because it is the governed of the world who pay the price for its malfunctioning and inequities. Markets that are best fitted to create wealth are, or should be, accountable to the publics of the world for the conduct of their private and corporate activities. Although this may necessitate only the lightest of touches, the test is not the weight of regulation but its appropriateness. Although companies and markets who lay the golden eggs also form part of the governed, their interests are not synonymous with public well-being. Genetic engineering, global warming, water scarcity, bio-diversity, novel weaponry – in short, the entire gallimaufry of universalized fears and phobias – may figure as public concerns demanding concerted responses. Novel as it might strike Metternich or even Kissinger, a concert of great powers may be compelled to raise its sights beyond the habitual check-list of power politics, to include husbanding the earth so that its rising populations have a chance of feeling at home in it. Whether in pursuit of aims of this unprecedented kind the great powers will put aside their rivalries, or merely permit new sources of hope and fear to become mingled with the more familiar 'agitations' of foreign affairs, remains to be seen.

If the consequences of change require ordering, and the work of arranging 'dykes and embankments', is the work of powerful orderers, those who engineer public decisions will do more than leave the marks of their labours on events. If successful they will, to revert to an earlier metaphor, be inscribing a new script for the world's affairs. It seems likely that the great powers will audition only themselves for the leading roles of authorizing the new 'shape of life' being uncertainly produced by changes increasingly stimulated by the growth of knowledge. Whether or in what form Europe will figure in this directorial company also remains to be determined.

Twentieth-century Europeans are suspicious of reasoning that leaves responsibilities in the hands of powerfully unaccountable states. It sounds like black comedy. In foreign affairs, the remedies promised by states risk becoming worse than the ills calling for or justifying their interventions. As a consequence, and without apparently realizing that their sentiments re-dress issues without redressing them, Europeans are more inclined to put their trust in FUN than consider the case for equipping the EU to play its part in foreign affairs as one among a small number of tutelary powers. They cling to the misshapen idea that UN co-operation between states is a substitute for actions by its most powerful members.

Antipathy to the arbitrary conduct of states in foreign affairs is noticeably reversed when attention is switched from the external actions of states to their internal affairs, where power is subject to law and responsive to the opinions of the governed. This bifocular perspective is especially important to supporters of ERE because it enables them to applaud the interventionist activities of constitutional states while maintaining opposition to external actions that smack of power politics. Both the states and shared institutions of the EU are most convincingly justified by reference to the public goods that political bodies are able to provide. It is accepted that states are able to pursue an extended range of purposes in ways that private concerns such as companies or single-interest groups are not. The authority of states allows governments to balance competing purposes and rival claims, and to take on several tasks at the same time. On occasion this may lead in directions later regretted, as when, for example, states set themselves up as comprehensive welfare agencies, stifle markets with over-regulation, or attempt to direct entire economies. Yet the same general capacities of states which may lead governments astray also enable them to make a legal order possible and with it other goods, such as justice. In providing for education and making it compulsory, states may stand out as vehicles of enlightenment. They may not be the only public or private bodies able to provide the good things that individuals want, but in post-war Europe its recreated law-governed and interventionist states have received consistent support.

The citizens of EU states are attached to public spending. On average it accounts for just under 50 per cent of GDP in EU countries. So long as it is representative and responsible, large government appears welcome. In this benign guise the state is acceptable. The picture changes sharply, however, when other features of states are identified and brought to the fore. Nowhere do attitudes change more radically than when attention shifts to the necessary fearsomeness of states both in connection with domestic order and external security. There is a strong desire to reject, often in the name of civil liberties, a feature of political rule without which its public and private benefits cannot be acquired or safely enjoyed. Some measure of fearsomeness is inseparable from states and essential to them. The 'policing powers' of states are necessary to the maintenance of public order. As Somalia illustrates, the collapse of government clears the way for lawlessness. Without some of the 'awe' described by Hobbes in his exposition of the state, even government drawn from the consent of the governed is unable to fulfil its essential tasks. With customary terseness Hobbes described the 'business' of the state as 'Salus Populi (the people's safety)'. But in the Europe of the EU, even where the force of this argument is reluctantly conceded so that the public 'sword' is admitted as necessary to the observance of private 'covenants', its extension to include the external corollaries of the same reasoning has become a logical forced march too far. The eirenic forces of CE and ERE are mustered to deny that states need power of any 'awesome' kind in order to safeguard their borders and external interests. Yet the fearsome powers of states that according to Hobbes, are necessary to the 'protection and defence' of civil man are needed in equal if not greater measure to provide for his external security. Without sufficient power in the conduct of foreign affairs, domestic order is exposed to the diplomatic equivalents of Machiavelli's 'violent rivers' in spate. Although this may not ring true in connection with islands or areas sheltered from events, an EU that is rich, large, vulnerable, and ineffectual is captive to power politics. Because it would disfigure its pacific and at times pacifist principles, ERE cannot, however, accept the austerity of this reasoning.

Once it has been recognized that a diplomatic system is likely to be composed of fearsomely armed states, and that Europe is implicated in the predicaments this poses, those who bow before the arguments of *Salus Populi* remain open to the charge of having rehabilitated power politics by the back door. The measures taken by one state to secure itself will excite fears in others, which in turn will justify yet more awesome defences. What appeared to be actions confined to the internal policing of states produces effects that perpetuate insecurity throughout the diplomatic system. The treadmill-like character of this situation renews the determination of ERE to forswear foreign affairs wherever they imply power politics. When for example, it is suggested that western Europe's Cold War tranquillity, which enabled its states to practise law-governed politics, owed much to the supreme awesomeness of US power, the riposte is duly made that MAMEE was at least half responsible for a nuclear balance of power that kept

Europe divided and its peoples scared half to death. When it is similarly urged, in connection with the wars of Yugoslavia's succession, that Europe's FNUs were insufficiently awesome to strike fear into Croats, Serbs and Bosnians, the discussion is diluted elsewhere. FUN is favourably alluded to until it is noted that the UN protection force's (UNPROFOR) 'humanitarian' actions on behalf of 'the international community' supplied Bosnia's warring factions with the material means of continuing their fearsomely savage fighting.

Part of Europe's predicament, therefore, is to have public support for states that ensure law-governed politics and welfare, but which dissipates when it comes to exhibiting their awesomness in foreign affairs. The preference seems to be for states which, although armed and at the ready, do not excite fear and whose consequent ineffectualness, when divorced from MAMEE, is seen as confirmation of the depth of Europe's post-war political reformation. Largely thanks to MAMEE, the radiance of this exemplary confusion has not as yet been darkened by events.

If Europe's liberal democracies are allergic to the awesome aspect of Leviathan, they are equally disdainful of the inequalities of power between states. Inside some EU states there are yet more modest versions looking for a way out. This desire reflects a widespread intention to disregard or condemn the advantages that accrue to great powers. Whether the attempt to wean Europe off power politics and school the world in improved ways will secure the EU and its peoples from the disorders of the world, or give the EU a sufficient voice in the management of the diplomatic system, is doubtful. Like mice in the hold of ships they must hope and trust that Their Highnesses, who steer the fortunes of Europe from the decks of great foreign ships of state, use their awesome powers for the best in what is not the best of all possible worlds.

## V
## THE SHORTCOMINGS OF CO-OPERATION

It is possible to argue that size is not everything. Safety can be had in numbers. If true then Europe's supposed need to play a part in the diplomatic system commensurate with its capacities appears already well-provided for. Since the EU alone has fifteen members and is keen to add to its tally, the call in the Treaty of Amsterdam for 'an effective and coherent' foreign policy appears unnecessary. In the form of its multiple FNUs, Europe already possesses, or so it might be claimed, advantages that are its real source of strength. Its unity is served by its diverse unities. Because nation states are robustly effective, hand wringing over the weakness of 'Europe' when its middling sized states are compared with the great powers of the future is uncalled for. Effective relations with the rest of the world are, it is said, assured by the tried vigour of Europe's independent states. Were not many of them once great powers? And do they not remain impressively well organized centres of decision? Perhaps the only modification made necessary by the exigencies of a more compressed world, and the existence of continental sized states, is one that Europe's states are also fortunately well-placed to make. If Europe's FNUs who value their separate standing in the world nevertheless need to co-operate in order to compensate for the modesty of their individual powers, they are perfectly capable of doing so without surrendering their independence.

Co-operation in foreign affairs among the EU's FNUs is likely to be easily and effectively forthcoming because it is almost second nature. The record of European diplomacy is packed with awareness of the usefulness of diplomatic alignments and alliances and their compatibility with the pursuit of national interests. The Treaty of Amsterdam therefore either rehearses a kind of co-operation practised for centuries among Europe's states or, where it invokes the need for powers of more unified decision extending beyond co-operation, it calls for what is unneeded. The desire for more 'coherent and effective' action in foreign affairs may also be criticized on other grounds. It may be foolhardy and a cause of weakness. Frustration with the many-pronged approach of separate foreign policies brought voluntarily into alignment, risks disrupting something of more surpassing importance. In whatever direction one looks – towards Russia, Turkey, the Mediterranean, the Middle East and yet farther afield – the alliance of EU countries with the USA is the mainstay and *gezamptkoncept* of their external, and perhaps ultimately of their internal, interests as well. An ill-conceived quest to raise the profile of the EU in the diplomatic system endangers the more fundamental and persistent need for MAMEE.

In the not-so-distant past the advantages enjoyed in foreign affairs by Europe's nationally grounded states were considerable. Their combination of fellow-feelings, industrial development and habits of organized statehood was such a source of strength that in the aftermath of a war which showed the destructive powers of states, action was taken to limit the most notable example. Wariness of nationalism led to a federally decentralized western Germany designed to weaken its external powers. Yet collectivized passions sap as well as enhance the effectiveness of states. Belgium is not the only country where rival feelings threaten to disjoint even a federal state, producing two, and, in the case of Yugoslavia, five bodies where once there was one. Smaller but more intense, Croatia and Serbia feel better able to be states even though their effectiveness in foreign affairs is limited by their size.

With rare exceptions, however, regionalization of the kinds carried out in the unitary states of Spain, France, and forthcoming in the UK, comes to a halt at external relations. With sixteen *länder* which for some purposes represent themselves in the EU, a united Germany never-theless has a single foreign policy. Although Catalonia's 'cultural and educational exchanges' with foreign countries hints at a foreign policy of its own, even the most devolved states maintain their unity *vis-à-vis* the diplomatic system. A single external policy is regarded both as evidence of statehood and entitlement to membership of the diplomatic system, and as a condition of effectiveness from which the components of a federal union reap rewards. A unified foreign policy is thought to be worth its weight in bargaining power. In the past many federal unions of states were created mainly, and sometimes solely, in order to combine disparate peoples and internally self-governing bodies against external dangers which none could deal with adequately when acting independently. The impetus behind even the loosest of confed-erations is the wish to go one better than an alliance in order to meet outside threats. *Salus Populi* is the *raison d'être* of *raison d'état*. In this sense, the EU is an oddity; the impetus for its development derived from the scheme of hitherto bellicose states to reform their mutual affairs, whose external aspects were, because of the Cold War and unresolved mistrust in matters of war and peace, taken care of the by the USA and by an alliance. The USA is in turn the most celebrated modern illustration of the adage that in hanging together, like-minded states best secure themselves against the risks of hanging separately. Although some, like Virginia, valued their separateness, the thirteen colonies were pulled together first to expel the British and then secure their prized freedoms. 'Safety from external danger', Hamilton wrote, 'is the most powerful director of national conduct'. [6] For as long as it survives, a political body can have only a single foreign policy. It took the American civil war to ensure that the USA would remain one state with an effective CFSP. When a state speaks with a jumble of voices, the dissonance announces either its impending break-up, or signals its internal and exploitable weakness to other countries. Although the EU is a political body in important domestic respects and in matters of external trade, its disunion in foreign affairs reflects the determination of its member states to maintain their own positions in diplomacy. From the standpoint of statehood and judged by the diplomatic system the EU is therefore at present an anomaly. In this it is not entirely alone. President Bush was informed of the creation of the CIS by Yeltsin and his collaborators, at a time when Gorbachev still thought he was governing the unified state of the USSR. Whether in their present indeterminate forms the EU and the CIS are sustainable in a diplomatic system that favours organized powers of decision and penalizes hydra-headedess is doubtful.

Confidence in the durability of Europe's FNUs extends to believing in the continued ability of their states to share government within the EU, while conducting their own foreign policies. Although all members formally agree on the importance of co-operation to produce a CFSP, the hallmark of voluntarism is that it surrounds each state with the right not to co-operate and thereby prevent action: or to set terms that reduce co-operation to the level of gesture. What thus appears to carry most weight is not the capacity of EU states to hold their own in power politics or their ability to co-operate convincingly, so much as the overwhelming need to preserve an independent voice in the diplomatic system without which their very existence as nations is feared for. For a people to entrust any but themselves with their foreign affairs is thus felt to be a greater threat to the fellow-feelings of national identity than practicing shared government in the EU. It is as if to share with others matters of 'vital national interest' that centre on the risks of war and peace is akin not only to suicide but to treason. Only the sons and daughters of the nation can be trusted to safeguard the links that bind 'those who are living, those who are dead, and those who are to be born'.[7] If – but only if – nations are like individuals, one only has to list the number of people, including close relatives, to whom one would trust one's life, to bring home the differences between bargaining in Brussels over the Common Agricultural Policy or policing common EU frontiers, and willingness to risk one's neck under CFSP command. Yet throughout the Cold War, the assumption was presumably made that, if necessary, the national components of NATO would kill and be killed at SACEUR's bidding, much as British and other allied servicemen took orders from Americans as the price of victory in 1945.

The passions associated with Europe's FNUs have subsided over the past half-century. In some countries recollection of them is now a source of self-hatred that inspires determination to create ERE. In others, patriotic sentiments have been siphoned into less mortal outlets, such as economic productivity, sporting events and the Eurovision Song Contest. The more general effect of Europe's two centuries' long submersion in nationalist passions has been to divest a civilization of awareness that, in spite of diversity, it constituted what Burke was still able to call 'the republic of Europe'. Although Europeans may now stand recognized in many parts of the world, their own sense of a common broader identity is thin gruel compared with the epaulettes of national identity. This remains true in western Europe even where nationalism is now widely felt, especially among the young, to be an incubus. The EU is itself undecided whether national feelings are the repository of all that is best in 'the family of Europe' or a mischievous reliquary that hampers political union and the cultivation of wider civil or collective sympathies with itself as their focus. The feelings of 'homecoming' in central and eastern Europe on being freed to join the mainstream of European life was for a time palpable. Although the notion of 'European nationalism' may be as contradictory as it is frightening to some, the sentiments aroused in eastern Europe by rejoining its western part saluted the idea of a 'whole' about which one could feel strongly. Whether sentiments of this kind will be disowned, reappropriated by national sentiments, or enhanced by membership of the EU has yet to be discovered.

The attachment of Europe's states to their own foreign affairs is grounded in habit. Past experience of representing their own interests in the diplomatic system makes consent appear the normal and necessary basis of co-operation. The misentitled European Political Co-operation (EPC) made its tentative appearance only in 1971 and, although it showed a desire to bring foreign affairs under discussion, it also demonstrated that its venue was to remain firmly outside EEC institutions where common policies were forever being mooted. Even though all agreed that consent and co-operation were procedurally in keeping with the national and alliance conduct of foreign affairs, when Maastricht registered the acceptance of a CFSP, foreign affairs were purposely assigned their own 'pillar'. The need was to make clear that ' common positions' and ' joint actions' were not devices to outflank national foreign policies. It was designed to get the utmost out of diplomatic co-operation, not remove it from centre stage. Foreign affairs were to remain a field for EU diplomacy and not shared

government. No FNU was to be dragooned against its sovereign will
and independent judgement by the use of qualified majority voting in
foreign affairs. This could only come into effect once agreement on
substantive issues had been voluntarily secured in unanimous consent.
And since the principle of consent, in the EU and elsewhere, leaves
the most reluctant with a veto on decisions, it allows those who uphold
co-operation to appear more eager for action than is often the case.
Unanimity as the condition for effective action favours those who
prefer the red to the green light. It is the essential safeguard of states
unwilling to trust others with their vital national interests.

More recently the Treaty of Amsterdam appears to overstep these
limitations by making provisions for majority voting, albeit subject to
restrictively byzantine conditions. The pith and marrow of policy
remains firmly in the Council of Ministers where the authority of
states is buttressed. Even though this does not preclude the formation
of common policies, in one way or another it allows all states to
protect their own views from being overwhelmed. Agreement to the
creation of a 'coherent and effective' CFSP is thus as forthright as are
its cluttered and throttling conditions. National foreign policies have
not therefore been outlawed, or subsumed within an EU ministry of
foreign affairs flanked by a parallel defence establishment. Under the
most recent provisions of the Amsterdam Treaty, the Commission
(which has long had its own interests in external trade, aid and EU
enlargement) is, along with WEU involvement, to be more involved
with member states in the formulation of foreign policies. The Commission has not, however, acquired the sole or even an equal right to
initiate policy proposals. Within the Council of Ministers' secretariat
there is to be a policy planning staff, whose head will enunciate policy
to the public. The powers of states and the consequent powerlessness
of the EU nevertheless remains largely unaltered. The French proposal for a political figure of stature to embody the EU's position in
world affairs, did not survive the Intergovernmental Conference
(IGC) that prepared the ground for Amsterdam. National feelings
were once more portrayed by governments as setting limits to the
possibilities of unified decisions in foreign affairs. Whether the governed shared the same reluctance to see their foreign ministries and
diplomatists edged somewhat into the margins, is not known. The
Treaty of Amsterdam also leaves the WEU at arm's length, ensuring
thereby that defence policy remains segregated from foreign policy,
and in any case predominantly the domain of NATO. In both cases the
effect of trying to convey an EU actively engaged in the diplomatic

system is disabled by the distribution of powers in several organizations. Where this does not instil incredulity among those with whom the EU and its states negotiate, Europe's polyphony ensures paralysed indecision. Resistance at Amsterdam to incorporating the WEU within the EU, was led by British fears for the well-being of the Atlantic Alliance, and by neutral states whose anxiety to remain untouched by power politics presumably includes everything or nothing. FUN is more to their liking.

Although no longer big enough to be considered global powers, the four largest EU states are most protective of their individual standing in foreign affairs. Neither Britain nor France is willing to surrender its position as a permanent member of the UN Security Council on behalf of unified EU membership. In defence of their seats both emphasize their lengthy experience of foreign affairs and responsibilities as nuclear powers. Each is willing to represent EU viewpoints so long as this does not compromise their individual standing. The pride of once great powers survives the conditions which raised them high. Britain and France cannot be forced out of their seats or be made to make room for additional permanent members of the Security Council without their consent. Membership of the EU appears to have little bearing on their determination to retain their privileged diplomatic positions. Their standing at the UN enhances the claim that they are most suited to guide the EU in foreign affairs.

Shouldering Britain and France is Germany. In view of its third place in the world's economics league, a united Germany holding pivotal economic and political sway in the centre of Europe has perhaps a more persuasive claim for recognition as a world power. Although Germany has painstakingly regained diplomatic respectability, strongly felt opinions both within and without remain opposed to a foreign policy that has any truck with the independent use of military power or indeed with any unequivocal assertion of German national interests. Even though 'Europe' and NATO have long been seen as the only acceptable conduits for its external interests, Germany is nevertheless the one European country that could foreseeably hold its own in the topmost division of power politics. Fears that, in spite of domestic inclinations hostile to the idea, Germany may find itself exercising independent power in foreign affairs is itself a powerful inducement to the formation of a credible CFSP within the EU. The logic of this reasoning that is echoed in the need for a 'European Germany' safely housed in confining institutions is not of course unique to foreign affairs. It is the *leitmotiv* of the entire post-war reformation of western Europe, whose latest expression is EMU. The difference, of course, is that whereas the EU has powers of decision in internal affairs, these are largely absent in matters of foreign policy. There it is MAMEE and NATO that supervise Germany and provide it with means of expressing its national interests in the diplomatic system. Even so, Germany's independent standing in foreign affairs has risen since the end of the Cold War. Although alliance with France remains the mainstay of Germany's policy this no longer means unconditional deference to Paris in external affairs. The voluntary basis of the EU's CFSP leaves ample room for an independent German diplomacy. Although advanced with a coyness reflecting the spirit of ERE, Germany's claims to a permanent seat in the Security Council are steadily advanced. For its part Italy considers its entitlement to a permanent seat in New York as no less worthy than that of the three other largest EU countries. The venture in Albania indicated a desire to be more prominent in foreign affairs which not all its EU partners endorsed. Italy's zeal for 'Europe' is no bar to asserting itself separately in the diplomatic system. By virtue of the size of its economy, Italy's membership of the G7 grouping of states, which includes Germany and France, is more secure than Britain's.

Each of the EU's four largest countries maintains a panoply of diplomatic representation in other states and at international organizations that embraces most of the world's capital cities. Especially in connection with multilateral bodies, Britain, France, Germany and Italy, along with other EU members, co-ordinate action and, where national interests permit, present a commonly agreed standpoint. In those places where the EU Commission has its own accredited envoys, at the IMF and the WTO, for example, need for yet further consultation exists. Below or, more diplomatically, co-adjacent to the four largest EU countries are others, like Spain, Portugal, Austria, Holland and Sweden, all of which recall past times when their countries were great powers. Except for Austria – though including Belgium and Denmark – these countries also acquired overseas empires, which has left their modern states with often close but ambiguous relations with their former colonies. Sweden and Austria, along with Finland and Ireland, are now neutral states. The presence of small states with principled opposition to power politics and active interests in FUN, adds its own debilitating complexities to the task of enacting a 'coherent and effective' EU foreign policy. The cast list of the EU's diverse representation in the diplomatic system, at present completed by tiny Luxembourg, will lengthen further with the enlargement of the EU to east and south. Some existing members, like Britain, see in an EU of twenty or more, a guarantee of their independent positions not only in domestic but also in foreign affairs. Nothing unified is capable of emerging from such diversity. A CFSP worth the name is thought to be impossible among so large a number of states. France appears more inclined to see an unwieldy EU as providing the opportunity, seen as a necessity, for French leadership in foreign affairs.

When it is suggested that the liking of states for their own foreign policies does not itself demonstrate their efficacy, the tendency of governments is to refer to the national sentiments of the governed. In democracies, one is reminded, the duty and interest of elected governments is to make sure that electorates are following their leaders. Although citizens are seldom consulted about foreign affairs it is then asserted that nations are opposed to the demotion of their states in the diplomatic system. It is one thing to co-operate in seeking 'common positions' and 'joint actions', and another to share, even with partners in the EU, decisions that may vitally effect their survival. Particularly in the largest EU states, the will of their peoples is said to be unmoveably hostile to the extension of political union beyond internal affairs and trade. When the arrow of policy points outwards the fellow-feelings of nations are said to be closed to the compromises of shared government. By way of emphasizing the folly of pushing too hard for a unified European foreign policy the dangers of provoking nationalist reactions are then alluded to. RDE is said to be the likely penalty of trying to squeeze individual states out of their entrenched places in the diplomatic system.

When it is repeated that the identification of a nation with its recognition by others as a separate state does not necessarily, or of itself, ensure the adequate protection of national interests, it becomes necessary to adjust the argument. Whereas the case for close co-operation in foreign affairs could be advanced as compatible with the independence of states, because it could commit them to nothing without their consent, it also implied the need to combine powers which were recognized as being individually too weak. It now has to be maintained that, even without co-operative alignment with other states, Europe's FNUs retain within their individual selves all that is needed to uphold their external interests. If necessary, the nations of Europe can each look after their own vital interests because the stalwart breasts of patriots are the most trusty shields of states. National sentiment, which was earlier adduced as setting limits to co-operation between states, now appears to make even partial reliance on others dispensable. France, Germany, Britain and Italy remain doughty enough to go it alone in power politics not because they possess individual power comparable to the USA, China, or other continental sized states, but by virtue of their national wills. To reason thus is, however, to put the cart before the horse. To focus entirely on the presumed attachment of Europe's states to their independence in world affairs has the disconcerting effect of largely ignoring the conditions that determine the effectiveness of a foreign policy. Because national identities and the collective sentiments on which they rest are allowed to fill the picture, the world of power politics to which states belong is obscured. Instead of beginning with the diplomatic system and its power politics, and then determining how best national interests are to be furthered, the matter is discussed the other way about, as if the world could be tailored by individual states to suit their individual interests merely because nations take pride in themselves. It can, of course, be objected that states do not come into existence as the result of diplomatic arithmetic and that nations value the modest measure of independence they are able to maintain knowing full well the limitations under which most of them are confined to playing minor parts in the diplomatic system. Many states are reconciled to having no more than walk-on parts. International organizations offer plenty of opportunities for holding high the flags of nations and for the envoys of states who lack power to flatter and console each other's sensibilities. Arguments of that kind cannot, however, be relied upon in discussing the place of Europe's states in foreign affairs because its largest nations vigorously deny that the price of their resplendent individuality is relative powerlessness.

Yet if all that states had to do in order to further their interests was to vaunt their existence and name the external circumstances most agreeable to them, there would not be much need for foreign policy. Wishes would be enough to father outcomes. Not even a superpower like the USA is in this position. To achieve its ends, its government has to do more than rouse national feeling in support of policies, important as that is. Even when the USA exerts itself to the full, it still cannot be sure that events are in its grasp. The USA has been unable to bring about a lasting peace in the Middle East. No member of the diplomatic system has the power to treat it like putty. Acting 'independently' or even in concert with like-minded states does not demonstrate that a country is the author of its actions. Where it performs to a script in which it has only a minor part, or where the leading actors ignore the existence of sub-plots, a state with its own foreign policy has little room for individual manoeuvre. At Munich in 1938, the independent and sovereign state of Czechoslovakia was not even allowed to appear on stage. As Churchill appreciated at the time, the heroics of Dunkirk were hardly evidence that because Britain possessed a strong sense of national identity this enabled it to determine events. At Suez, Britain and France were cowed by the strategic weight of Moscow and Washington. Fevered national feelings in London and Paris hardly affected the balance of power. The imbalance revealed did not imply that either country had forfeited its national identity or ceased to be self-governing; but it did expose a cavernous divide in power politics, which neither Britain nor France any longer had the means of bridging. The scope of their actions, their capacities to 'authorize' events, was henceforth (despite possession of nuclear weapons) diminished. During the Cuban Missile crisis, Macmillan and de Gaulle were consigned to the wings. They were consulted by Kennedy when he thought fit. An 'independent' foreign policy is thus one thing and its capacity to affect events another. For reasons of national sentiment many states conduct their own foreign policies irrespective of the meagre influence their actions can hope to have on the course of events.

A sheep is not made independently powerful merely by virtue of having an identifiable 'sovereign' body uniquely its own, and which only it has the means to propel quadrupededly in pursuit of vitalizing natural interests in grass. Constitutional sovereignty encapsulates no promise of power in the field of diplomatic forces. It is the expression of juridical authority and international status, which with good reason is silent on the relative diplomatic effectiveness of states. That silence is filled by power politics. The recognition by sheep of each other's distinct existences does not safeguard a flock of sensitive ewes from wolves. The attachments of Europe's FNUs to their distinct roles in power politics may persuade governments to reject a CFSP, but this is evidence of sentiment that only on rare occasions, when the wolf is at the door, can be translated into powers of stubborn resistance. For the most part and at present, Europe's states are not in that position. Their principal interest lies in a better ordered diplomatic system, yet memories of past influence and a continued sense of national worth do not supply from within themselves the means of bringing it about. Perhaps because of the sheltering illusions of MAMEE's shepherding, Europe's FNUs prefer to rely on their economic poundage to make their weight felt in foreign affairs. This may impress other sheep, but their teeth are unlikely to appear 'awesome' to carnivores who possess fangs as well as productive muscle. Even in Bosnia, EU declarations of concern and missions of mediation counted for little. When its states attempted to appear in wolf's clothing, they fell into a credibility crevice prepared by their own obliviousness of power politics. In order to exert influence in foreign affairs more is needed than what Hamilton called 'mere pageants of mimic sovereignty'. Countries attached to ERE give off the impression that in foreign affairs they have discovered the means of bringing influence to bear that circumvent the need to possess powers of effective decision.

The confusions revealed in Europe's attitudes to foreign affairs represent more serious defects than miscalculations. They stem from a prolapse of imagination. There is a refusal to recognize that *fortuna* has altered the balance and proportions of world power without abolishing power politics. Inadequate comprehension has little to do with processing systems of information. Many of the facts and figures germane to the USA, China, Japan, Russia and most other centres of decision are available on-line and in pocket sized books. Matters such as the size and performance of economies, governmental organization, military preparedness, scientific competence, the spread and intensity of interests, public support for policies, and the ambitions of rulers and ruled, may be harder to collate than is generally believed, but the difficulties of sifting information and deducing policies from it are not the nub of the matter.

The inability of Europe's present national statesmen to see the world from beyond themselves is not the first time this has happened. Although Machiavelli recognized the descent of the armies of France and Spain into Italy after 1494 as a disaster for the rich but small princely states of the peninsula, even this connoisseur of power failed to distil its widest significance. He saw that none of Italy's feisty rulers was able to resist the new scale of power represented by the French and Spanish monarchies. Perhaps because he felt so vividly that 'their barbarous tyranny stinks in everyone's nostrils'[8] he was unable to imagine that a vaster balance of power was then in the making for which Italy, like Europe during the Cold War, was to be the play-ground and the prize. He proclaimed that co-operation between Flor-ence, with a population of some 70,000, and other city states was strong enough to deliver Italy from a situation he believed reversible. Once the 'present extremity' was overcome, Florence and the others would, he appears to have thought, resume their former powers. Blinded by the desire to be rid of foreign domination, Machiavelli did not realize that the diplomatic system of fifteenth-century Italy had been brought to its terminus. It was to be absorbed into a new continental order of power politics taking shape before his eyes beyond the Alps.

Machiavelli's exhortation to the unity of Italy in the last chapter of *The Prince* fell on deaf ears. Would it have been better, and more in keeping with his thinking, to have aimed his salvo at the head rather than the heart? During the inter-war years following 'the great war for civilization' of 1914–18, cries of comparable intensity were addressed to 'Europeans' to set aside a fratricide that was doing their inheritance to death. Not enough rulers or ruled were moved. The states of Europe could not see beyond their nations. Aware of this failure, the leaders of post-war Europe's reformation preferred schemes based on interests to emotional appeal. Coal and steel, followed by a common market, would bring peoples together as material benefits showed up in improved standards of living. The rationale of interests would be a surer if less evocative means of instilling the advantages of gradual political union. Under the conditions of the Cold War, western Europe's external weakness produced NATO and dependence on the USA, not a union of European states based upon the principle of *Salus Populi*.

In the altered conditions that have followed the end of the Cold War there is little reason to believe that the influences which produced the EU will eventuate in an effective CFSP. Merely because a single market has succeeded in the creation of more wealth, this has not freed foreign affairs from the hold of nationally based states. In which country, it is asked, are rulers and ruled ready to have their armed forces placed under the command of fellow Europeans? And where are the replacement or parallel fellow-feelings of solidarity that, lodged in the EU, are capable of inspiring trust, self-sacrifice and loyalty? Even if reasoned argument is capable of suggesting that national interests now lie in and via a CFSP backed by European armed forces, it is likely to make no inroads on the veto of national feelings.

'No man', wrote Swift, 'was ever reasoned out of what he was not reasoned into in the first place'. One can catalogue the costs of Europe's disunion in the scales of power politics, without their enumeration undermining instincts nourished at the bosom of one's motherland. The supposed impossibility of maintaining national identities and serving national interests through the shared exercise of power is, however, rebutted by the evidence of Europe's post-war history. Had national sentiment been an insuperable barrier to combined action in foreign affairs, NATO would have been stillborn. Although the rejection of plans for an EDC by the French National Assembly in 1954 exposed the legacy of fears implanted by events, the failure to live down the past nevertheless immediately resulted in German rearmament within NATO's integrated and American dominated command structure. The USA made it plain that refusal to accept a German contribution to the defence of Europe and to rearm themselves would lead to an 'agonizing reappraisal', and in all probability to the withdrawal of MAMEE's protection against the USSR. Present fears and urgent necessities trumped all else. Faced with circumstances they were in no position to ignore, the European members of NATO agreed in advance to place their salvation as nations and states in the hands of SACEUR who was, and has always been, an American. In the event, holding fast to the inviolability of national sovereignty was not considered an effective response to the Red Army. In order to uphold national interests, NATO's European states were forced to swallow their pride and accept the consequences of their individual weakness. Their 'sovereignty' was preserved only by accepting severe limits on their independence in matters affecting their very survival. With the exception of Gaullist France, NATO's other members accepted that, in foreign affairs, their FNUs were of necessity compelled to follow the USA. National susceptibilities were accordingly adjusted.

Neither dependence on MAMEE for their security, nor membership of the EU seems to have been felt as an erosion of national identity or an infringement of national self-determination. During the Cold War the weakness of European states made it imprudent to resent the imbalance of power represented in NATO. The shift from self-government towards shared government that is to be seen in the EU, and which is likely to be furthered by EMU, was agreed to by the governments of states responsible to national electorates. Although governments may have lately come to complain about the pinch on their powers, the governed seem to have been untroubled by the development of the EU's internal powers of decision.

## VI
## MIGHTY AMERICA IN EUROPE

The post-war renunciation of war by the states of western Europe, which set the stage for political reformation, was not achieved unaided.

Pacification was prompted by fears that countries within the Red Army's sights were exposed to Stalin's mercy. Yet without the USA, the defencelessness of western Europe was not enough to overcome national divides left open by two wars within a single lifetime. Though In 1945 Germany had been occupied, its neighbours, and above all France, knew it had taken the combined powers of the USSR and the USA, aided by Britain, to overwhelm its mighty enemy. Fears of revived German power precluded the formation of a western European alliance against the USSR. Some questioned its necessity, interpreting the consolidation of Soviet power as a clumsily executed defensive measure directed against the predatory designs of American-led capitalism. Irrespective of who most accurately gauged Moscow's intentions, postwar western Europe was in need, as Joffe has aptly noted, of both a pacifier and a protector.

The USA answered both needs. The EU and the successful outcome of the Cold War both vindicated the Atlantic alliance created in 1949. In the absence of MAMEE, the states of western Europe would have remained too distrustful of each other to risk advancing beyond power politics; and only the USA wielded enough power to induce the USSR, and some of its more nervous allies, to accept the unification of Germany. The conclusion of the Cold War nevertheless led to suggestions that, as was earlier said of the British Empire, NATO's finest hour should be its last. Some were heard to say that although the USA had indeed been indispensable to the creation and security of political union in western Europe, which it repeatedly urged on, those days were now past. Altered circumstances produce different needs. Persistent US advocacy of Europe's integration had, it was said, succeeded so well that MAMEE had rendered herself redundant. The EU was depicted as a tribute to the wisdom of US policy; just as someone learning to swim has eventually to trust himself to raise the last toe from the floor of the pool so, in the form of the EU, Europe has at last acquired the confidence to strike out on its own.

A more careworn viewpoint worries not that the EU is unable to acquire the body and the brio to fend for itself in foreign affairs, but that the desire is misconceived. From this standpoint the Atlantic alliance is as vital as ever to Europe, as well as to more encompassing 'Western interests'. The time, it is counselled, to reinforce existing 'dykes and embankments' is when the waves appear stilled. While the former view stresses the distance Europe has come since the 1950s, and is impatient to plunge ahead, the latter opinion warns that since 1917 the USA has on several occasions had to rescue

Europe's FNUs from their repeated excesses. From this standpoint, the internal and external afflictions from which the twentieth century has suffered pleads the folly of agitating for a Europe that, irrespective of whether it succeeds or drowns in the attempt, risks severing its umbilical ties to MAMEE.

From Truman to Clinton US administrations have succoured Europe's reformation. Although American interests in more solidly reliable allies derived from conflict with the USSR over the balance of power in Europe, this did not lead to attempts by the USA to instruct western Europe to create a common market, or develop towards political union. Though principally designed to assure dependent European allies that NATO secured their countries against the USSR, the stationing of a third of a million American troops in western Europe also appeased fears that a Franco-German reconciliation which faltered, or proved too strong, might reproduce RDE. The reduction of US troops to nearer 100,000 since the disbandment of the Warsaw Pact leaves open the sore question whether, as in the past, MAMEE's presence is in part dictated by Europe's continuing need for a pacifier. If it remains true that the peace of Europe is secure only when policed by a foreign power from across the Atlantic, this naturally casts the progress of political reformation in darker perspective. It implies that the states of western Europe are less trusting towards each other than has been made out. A single market and the practices of shared government have not silenced the bogeys of national antipathy. The unification of even a liberal democratic Germany at the economic and political centre of Europe troubles Germans as well as their fellow EU citizens. The Brussels of NATO's 'sword', according to this Hobbesian argument, is therefore still necessary to the *'salus populi* or people's safety' of the Brussels of Europe's reformation achieved by the 'covenants' of Rome, Maastrict and Amsterdam. A withdrawal of all US troops from Europe, which is sometimes recommended on strategic and economic grounds, and which attracts support in Congress, would, in this view, so fibrillate the nerves of Europe's FNUs as to shatter the incipient body politic of the EU. Do the French, whose tetchiness over US domination of NATO has, since de Gaulle's days, been only diplomatically tempered, truly and in their heart of hearts look forward to the wee hours of the night after the last of MAMEE's sons and daughters have set sail for home? Will Poles in like manner feel more secure *vis-à-vis* Russia as their point of principal dependence shifts from Washington to Berlin? Are Greeks and Turks or Serbs and Albanians, likely to defer with the same discipline to the diluted compromises of fifteen EU foreign policies as to the commander in chief of the US Mediterranean fleet?

Trust is the most fugitive of political goods. Without it, political bodies cannot prosper. The rupture of trust when people refuse to be governed together announces secession, civil war or tyranny. Politics have for long been ruled out in Northern Ireland because neither of the 'two communities' could bring itself to trust the other with power. The 'consent of the governed' forks into rival sets of governed. In foreign affairs, the rules and conventions of a diplomatic system seek to reduce the disorder stemming from a manifold of self-governing states – whose members are often riven by civil disputes – who refuse to entrust their fortunes to the higher authority of what Burke called, 'the cold neutrality of an impartial judge'. Power politics are the result of this scantily regulated mistrust between states. Diplomacy both expresses and seeks to bridge the discord of states.

Being neither a state upheld by the trust of the governed, nor a regional diplomatic system of mistrustful states, the EU embodies the measure of confidence thus far achieved in Europe's reformation away from power politics and towards politics properly so-called. Its members no longer stand in fear of each other's fearsome powers. Their anxieties are mostly residual; hence their ability to test the waters of shared government. The enigma of political trust is not so much that it is largely uncomputable or cannot be manufactured to order, as that it is impossible to know in advance how far it can be relied upon. Have Europe's states moved far enough to trust each other and the EU with powers necessary to conduct public affairs? And is that enough to dispense with MAMEE as a sword-bearing pacifier?

Perhaps Europe's rulers and ruled will forever postpone trusting the durability of their covenanted reformation, so long as they rely on (that is, trust) the USA more than themselves. The most brazen supposition underlining belief in the feasibility of self-government is the liberal, and perhaps democratic, precept that trust is only likely to be forthcoming when put to the test; when responsibility *has* to be taken for one's actions. Peering from the side of the swimming pool is no substitute for the experience that only immersion produces. Had it been necessary to demonstrate in advance that the *demos* could safely be relied upon to use its powers with good sense, universal enfranchisement would have remained forever over the horizon. 'Trusting the people' with the affairs of states was for long opposed as irresponsibly risky because 'the people' was considered too incurably ignorant to learn as it began to exercise power. Decolonization of Europe's empires was justified by the argument that only with the achievement of independence, by entrusting themselves with the emancipation they had won, would the habits of self-government acquire the necessary opportunity to develop.

It may now be appropriate for Europeans to put themselves to a test in keeping with their own principles and which they have liberally recommended to others. Continued dependence on MAMEE to chaperone the good behaviour of Europeans encapsulates their own mistrust and makes it yet more difficult to lay it to rest. Reliance on the USA to superintend the domestic peace of Europe, while the EU launches ahead with ambitious projects like the EMU, prolongs schizophrenia. At the same time as EMU implies more shared government, the EU tantalizes itself with fears of RDE. This in turn prevents the growth of confidence that should be the reward for half a century of increased mutual dependence. The accumulated experience gained in the forty years since the creation of the ECSC, which should have buried memories of the first half of the twentieth century, is thus devalued. Europe's unwillingness to shoulder its own public affairs nourishes disbelief. The fault lies not in any desire of the USA to mastermind 'the matter and form' of Europe, but with the reluctance of Europeans to rid themselves of Cold War habits of dependency on MAMEE. The effect within the EU of impaled self-doubt is to hamper a political union that is about to risk producing a reserve currency for the world and enlarge itself, and which has increasing interests of its own in a diplomatic system that favours those powers that trust their own powers of decision. Although the pursuit of ambitious ends like EMU is bound to test nerves, the prize to be won by success is to scotch Europe's remnant fears that it is not to be trusted with power. The creation of political trust may be laboursome and not to the liking of the intemperate or faint-hearted, but its rewards are priceless. They enable those who come to be entrusted with powers of decision to exercise them with authority.

The loops of trust easily appear as seamlessly inconclusive as a figure of eight. Where the EU is their subject, following their contours supports the complaint that Europe spends too much of its energies checking its sociological pulse. This in turn justifies evasion of the lesson explored with remorseless logic by Hobbes and which Europe's entire post-war development exemplifies; prosperity and good government are inseparably bound up with security. The important part the USA played as Europe's pacifier is nevertheless of secondary importance to, or was in any case contingent upon, its role as Cold War protector. The superpower of the USA was alone sufficient to convey trustworthy promises of defence and security against the USSR. NATO was able to shield the fretful states of western Europe because in America's Supreme Allied Commander it possessed awesome powers of mass destruction that the USSR feared to challenge directly. What began in the late 1940s as a makeshift gesture to calm fears of Soviet expansionism has, fifty years on, developed into a military alliance of effectively organized commands.

A diplomatic system no longer moulded by superpower rivalry has nevertheless led to the belief that the continuation of a uniquely successful alliance is imperative. In foreign affairs, no version of Europe exists able to make promises comparable to those tested for half a century in the Atlantic alliance. Just as the EU and the WEU are no substitutes for NATO, so the global concerns of the USA likewise need helpmates it can trust to act alongside it beyond the confines of the organization's article five. As NATO is transformed from a Cold War regional alliance into an 'intervention alliance' able to deploy rapidly reacting force wherever it is thought necessary so, it is argued, the cohesiveness of the 'Atlantic partnership' is of greater rather than diminished value. In this view, the peace of the world may depend on NATO's effectiveness, and with it Europe's principal interest in the orderly working of the diplomatic system. If this means that the EU and the WEU must reconcile themselves to playing second fiddle to NATO, it is noted that Europe has no orchestrated external powers of its own. Were it to chance even a string ensemble, Europe's FNUs would, it is confidently predicted, squabble themselves to paralysis over the choice and manufacture of instruments, the choice of players and music, the nationality and powers of the conductor, its theatres of operation and, given the democratic and domesticated habits of CE, the costs of the whole meddlesome operation. The Eurocorps established by France and Germany, and since joined by Belgium and Spain, may, it is said, be a quartet with promise, but any more ambitious aims to create an effectively unified European defence force would appal ERE, whose preferences lie neither with a European Security and Defence Identity (ESDI) nor with NATO, but with supporting FUN's 'peace keeping' activities.

At the elbow of military schemes for an ESDI are matters of more imposing diplomatic difficulty. Throughout its existence, and deriving from both sides of the Atlantic, demands for a more equitable NATO have periodically arisen. The hardiest metaphor used in discussion plays on the figure of pillars. Although America's allies are unable to raise themselves to the same elevation as NATO's mainstay, a 'European pillar' would, it is regularly urged, help redress a transatlantic imbalance that has existed from the onset of the Cold War. On the eve of the Korean war, 'Europe' had little to contribute to the 'containment of communism' but, as European countries rearmed, a more balanced distribution of allied power between two, rather than fifteen or so points of reference, was thought advisable in order to silence complaints of MAMEE's highhandedness. This often produced American demands for Europeans to pay more for their defence while leaving the major military commands safely in their own hands. The USA has seldom been willing to entrust decisions or commands of importance to its allies. Since the Cold War, moves sponsored by France to appropriate the WEU as the EU's 'defence arm' have rekindled discussion over the need for a more equal Atlantic relationship. When, however, it looked as if some Europeans were serious about a defence 'pillar' of their own, which would be operationally distinct from NATO, argument appears to have sharpened. Protestations that an ESDI was compatible with NATO, and would indeed strengthen it, were met by Congressional retorts that if Europeans believed they could make a better fist of protecting themselves without MAMEE, the sooner they did so the better. When, however, Europeans caught wind of this mixture of American glee and distemper, many of them began to agitate with fear and trembling. Led by Britain, though including France as well as Germany, these countries became anxious to tell MAMEE that without her apron strings, Europe's FNUs would be reduced to relying for their security on the devices of HE.

Thucydides long ago described the upheavals that plague and frequently destroy alliances. The diplomacy needed to hold a revised NATO together does not therefore prove it is falling apart. Under circumstances where the USSR no longer sets warning limits to the dangers of allied rancours, NATO's internal ordering is bound to be diplomatically demanding. The EU's aim to create a 'coherent and effective' CFSP can hardly fail to stir passions as well as military argument. The most unyielding topics facing the Atlantic alliance are not the organizational provisions under which NATO's European members are to be at liberty to act without the involvement and endorsement of the USA. Citizens may indeed blanch when trying to grasp the links and connections under which European members will be able to use NATO's technologies of information, communications and command and control, while the Pentagon and American generals in Europe gaze forebearingly heavenward. Yet the most troublesome matters lie beyond administrative arcana. Until the substance of the forthcoming century's power politics have been adumbrated, devising 'architecture' to house disparate purposes is akin to setting up scaffolding in a vacuum.

The most difficult matters affecting Europe's relations with the USA have beguilingly simple labels. They also tend to incorporate answers mobilized during the Cold War and which, as the EU alters and the diplomatic system also changes, may no longer reply to the appropriate questions. The trouble, for example, with the 'the West' is not that it is a senseless or unimportant idea, but that it has been badly mangled by the Cold War. If 'the West' alludes to 'western civilization', then the point of reference which supplies it with meaning is presumably the great schism of Christendom between Rome and Constantinople traceable to the exchange of anathematas of 1054. The USA is thus deemed part of western civilization because its European forebears hailed from Protestant and Catholic western Europe. Where this reckoning leaves 'the West's' indebtedness to classical antiquity is left obscure, though since politics (as distinct from government) were invented centuries before the incarnation of God, omitting Athens and ancient Greece from a picture representing the importance of politics to good government is selectively weird. In more recent times, the centuries-long indifference or hostility of Roman and Orthodox Christianity to constitutional politics and civil liberties, has given way to a version of 'the West' adjusted to the Cold War. Under this treatment, the legacy of Periclean Athens and Justinian's digest of laws was harmonized with a Protestant view of Christianity whose essence was usefully discovered to include individualism and productive worldliness. The exigencies of the Cold War demanded that 'the West' was ranged against the Bolshevism of an 'East' identified with Russia and, with Mao's success in 1949, distended to include China. Although Marxism is as 'Western' or European as Liberalism or Democracy, for the purposes of the Cold War it was identified as the enemy of 'Western' freedoms. 'The West' was thus made to stand for individual freedoms, democratic government, the rule of law and, somewhat confusingly, also the collectivist right of nations to political self-determination. Although few seem to have done so, free nations that sided with 'the West' were expected to accommodate free individuals. Without demonizing the Cold War enemies of these personal and civil goods, it is doubtful whether in the mid-1940s the US Congress would have rejected isolationism and responded with such vim to

Soviet power in central and eastern Europe. In order to accommodate the strategic purposes of the Cold War, 'the West' was thereafter elasticated to include Turkey, Japan, Iran before the Ayatollahs, and almost any country or faction important to Washington. Lip service had everywhere to be paid to the political canon of 'the West' whose genius, it was explained, lay in principles and practices of universal applicability.

As the engine of 'the West's' prosperity, and the exemplar of individualist and corporate vigour, capitalism became integrally linked to 'Western democracy'. Free men, the rights of majorities, the will of nations and the liberating energies of 'free enterprise' were presented as 'the West's' endowment to the world. Europeans may at times have fiddled with hybrids containing dubious references to social this and socialist that, but this was excused as evidence of 'the West's' liberal and experimental diversity.

The collapse of the Soviet party-states in 1989–91 has left 'the West' in propagandist quandary. What public sense is to be made of the Atlantic alliance detached from its chosen formularies? And what solidifying meaning can 'the West' cling to in the absence of an inimical 'East'? One reply is that 'the West' still 'stands for' liberal democracy and market capitalism, and that it therefore 'stands against' tyranny, the denial of 'human rights' and economic malpractices, each of which offers plentiful if opaque grounds for 'Western' intervention. Advancing from the back foot of the Cold War to the front foot of its uncertain aftermath, these postulates of 'the West's' credo allow NATO to arm itself with 'ideological' purpose. In this view, even if it faces independent states, nations and religious passions that are lukewarm to its power and purposes, 'the West' must spread at least the semblance of democracy and use its powers to open the diplomatic system to global capitalism. Foreshortened to the rationale of a military alliance, this means that NATO must be equipped to intervene wherever principle and interest require it. Hence the need for rapidly reacting mobile forces to which European countries are required to adapt themselves. Where 'the West's' preparedness leaves the principles of national self-determination and self-government of peoples who decline to adopt enlightened 'Western' ways is not revealed; their fate appears to have been caught on the wrong side of history.

Whether this self-serving conservatism clothed in progressivist zeal is to the taste or interests of the EU is not self-evident. In a century notable for its triumphs, the USA may still have the desire and audacity to act as the world's moral midwife, but making NATO its forceps is likely to divide Europe and America. The Cold War effects of proselytizing the rival merits of 'Western democracy' and 'people's democracy' has not been to spread habits of good government, but rather to debase the entire vocabulary of politics and alienate the governed from its practices. No matter what its actual conduct, every member of the UN is encouraged to titillate itself with the name of democracy. The mendacity this authorizes saps beliefs that action taken by governments can be principled and that the best advertisement of principle is the example of practice. Europe has no interest in seeing the coinage it has spent half a century rehabilitating discounted as special pleading in the service of power. If the USA is incapable of acting in its own interests without discrediting the values of good government, there is no longer reason for Europeans to collude.

It is possible that few 'in the know' take seriously the public relations language of diplomatic justification. Soured by experience, they genuflect without pausing to bend their knees. For generations after the rulers of Europe declared their independence of God, most of them continued to represent themselves as the servants of their Lord. As memories of the Cold War fade, so the mission statements of its 'Western' victors may similarly pass without comment. Blandness of this kind is not harmless, however. It corrodes the things it pretends to uphold and obscures the important fact that Europe and the USA are more attached to constitutional politics than the use of propaganda shows. The EU *is* composed of liberal democracies, and as the greatest example of constitutional government the USA did indeed stand guardian over Europe's disarray while its countries recovered from the experiences of war, occupation and vile political regimes. These achievements are too important to be endlessly tarnished by the dreary habits of Cold War posturing.

Europe and the USA, along with Canada, Australia and New Zealand, share many 'resemblances ' and 'similitudes' which, when freed of cant, do indeed conjoin them in what may appropriately be described as 'the West'. They share attachments to a commonly derived inheritance. If 'the West' now means 'the Western democracies' that arose within 'Western civilization', this may indeed make for ease of diplomatic understanding and unforced sympathies, but this does not, however, prove or presage the existence of a single diplomatic interest. Merely because 'the West' upholds a particular idea of rulers and ruled, this does not demonstrate the existence of a political movement inching its adherents towards 'ever closer union'. 'The West' is not an entity of political, diplomatic or economic substance.

The USA did not declare its independence of Britain, spend its first century aloof from Europe's power politics and the second becoming the world's mightiest power, in order to reattach itself once more to Europe. Had the USA wished to absorb western Europe into its own federal union, the best opportunity presented itself half a century ago. NATO was not, however, a prologue to the incorporation of western European states into an Atlantic political body. It reflected the interests of a power determined to protect western Europe, not the desire of the USA to enlarge itself through extension until it included Copenhagen, Bonn and Ankara. Nor, should the boot now be on the other foot, has the EU's ambitions to expand its numbers produced a Commission proposal suggesting that the USA more easily fulfils many of the entry conditions than countries now standing in the queue. Has anyone suggested such a scatterbrained idea?

The name of 'the West' has, however, the effect of squeezing relations between Europe and the USA into the wrong parenthesis. Invoking the solidarity of the 'the West' suggests that because Europe and the USA have much of value in common, including variants of the same version of good government, this is sufficient reason to treat them as belonging to a single entity. The imputed common interests of this ocean-linked 'body' thus become grounds for maintaining powers of common decision which, as historical luck would have it, favour the superpower of the USA. The implication is that in its own interest Europe must accept and follow the lead of MAMEE for as far ahead as it is possible to see. Yet 'the West' is no more a political body by virtue of its historical antecedents than was nineteenth-century Europe, whose rulers had much in common and whose economies were also closely interwoven. What drew 'the West' together in NATO was not a civilization in peril or in need of integration, but an episode of power politics. The struggle spanned a civilization that included Moscow as well as Washington. The Soviet Union which produced the direst of totalitarianisms was nevertheless a 'westernizing' regime, whose aim was to out-industrialize and out-modernize capitalism by taking the forced route of 'democratic centralism'.

Since the Cold War has given way to a diplomatic system in greater flux than for half a century, it is necessary for Europe and the USA to acknowledge that 'the West' is not a political idea and that NATO is not a political organization. NATO is an alliance and hence a diplomatic concoction that arose within the diplomatic system in response to the 'actions and reactions' of power politics. With this steadfastly in mind, the EU and the USA may well continue to share important interests in adapting NATO to the future. The assumption that 'the West' is an entity enjoining a set of interests which needs integrated external action is, however, a misconceived way of preserving the Atlantic connection. Proceeding from the standpoint of 'Western values' obscures how the most effective alliances tend to be those that restrict themselves to limited purposes which usually revolve around security. Alliances do not require allies to see eye to eye on all subjects. Misrepresenting NATO as though it were more than an alliance is to burden it with unnecessary expectations. The pretence that otherwise seamless interests are spoiled only by mischievous national interests or 'lack of communications' makes it more difficult to gain agreement on those issues where combined action is mutually advantageous. American public opinion may demand rousing sentiments extolling universal principles in order to awaken it, but there is no longer reason why Europeans should sing along with MAMEE's favourite tunes.

Although the notion of the 'the West' is a straitjacket which stifles the identification of European interests, the discomforts of this confinement also provide useful alibis for Europeans with little inclination to burden themselves with thought and action in foreign affairs. Yet apprehensions over the effects of American defence company's growing domination of markets is but one illustration of what Europe stands to lose – and risk – should it become wholly dependent on US science, technology and arms manufacture. If the remedy is to create an integrated European defence industry, this also implies more than rejection of the idea that MAMEE's leadership entitles its companies to the choicest of economic pickings in an enlarged NATO; it suggests that here (as elsewhere) Europe's FNUs will be forced to combine in order to survive.

The practice of democracy in both the USA and Europe does not demonstrate a wider similarity of diplomatic interests. A shared predilection for government of a particular kind does not obliterate the significance of separate political bodies primarily interested in their own affairs. Nor does the capitalism practised on both sides of the Atlantic imply a convergence of even economic interests. The EU and the USA may co-operate to organize the trading regime of WTO, but the purpose of this body is to encourage competition and thereby emphasize differences. When the USA uses its superpower to threaten allies who defy its domestic claims to extraterritorial jurisdiction, the 'unity of the West' comes over as American hocus-pocus. The Helms Burton law may not be the thin end of a wedge, but the acrimony aroused by it is made worse by spurious American claims that those who invest in Iran or wish to trade with Cuba are damaging 'Western interests'.

Alliances are seldom composed of equals or insulated against change. A successful EMU will add to the EU's diplomatic weight in a globalized world economy, and make it more costly to subordinate its own interests, should they clash with those of the USA. Although the euro may complement the dollar, it may equally come to be its rival, and it is as yet unclear whether the USA has digested the implications of a scheme it has thus far supported. Even if the effect of EMU is to redress the balance of power between Europe and the USA, a more 'coherent and effective' EU is not itself a recipe for Atlantic harmony and durable equilibrium. Rather than realize equipoise among the 'Western democracies', a more self-trusting Europe might, for example, contest US policy in the Middle East with more independent vigour. A Mediterranean ablaze with conflict might suggest that rather than rely on MAMEE to pick its chestnuts out of the fire, EU countries should copy her ability to act. Just as the EU is likely to be shaped by the effects of its relations with Russia, Turkey and other countries, so the readily observable example of the advantages of well organized power ought to be constantly before the eyes of Europe's leaders.

Even if it is true that the headway in civil and military science enjoyed by the USA is increasing, it is by no means self-evident that this development is to be welcomed or accepted. The existence of a uniquely powerful state that is for the moment unmatched and unbalanced does not mean it will curtail its national interests on behalf of others. A world brought within reach of being governed by the will of a singe 'universal' power would not thereby be assured of peace. Europe's interests in a peaceful world do not therefore produce the unequivocal conclusion that they are best secured by a *Pax Americana*. They *might* be safeguarded by a US suzerainty under which important features of the diplomatic system were suppressed. The EU might even be enticed to play second fiddle in such a herculean and perhaps thankless task. With equal plausibility CE, ERE, and Europe's FNUs might hope to piggyback on MAMEE's broad shoulders. CE would naturally settle for any despotism that left undisturbed its preferences for horticulture. ERE would agonize as to how far an enlightened hegemon was compatible with its urge to improve and be of blameless use. Perhaps with Britain in their lead, Europe's FNUs might interpret being given something auxiliary to do in foreign affairs as evidence of their sovereign independence.

With better judged reason Europe's interest lies in a diplomatic system where the EU represents its members in foreign affairs and takes responsibility for its own actions. The wager of a diplomatic system is that order among states is available without succumbing to the domination of a single power. Although a plurality of armed states condemns all concerned to power politics, this is not necessarily a sentence to unrelieved strife. Under conditions of this arbitrary kind it is evident that diplomacy has to be ever vigilant, but wakefulness is equally necessary to sustain constitutional politics. In the absence of ceaseless activity by the governed as well as government, the tendency of all types of public life is to subside into lethargy, succumb to corruption by powerful private interests or lapse into civil conflict. Contrariwise, the wager of world government, or a ' universal monarchy' administered by a superpower, is that its rule would allow enough self-government to its regions, and liberty to the ruled, for the exchange to be worth the gamble. Yet even the most resourceful superpower might lack the means to restrain itself, enforce order, resist challenges or prevent its own internal withering.

One further possibility should be considered, which might enable Europe to avoid some of the hazards of both too little order in the diplomatic system and too little freedom to maintain its own interests. This would allow Europe to place its trust in neither a diplomatic system notoriously prone to disorder, and where the EU's present disunion in foreign affairs is a liability, nor in government by a gargantuan superpower. Although a proposal of this kind imposes the need for yet another acronym, its nature has already been signalled. Salus Populi Europe (SPE) would extend the internal reformation of the EU to embrace foreign affairs, thereby consolidating the achievements of the second half of the twentieth century. A Europe equipped diplomatically and militarily to bargain with the USA on terms of effective parity might trust more in its own powers, and hence be a more trustworthy ally.

Fears aroused by the exorbitance of US power can be turned upside down by anxieties of an opposite kind. The spectre of MAMEE averse to policing power politics, unwilling to exert itself except in its own backyard, or occupied with Asia at the expense of Europe, is perhaps a still more persuasive argument for SPE. Under circumstances where the USA was no longer dependably there to MAMEE it, *salus populi* would soon become the *suprema lex* of Europe, perhaps inducing greater willingness to share government in the EU than all the schemes for economic integration. Some of these might even be seen as a dangerous internal distraction from more fundamental matters. Even should its interest lie in doing its utmost to prevent US disengagement, a Europe in petrified obeisance to its FNUs might learn to its cost that disarray in foreign affairs made it impossible to dissuade the USA from turning its back. On more than one occasion in the life of NATO MAMEE has lowered her eyes in lachrymatory disbelief at Europe's internal pussyfooting. Were the USA somehow to be persuaded from detaching itself from Europe, a robust SPE, with its own denationalized armed forces and a single diplomatic service, might be a better ally in dealing with (say) Russia, or 'acting and reacting' to conflict over energy supplies in the Middle East or Central Asia.

The brooding of sleepless nights is not needed to foresee circumstances where even an SPE, organized with powers of credible decision, was unable to prevent the USA from leaving Europe to its own devices. The civil order of the USA is a wonder to Europe and a continuous reminder of the possibilities of political union, but not even its enviable capacities for renewal are safe from time and peradventure. The *fortuna* that for two centuries has favoured the USA may desert it overnight. Her inclinations are fickle as well as inscrutable. None can foretell how the people of the USA will respond to internal strife or political paralysis, both of which would soon have repercussions in foreign affairs. A superpower responsible for the rules of the global economy and pivotal to all the balances of power, but suddenly hamstrung by its internal affairs, would jolt the diplomatic system more than the unlamented demise of the USSR. Europe should not therefore place all its eggs in MAMEE's basket or allow the lullaby of NATO to rock it to incautious sleep. In its own interests, the EU should ready itself to 'act and react' to more than one severe agitation of the diplomatic system.

An overly self-assertive and unbalanced superpower may be no more to Europe's good than a USA grown impatient with the world, incapacitated, or denied its primacy. For its own sake, Europe should contemplate a diplomatic system in which the USA is too forceful or too feeble.

## VII
## THE MOTHER OF INVENTION

Consideration of the circumstances under which Europe's peoples would be better provided for in foreign affairs by being governed together is far removed from believing they are willing to bring this about. In private life, and even among friends, pointing to the good sense of a line of action is seldom enough to carry approval. Nor does mere assent to a scheme wondrously dismantle obstacles to its realization or ensure its effectiveness. When the company in question is nationally grounded states largely unpersuaded of the need to present a common front to the world, and instinctively wary of yielding the powers of government, the matter seems fated to hang suspended in the air.

The failure of exhortation earlier in the century to move Europeans to lay aside distrust has since been supplemented by other reasons for disavowing a Europe united in foreign affairs. Liberal democracies are averse to populist slogans repeating that 'unity is strength'. Although political parties of all democratic descriptions act on the assumption that the truism is a condition of electoral success, with their images of the masses totalized together the legacies of fascism and communism now make it necessary to reverse cautiously into one of politics' more straightforward precepts. Not much can be made of a media campaign admitting that Europe's 'disunity is weakness'. If exhortation is of questionable use, the enumeration of 'interests' also seems to run out of persuasive steam when it runs into the fellow-feelings of Europe's FNUs. Assent to a single market and EMU, whose benefits can be tested by citizens, producers and consumers, has failed to produce a groundswell of support demanding an effective CFSP. Governments have not wished to argue with much insistence that the EU's internal developments are bringing on the day when a corresponding foreign policy all of its own will become necessary. Europe's FNUs have thus far successfully drawn the line at diplomatic co-operation. Where bodies composed of nations and ruled by governments with strong interests in retaining their powers cannot be reasoned out of their habits by appeal to future interests, argument appears as unfruitful as exhortation.

A third inducement to the acceptance of change is said to be mightier than anything that can be put into words. Impersonal, remorseless and voiceless, 'the tide of events' that waits for none, shapes mankind to its movements no matter how loud men and nations splutter defiance. In Machiavelli's rough computation, '*fortuna* is the arbiter of half the things we do, leaving the other half or so to be controlled by ourselves'.[9] Although this assessment leaves ample scope for human actions, it also incises their powers of decision. In the guise of power politics, the impetus of *fortuna* may be drawing

Europe's states together despite the misgivings of governments and the sentiments of the governed; and the fate of those who defy her effluvial powers may be to sink separately into the mud of historical insignificance.

The well known trouble with warning messages posted by 'history', 'fate' and 'necessity' is that they are usually reluctant to speak with clear voices. *Fortuna*, philosophies of history and sociological forecasts of the future course of events, are unwilling to name outright the governing features of the impending future. In the absence of foreknowledge, one is therefore left with surmise. Even so, it is perhaps possible to detect lines of progression connecting the achievement of the EU's single market, EMU and enlargement, with pressures to make good these developments through whatever external actions are necessary. In the same vein a survey of Europe's neighbours might suggest that, in order to deal effectively with the USA, Russia, Turkey, and 'events' in the Mediterranean, the EU will be 'compelled' to act as one if it wishes to react effectively at all. Similar deductions can be extended further afield to include all occurrences in the diplomatic system affecting Europe's place within it. Although none of these undefined possibilities carries explicit instructions to policy makers, the exigencies of power politics suggest that, in order to respond to the turn of events, the time to make provisions is before rather than after their effects are felt.

The inscrutability of unfolding circumstances was in the past often highlighted by their resounding drama. Should this became less true of the future it will make it yet more difficult to focus attention on foreign affairs. Although some claimed to have heard the footfalls of 1914 a generation beforehand, the battlefields of Europe revealed events of unexpected vileness. Excerpts of this appeared in silent films. Half a generation later much of Europe is said to have felt in its bones that Hitler's rise to power spelled renewed war. The spectacle of Cold War MADness was sustained even as the curtain was lowered, with Gorbachev acting as if the USSR was reformable even as it collapsed about his ears. In contrast with previous events that left indelible marks and stirred awareness, the eeriness that has settled over power politics since 1989–91 has led to the suggestion that power politics have become less eventful and consequently easier still to ignore. Emptied of their customary visibility, foreign affairs are thought to be set on a new, less agitated course, and to be governed by different forces leading in unfamiliar directions. Less belligerently theatrical compared with what went before, this shift of mood is said to announce lasting changes to the diplomatic system. The purported 'transformation' of power politics into the happenings of 'the international community' is often explained by reference to the pre-eminence of the USA. Although a decade is a thin wedge of time on which to rest deductions, it is indeed possible that America's superpower will dissuade actions by other states that might otherwise disturb, or make for unruly 'events'. In this case, the rivalries of great powers may for a while cease to capture headlines. Yet although a less eventful diplomatic system may mean a more orderly state of affairs, it may equally indicate that power politics have incorporated novel features that may prove as intractable as the dramatic occurrences they are overconfidently said to have replaced. Some of these, which can only be alluded to, may be more difficult to deal with diplomatically just because they are of less arresting interest to foreign ministries than to the domestic anxieties of rulers and ruled.

When events come 'not single spies, but in battalions' they at least permit the effects, if not the intentions, of *fortuna* to be glimpsed. Terrorism is among developments that affect foreign affairs without the accompaniment of diplomatic fanfare. Whether or not spread by states, terrorism puts the diplomatic system to a different kind of test than when it is disturbed by the visible and clamorous conflicts of its members. Diffuse as it is, terrorism nevertheless keeps power politics active because it divides states over how great a threat it poses, and even more over the reactions necessary to counter it. Even as 'single spies', terrorism causes dismay to the 'battalions' of states, and since the grievances on which it thrives are legion and are regularly replenished, the EU is likely to remain troubled by it. If this is so, then measures necessary to combat terrorism will bit by bit oblige the EU to become more state-like. The effect of globalization on the mobility of terrorists will be to oblige EU states to organize themselves to act in unison and in co-operation with other states. Necessity will lead in directions that obliges states to yield some of their powers of independent decision.

The 'force of circumstances' that urges states to organize themselves to counter terrorism also applies to public anxieties over illegal immigration. After 200 years or so spent distributing its own peoples overseas, a peaceful and prosperous Europe is now a magnet to those seeking opportunity. As a direct result of the single market, this now directly implicates the EU both in the diplomacy of restraining the departure of migrants from other countries and in the domestic politics of policing entry to Europe. Here again globalization will reveal that, in order to shore up their own authority, governments of the EU's national states may bit by imperceptible bit have to cede powers of decision to SPE.

The same twist of events that appears to urge on EU action in respect of terrorism and immigration applies to trafficking in drugs and the crime that thrives on it. Although the mafia-like groups that organize this global business are hardly 'single spies', their activities have also made inroads into power politics. Because no international organization is vested by states with effective policing powers, the increasing borderlessness of the EU's single market once more makes Brussels the centre of decisions. Member states can no longer plausibly claim that the 'war against drugs' is a 'domestic' issue most effectively dealt with by national governments. With political and economic union, drugs and crime have become 'domesticated' throughout the EU. The step by step rungs progressively linking terrorism, 'law and order', illegal immigration, drugs, crime, globalization and foreign policy are cumulatively making the 'internal security' of EU states the subject matter of EU politics. As this development continues, the 'necessities' leading to the creation of SPE appear less the result of diplomacy taken in response to 'external' events set in motion by other states than as decisions increasingly forced on national governments by the political exhortations of their electorates. As Hobbes had reasoned, the 'business' of states is the security of their members.

It is false, however, to conclude that the turn of events of this kind that are bringing the internal and external affairs of the EU into ever closer union are thereby displacing older and more familiar aspects of power politics. As the difficult task of keeping tabs on which countries have nuclear weapons illustrates, governments are particularly unforthcoming about their military preparations. The 'peace dividend' that resulted from the end of the Cold War led to less spending on defence in Europe and the USA, but the same has not occurred elsewhere. The diplomatic system remains a system of armed states. The technological superiority of scientifically advanced states acts as a stimulus to others to purchase their products, or discover means of circumventing their advantages. Chemical and biological weapons are easier and cheaper to acquire and deploy than stealth bombers and satellites.

Having largely settled centuries-old territorial disputes, Europe's states no longer identify their well-being with acreage and volume of population. More nationally homogeneous than before, and more willing to devolve government to regional bodies, they measure prosperity by reference to economic performance. Lulled by this favourable condition, it is only an absent-minded step to assuming that all other countries of the world share Europe's plangent conservatism. Even though many parts of Asia and Africa are split over boundaries and by ethnic conflict, the comforting belief that these are little more than pains of induction to the modern world, which the more advanced 'post-modern' world may ignore or help to soothe, is readily advanced. The unfounded assumption is made that once these parts of the world have successfully caught up with 'the West' their states will settle down to the same kind of ordered life now favoured by Europeans. The implication is that a world of states composed of nations will become pacifically reconciled once generally accepted political boundaries have been universally agreed to. Such optimism does more than glance over the time and violence it took Europe to settle its national frontiers. It fails to recognize that so long as states claim to be subject to their own sovereign laws, and are bound only by those parts of international law that do not compromise their vital interests, the internal stability of states does not ensure a settled diplomatic system. Nor is perpetual peace the assured outcome of a world composed of liberal democracies practising market economies. The consent of the governed on which democracies rest is not that of abstract individual citizens with liberties and material well-being as their exclusive concerns. The willingness to be governed together is predominantly the assent of collectivities; of nations and sometimes religious groupings representing the combustible passions of fellow-feeling. Although public sentiments may be less manipulable than under illiberal regimes, there is nothing essentially pacific about collective identities. Liberal democracies are not coy in asserting their national interests or shy of demonstrating their patriotism.

Even if it could be demonstrated that democracies are more peacefully inclined than unrepresentative states, the attenuation of conflict associated with tyrannies no more removes all existing agitations from the diplomatic system than it can prevent fresh ones from arising. The reason why ethnically homogeneous China and Japan nevertheless follow every move in the balance of power in the Pacific is not because only one has a government accountable to an electorate. The fact that a democratic USA has no outstanding territorial ambitions in the Pacific has not produced diplomatic indifference to the juxtaposition of China, Japan, Russia and Indonesia. A liberal democratic China would no more remove power politics from the Pacific than a Russia adapting to constitutional politics can be counted on to leave Europe's affairs untouched by its national interests. A democratically inspired EU does not see eye to eye with the USA in the Middle East merely because both uphold the importance of constitutional government.

Power politics may be primed by territorial and ethnic disputes, by ambitious governments and volatile peoples, by dislocations in the world's economic affairs, and by all manner of affective grievances; none of these is, however, necessary to keeping the 'actions and reactions' of the diplomatic system 'in continuous agitation'. As with many other desires, power is its own stimulus and objective, and nowhere perhaps is this more jealously demonstrated than by states whose arbitrary powers in foreign affairs are largely ungoverned by law.

Europe's reasons for being wary of power politics have been acquired at such fiendish historical cost that disinclination to play an active part in them as a necessary consequence of political union is not difficult to understand. Its states are no longer great powers urged on by unfulfilled ambitions and the desire to command events. Territorially sated, their governments and governed are absorbed by domestic affairs and the EU. Interest in the rest of the world extends to the pursuit of wealth, pleasure, conservation of the earth and periodic help to the less fortunate. The unassertive states of Europe thus have no wish to appear awesome to others. None of these sentiments, however, justifies the pretence that Europe can safely turn a blind eye to power politics, or expect its own reformed and peaceable example to purge the world of conflict. Perhaps unfortunately for those possessed of sedate passions, the desire to enjoy them in peace and security does not entitle them to a safe ride on the treadmill of power politics. A Europe with an especially large stake in order, and easily made anxious by fears of what might disturb it, cannot afford to rely on the antics of HE or, like CE, on the beneficence of a matronly despotism. Faith in the favourable turn of events is not a politically prudent way to acquire confidence in the future.

If Europe's interests lie in a stable diplomatic system, the surest way to achieve this is by taking responsibility for actions that may bring it about. The consolidation of broadly conservative interests thus implies the opposite of passivity, but it also comes at a price that many Europeans consider too steep. The route to making Europe's place in the world more secure lies through power politics. There are no bypasses or lay-bys, and schemes to devise them are littered with frustration. Only by engaging fully in the diplomatic system, and with power commensurate to its interests, can Europe cyber-dyke and cyber-embank itself against adversity. Yet the impetus of 'events' and 'circumstances', which may drive home the necessity of Europe acting as one in foreign affairs, may equally well be resisted. Europe's peoples may choose to stare the mother of invention in the face, damn SPE as too compromising of past national glories, as too dubiously risky, costly and burdensome – and turn their backs on it. They may prefer to trust whatever is to come rather than trust in their own powers of action.

Although refusal to forearm against the forewarnings of power politics has implications for the present conduct of foreign affairs, other more far reaching consequences also follow. It is one thing to oppose measures that would erode the scope for individual action and quite another to discover that the wider effect of disunion is that Europe plays an insignificant part in devising the diplomatic system of the future. For the largest parts in authorizing the script of foreign affairs are claimed, if not seized, by those with the most commanding roles. Paris in 1919, Yalta in 1945, and the superpower diplomacy of the Cold War, reiterated in this century what appears true of all diplomatic systems: authorship in power politics can only be successfully acquired by the principal actors who have placed themselves at centre stage. Supplementary members of the diplomatic cast, like Europe's FNUs, may crowd the stage and solicit attention, but it is the stars (or superstars) who transcribe the action and in doing so produce the plot. This has naturally struck many audiences, critics and would-be playwrights as unjust, but despite their dissent it is the great powers who deploy means able to consign an existing script to the shredder, and authorize a fresh one. If Europe cannot bring itself to claim a leading part in shaping the foreign affairs of the world, its FNUs should not be surprised if one day when they turn up at the stage-door they discover they have been written out of the script. Their individual performances may continue to be a source of self-absorption while leaving the rest of the world unmoved.

Hence demands for a stable diplomatic order as well as calls for its replacement by a different 'shape of life' lead ineluctably back to the question of means. When these are inspected, it becomes evident that they cannot for the most part be separated from the activities of power politics. Power is the condition of effective action. The reason for this is as plain as it is blunt. States with most power have the largest say both in framing events and determining the rules by which power politics are conducted. In the twentieth century, Europe was shaped

above all by the power politics of its great powers and by the superpowers of the Cold War. Distasteful as it may be to many Europeans,
their fortunes in the century about to begin will likewise be shaped by
power politics. Hence the plea that supporting roles are quite sufficient to the needs of Europe's states is defensible only if its advocates
recognize the full implications of their arguments. It is possible to
prefer the continuation of individual states, each with its own foreign
policy, even though this reduces the scope for influence; but it cannot
be maintained that a refusal to share government with like-minded
states ensures influence in a diplomatic system dominated by great
combinations of power.

If the entire diplomatic system is considered objectionable because
it prolongs power politics, even minor roles for Europe's states may be
resisted. Where this happens the question of foreign affairs then
divides. In one direction lies a penitential response to foreign affairs
that urges abstinence from everything touched by power politics. This
is the humble yet lofty ground on which ERE is sited. Europe must
become a beacon to the world, showing by example and assistance to
others that the power of the diplomatically powerless can be a force
for good before which armed Leviathans will eventually yield. Another
path thickens with schemes to displace the entire diplomatic system
with a government of mankind that avoids states. In the former case it
is improbable that governments and peoples, as distinct from individuals and private groups, can disown the consequences of inhabiting a
world with pronounced needs for orderly and just rule and a genius
for generating power. Even the aid agencies that went to Bosnia and
Rwanda with blameless motives, found themselves drawn into conflicts of interest and passion they wished only to offer 'humanitarian'
release from. Those of the second persuasion, who glisten with impatience to overthrow power politics and reorder the world, are usually
silent both about the awesome powers needed to displace great
powers and nearly 200 states, and about the powers of the bodies
that would thenceforth govern the world. Some, of course, hope that
'economic forces' will remove the need for political and diplomatic
action, without acknowledging that faith in the unifying powers of
globalization only transfers to the hidden hands of markets the impersonal capacities otherwise ascribed to *fortuna* and the 'force of events'.

Even shorn of speculative asides, the dilemmas surrounding Europe's place in the world are troublesome. Its present position in
foreign affairs is a caricature of influence that raises the diplomacy
of FNUs to a stage act worthy of Houdini's escapology. Failure to

equip the EU with powers to shape the diplomatic system to Europe's purposes may also have dire repercussions on its internal affairs. A Europe at sixes and sevens over foreign policy may find that in the eye of a diplomatic storm reliance on the eclectic diplomacy of co-operation subjects the EU's political union to severe strains. Were this to happen the accompanying alarums would be those of RDE. In the absence of SPE, the power politics of the world may reappear among the states of Europe, wreaking havoc on the foundations of Europe's post-war reformation. This would disturb even CE. When its virtues were discovered to be in hock to the vices of the world, ERE would likewise be as perplexed. The worst consequences of external events that threatened to undermine the EU's internal order would, however, be reserved for Europe's FNUs. Their representatives would have to explain how being wise after events that had exposed the limitations of 'national sovereignty', the 'independence' of ineffectual national states could still be vindicated. They would have to hope that MAMEE was in dependable mood and willing once again to defend Europe from the consequences of its illusions. A Europe that had declined to put its house in order might not, however, be a property worth risking American national interests to secure. Were the USA nevertheless to uphold Europe, this would no doubt be cited as evidence that the Atlantic alliance was in trustworthy working order. Europe's FNUs would then be able to repeat that SPE remained unnecessary.

Should, for whatever reasons, Europe find itself abandoned by MAMEE, or in conflict with her, its peoples would then be forced to hope that everything would be for the best in a part of the world deprived by its twentieth-century history of belief in providence and progress. In the aftermath of diplomatic events that episode by episode had exposed Europe to the penalties of disunion, it is conceivable that the governments of its FNUs would persist in ignoring where the true interests of their countries lay. Even as their voices came to count for less and less in the councils of the world they might, like horses taken to the water's edge, refuse to drink. One reason for obduracy of this kind might have little to do with serious belief in the effectiveness of individual action or the adequacy of mere diplomatic co-operation. It might have more to do with rulers having forgotten how to explain to the ruled the extent to which the tranquillity of domestic affairs depends on external circumstances. And that the enjoyment of peace and prosperity is no more secure than the willingness to take responsibility for shaping foreign affairs as best they are able. Perhaps even more alarmingly, the reluctance of governments to admit publicly the limitations of their own powers might prove of considerable electoral advantage. Having come to expect 'peace dividends' from the end of the Cold War, it might prove more acceptable to the citizens of Europe's liberal democracies to be left alone in their gardens, believing that the manifest harmlessness of their productive pursuits was enough to secure the fruits of their labours. If both governments and governed prefer a quiescent existence on the temperate slopes of power politics, who is to say that no such safe haven exists?

To settle for the 'decent drapery' and 'pleasing illusions' of national independence has powerful attractions, though not in the sense described by Burke. He did not intend to eulogize self-deception. He believed that it was necessary and possible to civilize power and raise it to the level of authority. The need to clothe power in the products of convincing moral imagination did not mean that weakness could be substituted for strength merely by adroit tailoring. The debilities in foreign affairs suffered by Europe's national states are not therefore curable by the fanfare that 'independent nation-states co-operating in the EU and NATO' effectively represent Europe's interests abroad. Such pretences reveal foreshortened imagination as well as contempt for the common sense of citizens.

Paine criticized Burke on precisely these grounds. He said of Burke's devotion to the *ancien régime* of Europe that he 'pities the plumage and forgets the dying bird'. In similar vein, and in spite of having agreed to political union, the governments of Europe's FNUs are still spellbound by the figures they once cut on the world's stage. They have pride and position to lose by admitting that their separate foreign ministries and defence establishments, their pleasing embassies and decently draped generals, have been diminished by the scale and reach of power politics. Meanwhile the national interests of their countries do not derive much sustenance from a self-deception which raises narcissism to a governing principle of public life.

Paine saw more clearly than Burke that the American and French revolutions heralded new 'shapes of life' that were destined to revise long accepted conceptions of states, nations, economics, government, law, education, science, art and thought. He also understood something Burke also conceded; that only those willing to adapt to changing circumstances would be able to secure their well-being by influencing the course of events.

What would perhaps have astonished both observers of the *ancien régime* was how so many of the innovations that consigned it to the past were not only absorbed within the diplomatic system that took shape after Westphalia, but strengthened its components. States and their disorderly system of foreign affairs did more than survive the upheavals of 1789 and Napoleon's imperial rule over much of Europe. The industrial revolutions of the nineteenth century that knit the economies of Europe ever more tightly together, and extended their grip throughout the world, added to the internal and external efficacy of states. A turbulent twentieth century has similarly failed to dislodge states from centre stage. The great powers of the present, and above all the superpowered democracy of the USA, are incomparably more awesome than those looked upon not only by Burke, Paine and Hegel, or by Clemenceau, Lloyd-George, and Woodrow Wilson, but by Roosevelt, Stalin and Churchill.

It is this work of *fortuna* that has come to belittle Europe's states. Their half-achieved political union is an incomplete response to the turn of events because, although the EU is a reaction to what had befallen Europe by mid-century, it has not digested what has since transformed the rest of the world. If the governments and governed of Europe's overshadowed states fail to recognize that foreign affairs are set to remain dominated by a handful of global powers, they may live to regret the failure to prepare the EU to become one of them. Having chosen instead to pass the time recomposing their individual tail-feathers, they will have none but themselves to pity when cast aside by the agitations of events they are unable to prevent, bar or direct.

## Notes

1.  Voltaire, *Candide* translated by John Butt (Harmondsworth: Penguin 1947), p.142.
2.  Ibid, p.144.
3.  Ibid, p.141.
4.  This issue is further discussed in my 'The Liberal State and Nationalism in Post-War Europe', *History of European Ideas*, Vol. 10, No.6 (1989), pp 689–703.
5.  *The Economist*, 3 January 1998.
6.  *The Federalist Papers* (New York: Mentor, 1961), No. 8, p.67.
7.  Edmund Burke, *Reflections on the Revolution in France* (London: Every-man, 1964), p.93.
8.  Niccolo Machiavelli, *The Prince*, translated by George Bull (Harmondsworth: Penguin, 1961), p.137.
9.  Ibid, p.130.

# 6 Occlusive Albion

Along with other countries of Europe's Atlantic seaboard, England prospered in the wake of the great naval explorations that in the sixteenth century opened the world to traders and settlers. By the close of the following century London was set to supplant Amsterdam as the financial hub of Europe. Yet if the Americas and Asia were the points of reference for maritime wealth, it was as a member of the diplomatic system of Europe that Britain became a great power. From the time of Marlborough's exploits in the heart of the continent during the War of the Spanish Succession, until the two plus four negotiations of 1990 that endorsed the reunification of Germany, Britain has been one of the five or so 'powers' around whose actions Europe's power politics have turned.

Even at the height of its Imperial sway, when 'splendid isolation' depicted a country rich and secure enough to disdain the balance of power on the continent, Britain's naval superiority did not leave it unaffected by events across the Channel. Britain's far-flung rivalries with France and Russia affected the affairs of Europe as, in different and eventually more decisive ways, did the consequences of German unification in 1871. Despite proverbial hostility to any continental power dominant enough to 'point a dagger at the heart of England', it was only when Bismarck's successors added *weltpolitik* to their ambitions that Germany's precocious industrial achievements led to Britain's tentative diplomatic realignment alongside France and Russia. Whereas Paris and St Petersburg were drawn into alliance by fears of Germany's mastery of the continent, Britain's anxieties were fed by the prospect of a rival naval power able to compromise its world-wide possessions. When the balance of power failed to ensure a limited conflict in 1914, Britain felt the full force of prolonged warfare. While Russia was knocked out of the struggle and into revolution, the combined powers of Britain and France were unable to expel Germany from France and Belgium. At the armistice of 1918 the country that 'tipped the balance' and induced Germany to sue for peace had its home and fortune in North America. There it had expanded to become the largest industrial economy in the world, so that by the conclusion of war in 1918 the USA had eclipsed Britain as the leading creditor nation. Within a few years Britain lost its naval position not to Germany but to the USA. If one visible effect of the Somme and Paschendaele was to people every village and town in Britain with war memorials, the diplomatic consequences were felt at Munich in 1938, when aversion to renewed land warfare tugged against the historically engrained sense that Britain's interests riveted it to the European balance of power.

Powerless to prevent the forcible unification of much of Europe under the Third Reich, Britain's role in the Second World War was to sustain opposition at a time when other countries had been defeated, occupied or in part reconciled to German dominance. Hitler's grip was lifted first by the resistance of the USSR, which made Stalingrad the decisive military event of the war in Europe, and then by the mobilization of the vast resources of the USA. At Yalta and Potsdam, Britain's fortunes had come to depend on these two great powers alongside whom, as Churchill realized at the time, his country and its empire could no longer be reckoned an equal. In the subsequent Cold War rivalry over the exhausted carcass of Europe Britain unequivocally aligned itself with its mighty Atlantic offspring because only the USA could succour the countries of western Europe, (including Britain), pacify fears of a resurgent Germany and safeguard them from the effects of Soviet power in central Europe. With the establishment of the 'iron curtain' Britain's impulse was to stabilize the most recent twist to Europe's balance of power, while using its continuing pre-eminence among European countries to explore possibilities of 'peaceful co-existence' between 'East' and 'West'. Through close alliance with the USA in NATO, Britain's part in the Cold War kept alive a sense of diplomatic importance that squared deceptively with its wavering economic performance and hurried relinquishment of empire.

As the economic momentum of western Europe strengthened in the 1950s and the infant institutions of the EEC took shape, Britain sought a position from which its rickety economy might benefit and from where it could monitor the wider ambitions registered in the Treaties of Rome. While Britain welcomed moves that encouraged better relations among the six, and above all between France and West Germany, it neither shared their conception of the need for a political re-ordering of western Europe nor treated the idea as something likely to succeed. Yet the realization of the Schuman Plan in the ECSC had already undermined the presumption that European affairs could prosper and develop only with London's approval. Britain seemed unaware that the USA had replaced it as the country on whose future western Europe most depended and evaded signs that Washington not only backed the ECSC and the Treaties of Rome, but had few qualms about a Franco-German reconciliation from which Britain was absent. For its part Britain continued to see its external interests within the widest setting of power politics. Despite the decline in its world power represented by Suez, the Cuban Missile crisis and speedy withdrawals from empire, Britain's unique position within the Atlantic alliance suggested that, so long as the Cold War lasted, the fundamentals of its position in the diplomatic system needed little reappraisal.

Whereas the countries of western Europe were shunted by the effects of war and its Cold War sequence towards recasting their relations in the direction of renunciation and reformation, Britain felt no comparable need for root and branch re-thinking. Its rulers persisted in habits of thought and action that appeared vindicated by Britain's less traumatic experience of twentieth-century events. In the Allied victory over the Axis, Britain stood out as a liberator among the liberated of Europe. Its body politic, if not its economy, survived the war intact, binding its citizens with renewed pride yet more tightly to their institutions. Experimentation with a welfare state was careful to leave the most visible features of its political inheritance undisturbed. Against this background, the Cold War provided further encouragement for the belief that Britain's post-war prominence in foreign affairs represented and justified continuity of outlook. Although less powerful than the superpowers, and heavily dependent on one of them, the middle decades to the twentieth century did little to ruffle the assumption that Britain's past experience of foreign affairs remained its most dependable guide. Even though the needs of trade and security had taken it closer to the countries of western Europe, Britain's relations with the continent remained, as they had for centuries, the domain of foreign affairs, subject to the precepts of the balance of power and the practices of diplomacy.

It was from this traditional standpoint of a great power that Britain viewed the stirrings of political reformation in western Europe. Economic arguments for joining the 'common market' were fitted into a picture in which, far from being compromised by involvement with newfangled institutions linked to woolly political notions, Britain's position as an independent state would be refurbished by the stimulus of enlarged opportunities. By helping to remedy its economic sluggishness, the 'common market' would strengthen Britain which would thereby be made more sturdily independent. Its capacity for self-government would thus be enhanced rather than curtailed by compliance with institutions of continental devising that unavoidably went with the chance of increasing the country's rate of economic growth. Perhaps most significantly, membership of the 'common market' was confidently thought to leave undisturbed Britain's long practised habit of regarding the states of Europe as foreign countries with whom relations were governed by the precepts and practices of diplomacy. Economic necessity, decolonization, and the Cold War that drove Britain into closer relations with the continent were not thought to call in question the fundamental nature of its long standing relations with European members of the diplomatic system. Hence the suggestion sometimes made, that British governments misjudged their powers to halt developments in western Europe they were opposed to, is not the nub of the matter. The handicap from which Britain suffered most had more to do with the failure of its rulers to recognize the evidence of their senses than with the power at the disposal of governments. Britain's reduced post-war powers as a state were badly served by yet more fundamental defects of political imagination that led Britain to misjudge or discount the objectives of the six original signatories of the Treaties of Rome. The supposedly economic grouping to which Britain sought admission within a few years of its creation was composed of states who were set on reconstituting relations with each other away from the disastrous habits of foreign affairs in the more controllable and pacific direction of domestic affairs. The weight of Britain's island experience of Europe's foreign affairs, which its recent, as well as the more distant past, seemed to endorse, made a political undertaking of the kind proposed by the six so incomprehensible as hardly to raise the question of its acceptability. The fact that the authors of Europe's political reformation were themselves unclear about their objectives, and the form their realization was to take, allowed Britain's bafflement to justify incredulity.

Peering at western Europe through a prism that revealed only foreign affairs and diplomacy left Britain's relations with the EEC a casualty of occluded imagination. It failed to register a political experiment designed to dissolve power politics in a customs union. Britain's perspective was dulled and sanctioned by an outlook governed by an inherited experience unsuited to appreciating the fresh direction of events. Britain was accustomed to seeing 'Europe' as either a diplomatic system composed of states, or as the setting of attempts by a continental great power to replace their fractious independence with a forcibly imposed order. Britain was unable to draw on precedent to

help make sense of a voluntary coming together of states for the
indeterminate but irreversible purposes of 'ever closer union'. Unlike
the countries of continental western Europe who accepted, albeit with
varying amounts of fear and trembling, the need to reform their
relations down to the very rudiments of statehood, Britain remained
attached to stratagems that had not resulted in the humiliation of June
1940 for France and the disaster of May 1945 for Germany. Little
wonder, then, that when Britain sought to make sense of membership
of the EEC its trusted ways of thinking about the affairs of Europe
were unable to make sense of what was unfolding on the continent.

   The debates accompanying Britain's admission to the EEC tirelessly
reiterated its view of Europe as a field of diplomatic forces presided
over by independent states. Assurances were laboriously given by
government spokesmen that ratification of the Treaties of Rome and
compliance with their provisions entailed 'no question of any erosion
of essential sovereignty'. Britain's forthright intention was to benefit
economically without membership of the EEC affecting its powers of
independent decision. Equipped with only a single interpretative viewpoint of the Rome treaties, it assumed that its own reading of them
was shared by other signatories. As an 'association of states' the EEC
might possess certain diplomatically odd-looking features in the form
of a court, assembly, supranational commission, and provisions for
'common policies', but in the round the picture of a glorified customs
union was framed within a view of events that placed developments
under the control of states. The terms of Britain's admission were
devoid of any explicit proposals to create a new centre of power in
western Europe that might jeopardize Britain's independent role in
world affairs. Since the authority of states appeared unimpaired, the
permanence of the EEC was no more cause for alarm than mention of
'ever closer union'. As with all alliances and diplomatic undertakings,
nothing could prevent states from revising their irreversible commit-
ments should national interests require it.

   As the EEC developed towards the EU, Britain held firmly to its
view that 'ever closer union' was either diplomatic fluff or diplomatic
manoeuvring in the grand manner of *raison d'état*. The clue to events
was to concentrate attention on the motives and actions of states.
From this angle of understanding, 'Europe' was an intelligible stratagem of French foreign policy designed to institutionalize its fortuitous
post-war eminence in western Europe. Circumstances resulting from
the war had produced a divided Germany that permitted France to
befriend its western part on terms that relieved *la grande nation* of

fears concerning German power. British understanding of French national interests did not, however, imply that they coincided with its own or that London had reason to support schemes whose effect would prolong French ascendancy. Britain's economic needs which had led to membership of the EEC were not thought to include condoning or being hoodwinked by 'political' ploys dreamed up in the Quai D'Orsay. In later years the acceptance of a reunited Germany entrenched within the EU was seen from London as one means by which German power could be accommodated with reduced risks to its neighbours. Whether the focus of interest was France or Germany, the principal feature of the EU from the standpoint adopted by Britain was the alliance between these two countries. Even though this important diplomatic rapprochement is decently draped in unusually lavish institutions, this shouldn't, according to this interpretation, be allowed to distract attention from the 'fact' that 'at the heart' of the EU lies a variation on the familiar theme of alliance between independent states. In addition to the economic advantages of a common market, Britain therefore had traditional reasons of state for securing a position within Europe close enough to the centre of events to ensure that a balance of power dominated by Franco-German alliance was compatible with its interests.

The error represented by this way of construing the EU is not that it sheds no light, but rather that its single-minded perspective is unable to pick out anything that falls outside its beam. France and Germany do indeed dominate the EU, and neither country has renounced its national interests. It does not necessarilty follow that this is all there is to their combination or that the institutions and policies they have developed in tandem are mere window dressing. Understanding the origins of something may be the place to start, but if nothing inconsistent with the beginnings of a scheme could ever be created, hardly anything describable as change or purposeful development would exist. France and Germany have achieved more than an alliance that temporally composes their foreign affairs. They have moved beyond the mutual wariness typical of even stable diplomatic relations towards the kind of trust that acts as the yeast of politics and indeed makes their practice possible. Over a generation they have produced a reformation in which their conflicts of national interest are subsumed within a constitutional order and have become subject to horse-trading of a kind more typical of the internal affairs of single political body. It is the governments of these two countries that practise and promote the sharing of government, and it this development that a resolutely

single-sighted diplomatic perspective of European affairs systematic-
ally fails to acknowledge. France and Germany have not abandoned
their interests, let alone their national identities, so much as arrived at
a willingness to share government as the means of assuring them. In
agreeing to subject themselves to law and man complex institutions
endowed with substantial powers, both countries have stepped beyond
the confines of traditional alliance, or indeed beyond anything recognizable under the heading of that oldest of diplomatic terms.

Perhaps because for centuries it has been part and parcel of Europe's diplomatic system of shifting alliances, Britain has not been able
to fathom the post-war determination of its old associates and rivals to
re-order the affairs of Europe away from power politics. Even so,
Britain has no dearth of experience of transformed relations between
states. As its own Empire turned into a Commonwealth of Nations
much was made of how self-governing independent states were able
to remain bound closely together. Something of a similar kind developed as a result of wartime and Cold War co-operation between
Britain and the USA. In neither case, however, was the idea of a
'family of nations' or the 'special relationship' considered a prologue
to political union. The Commonwealth was a rejection of the enforced
unity of imperial rule. If relations between Commonwealth states are
not 'foreign', their distinctive character has not made them 'domestic'.
Although Anglo-American relations show periodic evidence of intimacy unusual in diplomacy, this has never presaged a movement for
the creation of a single political body straddling the Atlantic. Perhaps
Britain's experience of close Commonwealth and Atlantic ties of
language, thought and political habit have hidden from its view similar
ties of sympathy and solidarity that have reappeared in the second half
of the twentieth century on the continent of Europe. Peoples with
vivid national differences have largely ceased to treat each other as
foreigners and prospective enemies, and now recognize each other as
more like fellow-citizens. Despite Britain's attempt to interpret the
EU as a means of exploiting a single market, or a way of cementing
diplomatic relations, the attempt has left it trying to make sense of, or
disown, changes that refuse to fit into either category.

The Cold War deferred Britain's need to reach a truer understanding of the political purposes of its European 'partners' The external
affairs of most importance to London were thought to reside in
NATO, whose focus was not Paris and Bonn, but Washington and
Moscow. Measured along the scale of world affairs, where Britain's
imperial reach had for so long assured it of prominence, the EEC was

a regional sub-division of the diplomatic system. Whatever the 'common market' might do to invigorate western Europe with a new form of peaceful and prosperous life was of only marginal significance to Britain compared to the standing conferred by its privileged position in Washington. This disposed Britain to misread developments on the continent, even as it exaggerated the sense of its own 'freedom of action' upon which much of its attitude towards Europe rested. The purchase of nuclear missiles from the USA concealed Britain's decline from power and reminded France that no other ally of the USA was the recipient of equal trust. Although the war against Argentina suggested that Britain was henceforth unlikely to use force without allies, it made it even more probable that in future it would rely most heavily on the USA. Matters as central to the peace of Europe as Bosnia illustrated Britain's continuing dependence on Washington. The ineffectual conduct of the EU, for which it was in part responsible, justified Britain's assessment that the achievement of a single market lacked political significance and demonstrated the inherent implausibility of a common European foreign policy. The conclusion was drawn that the only power in Europe capable of decisive action was MAMEE, without whom Britain would not venture.

Britain's reliance on a single theme to explain relations with 'Europe' reflected feelings of national pride that emphasized its continued political self-sufficiency. Britain is among Europe's most shameless FNUs. 'Joining Europe' was presented in ways that went to uncanny lengths to persuade the governed that economic benefits did not have to be purchased with sharing of political powers with other countries and compliance with common institutions. More than in continental countries, a fear seemed to lurk that anything that impeded Britain's independence as a state would threaten its national identity. In a country so apparently sure of itself, the idea that a collective identity composed of several nations would flake away unless its government remained wholly under its own control seems difficult to explain. Whatever changes Britain was obliged to accept – in agriculture, for example, or in matters of foreign trade – were nevertheless represented as entirely in keeping with self-government. The English disposition to portray even radical change as proof of continuity can be traced at least as far back as the 'glorious revolution' of 1689 whose constitutional linchpin was a political union between England and the United Provinces under William of Orange. This was brilliantly entered into national history as the preservation of an established form of inherited rule only temporarily disturbed by a personal dislocation. Three centuries later, adaptation to the 'common market' was similarly depicted as constituting no irreversible departure from the past. The most widely distributed explanation maintained that membership of the EEC was compatible with Britain's traditions of self-government at home and independent foreign policy abroad. No uncharted territory was being entered because between those two bastions of national experience no such place could be envisaged or admitted. Merely because Britain was obliged to adapt to earning its living under altered conditions, it did not mean that either constitutional novelty nor political adventurism with foreigners was being risked. Just as the monarch would continue to occupy her throne, so the powers of Britain's cabinet government would remain similarly sacrosanct.

In this manner the 'force of events' that impelled Britain to seek entry to a body whose French methods of work it had played no part in fashioning, and which committed it to a new realm of law, unfamiliar decision-making procedures and common policies, were passed off, if not over, as an exercise in foreign policy. Different as the 'common market' might be in content from other international organizations to which Britain belonged, the Treaties of Rome no more mutilated 'sovereignty' than did membership of NATO and the UN. In a famous fracas over the supranational political ambitions of the EEC in 1965, had not de Gaulle established by the 'Luxembourg compromise' that the ultimate safeguard of a country's 'vital national interests' could not be removed by any formulaic of majority voting? With this apparent bulwark of every member state's 'right of veto', Britain's membership of the EEC was advanced with a mixture of economic argument and diplomatic calculation. Against this background, where no shadow of political union appeared to cast its incoherent features, accession in 1973 required no special kind of reasoning from unhistorical principles to account for the decision taken on behalf of people used only to the assurance of continuity. The rulings of the ECJ, which nearly a decade before Britain's accession had proclaimed in *Costa* v. *E.N.E.L* the primacy of EEC law in matters covered by the treaties, were left in unanalysed limbo, along with the evidence of political and legal intent.

The extent to which British governments have misconstrued the EEC/EU, and the costs this has incurred, are well illustrated by the SEA. The one important initiative taken by a British government, the creation of a single market soon came up against the 'practical' needs to get decisions taken. The end of increased wealth justified the use of qualified majority voting, which, despite its palpable political character, met with British approval. Yet these procedures were conveniently or absentmindedly divested of any political significance under the apparent belief that economics is a self-contained order of activity that governments can be midwives to, but which thereafter prosper best when left to autonomous market forces. Even when a single market called for 'administration' to ensure the free movement of goods, capital, persons and services, among 375 million people, this was deemed by Britain to leave unaffected the powers of national governments. No shared government was apparently involved and hence no precedents were being set. Although decisions were taken by governments acting together and with the Commission, they were explained as somehow 'technical' rather than political. Has it ever made sense to describe Britain's annual budget as a 'technical' rather than an intensely political occasion? How much the determination to deny that qualified majority voting (QMV) and a single market were political decisions, owed to the *laissez-faire* anti-political thinking then fashionable in government circles is impossible to say, but the separation of economics from politics beloved of classical liberalism seems to have encouraged the belief in Downing Street that the advantages of markets were available without encroaching upon the territory of politics. When the SEA immediately spawned the Delors plan for EMU, and German unification led Kohl to press for further political union, these proposals were greeted in Westminster as if they owed nothing to their own actions in furthering a single market. Even though QMV had been authorized with Britain's consent, the Council of Ministers was, in the view of London, still a diplomatic forum that had successfully turned its hand to legislative activity. The fact that the SEA ensured that the substance of matters coming before COREPER thereafter bore more and more resemblance to the itineraries of domestic politics was discounted as of no lasting or political significance.

This viewpoint has left Britain with only a warped representation of western Europe's political reformation. Yet developments that threaten its reliabilty have been resolutely dismissed as either nonsense or continental attempts to alter the terms under which Britain 'joined Europe'. In this way, Britain has come to see itself as the protector of national interests and with the duty to oppose, and where possible neuter, the 'political integration' of Europe. With Britain at their head, Europe's FNUs are to be saved from follies which Britain persuades itself formed no part of the original idea because its rulers could not imagine that anyone took their espousal seriously. Britain's twofold predicament however, is that it has persistently lacked the means – the power – to resist European developments that in any case it can only with difficulty recognize as taking place.

Other than in matters of economic opportunity, Britain has not wanted to see the EU as a novel experiment whose generative nature lies in what it might become. It prefers to see 'co-operation in Europe' as providing support for long standing states and the enduring nations they exist to secure. Such un- or anti-political thinking ignores the possibilities of creating something new out of old materials. In the case of Europe, the effect is to misrepresent the nature of what began as a localized scheme to deal with the military significance of iron and steel, but which ripened into Common Agricultural Policies which, to the consternation of many, have taken on lives and exorbitant costs of their own. Out of modest beginnings in diplomatic and economic calculations have emerged single markets, common citizenship, EMU, policies governing the quality of water, the habitats of wild life, and laws enforceable in courts that distinguish milk chocolate from the real McCoy. This is not either diplomacy in updated guise, or the independent logic of market forces; it is a mixture of the deliberate and wayward consequences of politically intentioned actions. Britain has not wanted to recognize this. It has instead wished to enjoy the advantages of a single market without finding itself caught up in a political experiment with far reaching though unspecified constitutional implications. The way that the one is bound up with the other has never been adequately addressed by British governments because it has proved impossible to face the possibility of political union.

It does not, of course, follow that had the political direction of EU membership been adequately aired, it would have led to willing or even reluctant acceptance of political union. A more forthright recognition of what the EU is might have led to prompt rejection of Britain's part in it. The pretence that the EU is the administrative agency of a single market has, however, left Britain in a position where the true and unique character of the enterprise cannot even appear at the centre of national debate. Because of the way Britain's relations with Europe have been conceived, questions that matter are only squinted at. If the EU is, and is set to remain, an 'association of nation states', what of importance is there to deliberate? Yet although it is difficult to think of many things more central to a political body than a Central Bank, including the role of the Bank of England in Britain's own historical emergence as a state, EMU is represented by government ministers in unblushingly economic terms.

The effect of obtuse thinking is to leave Britain on the back foot, continuously reacting to events which none the less carry it reluctantly forward. Although movement seldom slackens in Brussels, it is accompanied in London by the inability of British governments to admit to themselves or explain to the governed what is taking place. Because it is impossible to admit that the EU is a political body of which Britain is a part, confusion finds expression in bouts of biliousness. Because in the eyes of British governments Europe is precluded from having a 'public interest' to which its own experience of politics might contribute, its people are denied fresh outlets for their energies. Having lifted not a finger to create EMU or ensure its success, Britain is nevertheless biding its time to see whether the risks undergone by others succeed well enough to make its own accession prudent. As citizens of the EU it is difficult for Britons to know what they are members of because the incipient *res publica* to which they half-heartedly belong can only be referred to in the language of foreign affairs or as a sequence of business opportunities. The meagre and misleading terms employed in discussion of Europe ensure that Britain is paralysed by confusion, while changes occur that it cannot entirely thwart and which might be to its advantage. As relations with Europe become denser and imperceptibly more detailed, so government disclaimers that national powers of decision are being shared with other EU governments and with common institutions rise in inverse ratio to their credibility. Denunciations of 'federalism' grow in vehemence as the reality that Britain credits itself with having stopped in its tracks edges onwards. The Maastricht treaty that advanced EMU but left two inter-governmental pillars of 'home affairs' and 'foreign affairs' has only five years later been supplemented by the Treaty of Amsterdam which moves the former if not the latter within the realm of the EU's internal and domestic affairs. Despite 'subsidiarity', 'flexibility' and 'opt-outs', both treaties extend the meaning and scope of the EU as a political body. If it does not founder, EMU will add fresh impetus to the same direction. Should it succeed, the euro will bind citizens as well as the single market closer together and draw the attention of the world to Europe's added substance.

As British governments are at a loss how to justify the EU without misrepresenting its character, it looms as an alien and furtive force, dominated by foreigners with whom we have somehow become nominal fellow-citizens. Because Britain is not party to the Schengen accords, its nationals find themselves on a different footing from most other members of the EU. And because the EU is persistently slipping the ropes of its supposed category as an 'association of nation states', its indescribable and immanent nature also appears threatening. Not for the first time nationalists are the beneficiaries of confusion that leaves patriots on the defensive. Because no irreversible engagement of a political kind has ever been officially admitted, no line of defence can be drawn at Dover, Plymouth Hoe or anywhere else, beyond which Britain might say either 'yes' or 'no' to more political union, The effect is to make it impossible to argue with any clarity of purpose over what most other countries of the EU appear to take for granted: that national interests now lie in sharing important measures of government and that European political union represents no threat to the collective identity of nations. In Britain's case the attempt to embrace this deduction collides with the axiom of foreign affairs which sees anything going beyond conditional and hence reversible co-operation among states as undermining their existence.

So long as it is impaled by these false antinomies, Britain's alternatives appear stark. It must either exit from the EU on grounds that Brussels has acquired political purposes not present in the treaties it signed, or negotiate for itself a position from where, although it would have less influence on the EU, it would continue to recognize itself as a self-governing country. It might then hope to enjoy some of the advantages of the single market while conducting the bulk of its relations with the EU on the basis that it was dealing with foreign countries. Were, however, the EU to become a political body with its own foreign policy, Britain would then find itself in a position of having to deal with a continental power of considerably greater resources than its own.

II

Although a better understanding of the EU might bring home the choices that lie before Britain, it would not make the task of resolving them painless. Rather than indicate in which direction the country's future lay, more forthright deliberation might produce rigor mortis in the body politic of the nation. Unable to hold the line at co-operation between consenting states, or make a virtue of the necessities impelling it to adjust to developments it does not care for, for most of the time since 1973 Britain has in any case been left chasing the tail of events.

At Maastricht Britain acceded to the idea of a CFSP in the belief that the terms of agreement would allow it to confine developments within the accepted diplomatic practices of voluntary co-operation. Although it was accepted that any matter could be discussed in the Council of Ministers, the ability of states to conduct their own foreign policies and to veto action by the EU remained intact. Co-operation did not compromise the right of all members to dissent and therefore prevent or distance themselves from combined action. This protection of the right of states to pursue their national interests as they see fit was of course the prime British justification for placing itself at 'the heart of Europe'. From within the EU Britain would be in a position to slow its pulse and apply a tourniquet to proposals it did not favour. Deployed at Maastricht and again in the IGC that preceded Amsterdam, this stratagem has been the standard fare of Britain's bargaining position. The drawbacks to this approach nevertheless amount to a précis of Britain's entire experience in Europe which illustrates the defects of acting on the basis of diplomatic assumptions within a setting where other countries are cautiously removing themselves from the domain of power politics. Although Britain baulked attempts at Amsterdam to incorporate the WEU into the EU, its lack of choices – that is its limited powers – produced not forthright opposition to making a CFSP more effective but to shilly-shallying. Presented with proposals by nine EU members, including France and Germany, Britain, with the support of neutral countries, had to say something less than no, in the hope that a Micawber-like something or other would make its negatives appear positively constructive. While winning reaffirmation of NATO's crucial importance, Britain acknowledged that in principle, though not yet awhile, a European voice in foreign affairs, backed by armed forces under European control, might eventually be forthcoming. This was conceded by a new Labour government whose 'mission statement' reiterated that Britain's idea of Europe remained what it had been on the day the country joined the EEC in 1973: an 'association of independent nation states'. Once again a diplomatic conception was used to disown the existence and extension of political union that Britain dare neither openly recognize nor reject too abruptly.

As a method of safeguarding national interests, irresolution produced by confusion differs hardly at all from appeasement. The initiative is left in the hands of those pushing for change, so that with each shove forward those opposed are left examining what choices are left to them. When forced to reflect on the consequences of splendiferous isolation in Europe this produces a picture of Britain's independent 'freedom of action' so starkly limited that ground is reluctantly conceded. When the bluff of pragmatism is called, British policy in the EU dissolves into nothing more principled or effective than living from hand to mouth. Let down by the failure of the EU to be merely a peaceful and prosperous version of Europe's diplomatic past, taking one step at a time in Brussels proves a mistaken way of staying in the same place.

At the very time when the recomposed and unstable power politics of the diplomatic system suggest the wisdom of a strong Europe, Britain's governments appear to hope that the 'tide of events' has turned against further political union. Support for the belief that Europe is best considered a 'family of nations' in voluntary association, but otherwise unrestrained by shared government, relies on the prospect that Europe's FNUs will become increasingly surly if drawn against their wills into tighter political union. Perhaps without quite being able to say so, even to itself, Britain appears to depend on the resurgence of nationalist sentiments to halt, if not reverse, political union. This is to hope that the collectivist passions of this century that have bedevilled European life can be both used and kept under control by national governments without their rekindling the power politics they have repeatedly inflamed.

Although the failure of political union would not necessarily return Europe to its former divisions, it would place Franco-German relations under greater strain than at any time since Germany was last the strongest of the two countries. Fears of RDE would grow with every hint of conflict between Paris and Berlin. As these took hold the trust represented by the EU would seep into the ground. Since there is nothing in the institutions of the EU, or in any political association, able to withstand the subversions of fear, and the rubbish bins of history are stuffed with the detritus of failed political unions, the prospects for the future of Europe would be bleak. Perhaps sanctioned by the democratic wills of sovereign nations, the disintegration of the EU might be proclaimed as the liberation of a people's Europe from the awesome tyranny of a superstate. Politics, law and a European civil order are dead. Long live power politics, diplomacy and armies at rapidly reacting readiness!

Providence would not ensure that Britain escaped the effects of reversion to generalized distrust in Europe. The balance of power would be restored as the principal topic of British foreign policy at the expense of wider diplomatic interests. Though some might welcome a renewed chance for Britain to demonstrate its prowess in a regional pool where it was among the biggest fish, not since the 1870s has it been powerful enough to hold the balance of Europe unaided. Over the succeeding century Britain has not acquired greater powers or a network of dependent allies. In the scramble for allies in a Europe once more at loggerheads, the single market might be among the minor casualties. Sooner rather than later Britain would rediscover that a 'Europe of nation states' in unstable and untrusting relationship with each other, once more threatened its own national interest.

To one side, MAMEE might wash her hands of RDE altogether. Given its global interests in the balance of power, a more likely result would be for the USA to align itself with European countries of most use to itself. A united Germany holding sway in the centre of Europe would make Berlin of at least as much value to the USA as Britain. East of a powerful Germany, Russia might see in *mittelEuropa* reason for alliance with either Germany or France. Kept anxious by pondering in whose hands their security lay, the countries of central Europe would be returned to their harrowing pasts. With its strategic eyes on both ends of the Eurasian landmass, the USA might aim for alliance with Russia and Germany as the means of denying China diplomatic support. At Yalta Roosevelt looked forward to policing Europe in partnership with Uncle Jo Stalin. Although once indulged in, the rehearsal of possible diplomatic alignments needs little to fuel it; geopolitical speculation is less the product of chessboard chatter, than extrapolation from the nature of the diplomatic system. The dispersal of power among many states makes combinations among them a condition of survival and instrumental to the furtherance of national interests.

If Britain's twentieth-century experience of power politics supplies ample reasons for not wishing upon itself a fractious Europe envenomed with nationalist passions, an equal source of agitation may lie in a continental political union that goes from strength to strength. Were the EU to pass the tests of EMU and a serious crisis occurred in the Mediterranean that forced it to act decisively, it might begin to act as a great power in the foreign affairs of the world. No doubt under the direction of countries most responsible for its effectiveness, an EU of this kind, in which the problems of effective organization were overcome by the dictates of necessity, would leave Britain in less than sumptuous isolation. Were something of this kind to occur, Britain would have more urgent things to resolve than ruminating on how the emergence of a continental power, able once more to point a dagger in its direction, had been furthered by its own insistence on facing the future as if it could only be a replay of the past.

Possibilities of this lurid kind do not demonstrate that the only wise course for Britain is to accept political union of no matter what kind and play a part, from the inside, in determining its external actions. Plenty of countries smaller and more exposed than Britain co-exist with mighty neighbours, and some do so in prosperous tranquillity. What Britain could not, however, expect from a position of self-marginalization would be an influence in the foreign affairs of its environs comparable to the EU. The balance of power between Britain and Europe would be a euphemism for imbalance. Britain's national interests would remain under the sole authority of its own government, but its power to uphold them would reflect the relatively limited means at its disposal. From within the EU, Britain might have a better chance of shaping its future and hence of bringing its own conceptions or an orderly world to bear with greater weight.

Should the EU survive the trials of EMU, enlargement, modification to its institutions, overhaul of the budget, the Common Agricultural Policy and regional aid, as well as determining relations with the WEU and NATO, there are likely to be many sore heads and short tempers throughout Europe. Somewhere along the line it may all prove too much for Britain. Unable to stand the pace or accept the direction of change, the pretence that political union was not already far advanced would perhaps finally be set aside. Attempts to square self-government in London, devolution to Edinburgh and Cardiff, and incipient civil war in Ulster, with shared government in Brussels and Strasbourg, may debilitate one of the world's most unitary states. Under circumstances where the solace of continuities was in short supply Albion may settle for conditional estrangement from the rest of Europe. This might be achieved under the rubrics of 'flexibility' or as the cumulative effect of repeated 'opt-outs'. The recovery of national independence from the maws of Brussels would, however, be only the heroic and negative part. What would subsequently have to be resolved would be Britain's future, in relation to both Europe and the rest of the world. Having reclaimed 'freedom of action', adequate means would then have to discovered for asserting Britain's own voice within a diplomatic system attuned to powers much greater than its own.

The national and democratic appeal of bulldog self-reliance might be strengthened by arguments that in a globalized world, where markets have repeatedly reduced the importance of states, a modestly sized trading nation could look forward to peace, prosperity and self-government. Britain would thus appear in the vanguard of a world emerging from power politics and in which influence would no longer be monopolized by the most awesome combinations of power. While Europe remained a muscle-bound behemoth, Britain's less encumbered proportions might allow it to loose its sails before the winds of change and, when necessary, tack single-handedly against them. Did not Elizabeth inform her loyal subjects at Tilbury in 1588 of the 'foul scorn' she felt 'that Parma, or Spain, or any prince of Europe dare invade the borders of my realm'? Since Albion prospered before it rose to be a great power, it might do so again after it has ceased to be one. Britain could face an uncertain future by returning to tales of indomitable independence. Yet the truth is less stirring than myth. Even though Britain is no negligible power, and possesses an enviably robust sense of collective identity, it does not follow that puckishness is a dependable counter to the gyrations of power politics. Charlie Chaplin may have cut the great dictator in Berlin down to size, but a memorable showing on film was not quite enough to dispel the power of the Third Reich. Nor does globalization promise to rid the diplomatic system of agitations that middling states can hope to ride out if only they show sufficient aplomb. The arbitrary and now foreshortened 'actions and reactions' of foreign affairs are remorseless; they are now moved by weight of resources, scale and solidity of political organization and increasingly by technologies of wealth and war based upon science. There is a place in the world for countries that do not possess these ingredients, and who decline to become politically attached to those who seek them; but it is to be found on the reacting and receiving, not the acting and decisive, end of power politics. To pretend otherwise is to add misrepresentation of the diplomatic system to the misreading of Europe's political reformation.

Situated on the outskirts of a united Europe Britain will stand in relation to it as a familiar though foreign country. To wish to have it every which way, to be part of Europe, but not too much so or beyond recall, Britain would need to possess independent powers which for half a century its rulers should have been aware their country no longer commanded. In power politics a sustainable balancing act requires more than the poise of a trapeze artist. To attempt a conditional positioning towards the EU with an economy no larger than France's or Italy's and close to half the size of Germany's, and from a manufacturing and scientific base no longer able to support the independent manufacture of modern armaments, is not to choose national independence, self-government and the continuities of a treasured inheritance. It is to condemn Britain to be governed by the deluge of events and by powers over which it has resigned itself to have less influence than otherwise it might. For a while the effect of diminished external influence might be of less importance than the retention of Britain's sense of itself as a nation. But in the longer term a Britain for so long used to exercising influence in world affairs would risk losing sight of itself as lack of power removed it ever further from centre stage. Sharing government in a Europe that ranked among the world's principal powers might preserve Britain's national identity better than holding on to a view of self-government that condemned its 'national independence' to increasing diplomatic irrelevance. In deference to a well-plumed past that is beyond resuscitation, this would be to crop the nation from its future.

### III

Isolation is not the fateful sequence of independence. Lack of national power can be compensated for through alliance and diplomatic alignment with other countries. Distanced from Europe's political future, Britain would veer unambiguously, some might say naturally, yet further towards the Anglo-Saxon superpower across the Atlantic. What gladder fortune than that the country upholding a trading regime congenial to Britain, and which twice this century has rescued it from European wars, is now the preponderant state of the diplomatic system. Since the collapse of the USSR, and not withstanding China, the USA bestrides the world. Perhaps its command of power derived from science is set to increase. What more succinct future for Britain than alliance with a country of 250 million, whose habits of thought and feeling lie so close to its own? While remaining true to itself, Britain could acquire the security it can no longer ensure single-handedly and look forward to earning its keep.

One weakness of this argument is that Britain is in no position to negotiate terms of equal alliance with the USA. Montgomery served under Eisenhower not the other way about. Since mid-century, the Atlantic partnership has become ever more lopsided. Just as the USA was crucial to Britain's wartime salvation, peacetime recovery and Cold War protection, so the substance of their future association will also be determined in Washington rather than London. While the imbalance between a superpower and a once great power can be decently draped in diplomacy, its marked disproportions have for long been the governing factor in Anglo-American relations. Particularly in moments of crisis, the USA may value a tried and trusted ally and listen to its counsel with unusual attention, but when an American Secretary of State refers to their two countries standing 'shoulder to shoulder' *vis -a-vis* Iraq, the flattering perspective is at variance with any known physiological or military register. Although ease and effectiveness of co-operation between two English-speaking peoples are notable assets, neither can camouflage which country leads and which follows. It is possible that British interests are not infringed by the pride of place given to American national interests, but the fact that followers are seldom choosers makes it difficult to argue the matter. Although awareness that Britain has no alternative to dependence on the USA in foreign affairs may be bowing before the inevitable, such reasoning cannot in the next breath be used to affirm that intimacy between London and Washington demonstrates and ensures Britain's national independence and 'freedom of action'. For the same reason it can hardly be maintained that, compared to the constrictions of the EU, where Britain is among countries more nearly its own size, alliance with the USA is a surer safeguard that its national interests will not be swamped. With the exception of the Falklands War, it is difficult to recall an important USA foreign policy whose formulation was shaped by the need to adjust America's own interests in order to accommodate those of its British ally.

Whereas the tail has seldom wagged the dog, the USA has constantly urged Britain to move closer to Europe. A solid NATO and a prosperous European common market, with Britain active in both, has for long been considered in MAMEE's interest. And with the Cold War no more and NATO rejigged to intervene beyond its previous sphere of interest, the White House may find it diplomatically useful to exhibit a British prime minister before Congress and the cameras. For its part, Downing Street may welcome the chance to 'beacon' intermittently from centre stage. Acting alongside the USA to maintain a diplomatic system stamped with the power of the latter may persuade Britain that effective powers of decision in Washington are preferable to the EU's dithering CFSP. How far the latter is due to Britain's disinclination to sink its fortunes in Europe is a circular and therefore unanswerable question.

Doubts that Britain may harbour over the wisdom of dependence on the USA may be enlivened by memories of its own conduct as a great power. At the height of its empire Britain revelled in the choices made available by its naval power, one of which was the belief that, despite their usefulness, allies could be dispensed with. For reasons of domestic politics, the USA may persuade itself that allies are desirable, yet for Washington allies are similarly a diplomatic convenience. Where, as in NATO, they are essential to American interests, backsliding or piggybacking by allies can ultimately be corrected by the reminder that American power is separable from MAMEE. At a pinch the USA can wash its hands of NATO, leaving European insecurity to Europeans. An anarchic Europe would doubtless complicate the global balance of power, deprive the USA of allies and ruffle markets, but these are peradventures that a superpower of continental proportions, with the Americas, the Pacific as well as the Atlantic subject to its naval power, can absorb.

For a Britain uncertain of its place in the EU, the dissociation of the USA from Europe would necessitate the rethinking of its entire position in the diplomatic system. The effect of years of dependence on the USA is to make discussion of British interests similar to observing a puzzle to which the solution is endowed with the status of the revealed truth. Only when Anglo-US relations are agitated is there cause for concern. Because Britain has drifted into a position where some of its leaders might be more at home within the American than the European union, attachment to the 'the mere pageant of fictive sovereignty' is stressed more in relation to Brussels than Washington. Naturally enough the USA applauds the devotion shown to its interests by another country whose 'independence' it is able to salute while at the same time advocating 'European integration'. The main advantage to Britain of alliance with the USA over closer relations with the EU is that, although NATO embodies British dependence on another country for its security, and hence reveals its lack of independent power, reliance on MAMEE does not call in question the constitutional authority of British self-government.

Since it has placed its eggs in one basket, Britain's guiding interest is to make sure that MAMEE does not release her grip from the handle. At the Madrid meeting of NATO in July 1997 most of the USA's continental allies favoured a wider enlargement than the three countries supported by Washington. On this issue Britain once again sided with the USA, confirming that the two countries usually see eye to eye. It does not, however, follow that Anglo-American co-operation is the sole or most fundamental reason for NATO's existence, or that were Britain to sideline itself from continental Europe, USA interests in Europe would wither. This would be to confuse Britain's value as an ally with the circumstances of power politics that explain American interests in European security and EU prosperity. Britain became of importance to the USA because of the latter's balance of power interests in stabilizing a Europe divided by the Cold War. Although in order to strengthen the 'Western alliance' Britain was constantly prodded by Washington to take an active part in European affairs, London's unresolved hesitancies over 'joining Europe' were, though regretted, largely ignored by the USA. By default and then by design, American policy in Europe came to concentrate on the continental capitals and the institutions they were busily creating. However attached it still wishes to be to the USA, a Britain detached from Europe's political fortunes is therefore likely to be of less significance to Washington. The USA is quite able to absorb Britain's Atlanticism, which costs it little, while adjusting its main centre of interest to whatever new and more effective constellation of power takes shape on the continent. The logic of power politics would not suggest otherwise. In important respects, such as trade, USA statecraft has already recognized that with or without EMU and further enlargement, the EU is its principal interlocutor in Europe. The reasons for this no doubt have much to do with the EU's single market, but they include an awareness, that appears to go unnoticed in Britain, that as the EU demonstrates increasing powers of decision, 'it' (rather than the 'they' of its member states) will increasingly become established as the focus of US diplomatic action. The effect of US interest in ensuring that NATO and EU enlargement remain in kilter is likely to be more attention to both centres of decision in Brussels and correspondingly less attention to countries less than fully committed to the EU. Rather than recollections of wartime and Cold War co-operation, it is surely calculations of this kind that are bound to count for most in the future policies of a superpower. Given its aptitude for interpreting even the affairs of the EU as variations on the themes of balance and power between separate states, it is odd how British governments have clung to the mythos of a 'special relationship' able to withstand changing circumstances.

From the periphery of the EU, Britain's dependence on the USA will become more pronounced even as its usefulness as America's most trusted link with Europe declines. In response to an EU able to bargain with the USA on terms of greater equality, it is difficult to envisage what role would remain for an intermediary needed by neither side. An Atlantic alliance between the USA and the EU would no doubt differ from the present day NATO, but its success would scarcely depend on which side Britain was most aligned with. It is more plausible to imagine Britain exerting greater influence on the USA from within an EU equipped to act as an independent power, than from a position where its complementary support is largely taken for granted in Washington. In the event of conflict between Europe and the USA, that may arise over trade, environmental issues, or policies in the Middle East and Mediterranean, Britain might fancy itself well placed to broker understanding; the idea might even be raised to the level of a future role in foreign affairs. Yet given the proportions of power involved in the equation between the USA and an effective EU, Britain's ability to mediate between a hammer and anvil would be more akin to an acorn caught unenviably between them. The make-believe that Britain might prosper as the balancer between the USA and the EU, with London's diplomatic footfalls tipping the seesaw now this way and now that, is to indulge balance of power thinking to the point of delirium. Without absorbing the intervening changes that have occurred in power politics, this blithely transposes to present times the powers of diplomacy once disposed of by a great seaborne empire of the nineteenth century.

Britain's trust in the USA may be the reverse side of its misgivings over Europe. Perhaps self-exclusion from Europe causes little concern because the EU is expected, with assistance from London, to remain diplomatically ineffectual. Alliance with the USA might consequently protect Britain from the worst consequences of stalemate or disunion on the continent. What security Britain would enjoy faced with RDE would of course be for Washington to determine. While a disorderly Europe would lead Britain to shuffle yet closer to the USA, those in charge of American national interests might reach inconvenient conclusions. In the absence of a powerful Russia, or thanks to more pressing engagements at home or elsewhere, the USA might decide the time had at last come to cut its losses in Europe. Having spent half a century fostering amity, American public opinion might regard the old world as incorrigible and leave Europe to its recidivous habits. As with the EMU and much else, Britain might rue the days when, instead of putting its weight behind political actions of benefit to the country and helping thereby to shape and secure their success, its governments expended diplomatic energy preparing to deflect the consequences of failure.

Over the last half-century it is difficult to identify a Britain at serious odds with the USA. Suez was made up, and throughout the Vietnam War Britain looked the other way. It may now be part of *fortuna*'s 'cruel and steady malice' that this legacy now encumbers Britain's future. The interest of the USA in keeping a willing auxiliary in amiable tow may be at cross-purposes with Britain's interests. The good habits of dependable alliance may have unwittingly been turned by shifting circumstances, into the bad habit of resisting the need to adapt. The American shield held in front of it throughout the Cold War now masks Britain's relations towards Europe. Among the ironies contained in Britain's over close relations with the USA is that Americans often seem to have understood its ally's dilemmas better than itself. The Anglophile Dean Acheson is not the only person to have been bewildered and saddened by Albion's occlusiveness.

Anxieties over Europe dwell on the sinuous links between the fellow-feelings of national identity, self-government that raises issues of constitutional authority, and independence that turns on how much power a country has. Yet these self-interrogations inspired by Britain's relations with Europe are prolonged without being resolved by unthinking belief in the 'special relationship' as the irreplaceable buttress of Britain's place in the world. The effect of continuing reliance on reflexes induced by the experiences of half a century ago is to make equivocation over Europe appear sustainable and even diplomatically astute. What this produces, however, is neither perfidious nor principled opportunism in the best traditions of power politics, but mutual incomprehension between Britain and its EU 'partners'.

## IV

Between the devil of European unity and the deep blue sea of the Atlantic superpower, some espy room enough and opportunity for Britain's FNU to prosper on its own. For a country diplomatically recumbent after its decline as a great power, the effort of standing on its own national feet may be considered bracing enough. As a trading nation again reduced to its homelands Britain should, according to this prescription, set its sights no higher than paying its way in the world, leaving to others the management and scripting of the diplomatic system. Let Britain be an island exemplar of CE. Discussion of how independent and influential a self-governing country it is able to be can in this view be dismissed as outmoded. The affairs of the world are shifting, so this line of argument would have us believe, against the male-inspired posturings implicit in metaphors of power, prestige and armed hierarchy. The future lies not with cranking the futile treadmill of power politics, but in exploiting the vivid and unifying energies of a world economy which unaided by diplomacy and in defiance of great powers, is busily producing a different and better world.

Britain accordingly has no need to exert its public self, join or reject a powerful Europe, ingratiate itself with the USA or add its own counsel to the diplomacy of security in the UN. Its business is to make the best of assets that include a language used the world over and the current reputation of Britannia as a centre of 'cool' enjoyment. Global markets are now the place to catch the conscience of world and prod it in unpolitical and undiplomatic directions. There is nothing little or grey-haired in helping to bind the world together in the pursuit of gain and entertainment. Without public fanfare or government involvement, an independent Britain immersed in civil and commercial affairs can, according to this lyrical version of its future, have more influence on the 'shape of life' now unfolding throughout the world than by attaching itself to combinations of power and diplomatic entanglements.

This roseate picture in which Britain has conveniently detached itself from power politics has not, however, rid itself of blights present in its previous formulation by proponents of a more austere Victorian version of *laissez-faire* liberalism. The desires of producers and consumers to be left undisturbed by power politics has not once proved sufficient to ward off their agitations. The global capitalism that promises to spread wealth about the world is likely to produce new conflicts over might and right and cause fresh alarms over man's attempted mastery of nature; it will also be grist to human passions and to those who dote on power. Globalization provides no sanctuary for Britain because the growth of knowledge and the spread of worldwide markets is not taking the wind out of large states. The USA goes from strength to strength and its example is pored over by others. A Britain indifferent to power politics yet global in its pursuit of wealth would not thereby acquire, as if by special unhistorical dispensation, a safe haven in the diplomatic system.

Even so, the democratic will of the nation may give popular support to the idea of Britain as a 'garrisoned sea-town' (as Burke once described it). In spite of the risks, or perhaps left innocent of their existence, the British may prefer to stake their future on the chances of easeful self-government and gratifying prosperity, unburdened by diplomatic exertion. Whether, with few inclinations to engage in foreign affairs, though still more exposed to their buffetings, Britain would for long recognize or value its own peculiarities is another matter.

## V

In Britain's unhurried transition from monarchical via aristocratic to democratic government, foreign affairs have seldom been put to the people. Justification for the inability of parliament and public to control decisions that go to the heart of a state was provided by the man most associated with the liberal proposition that good government required the consent of the governed. Alongside executive powers dealing with domestic affairs, John Locke distinguished 'the federative power' whose object he described as 'the management of the security and interest of the public without'.[1] Although in practice these two aspects of public affairs are conducted by the same people, Locke noted that, in foreign affairs, there existed no 'antecedent, standing positive laws' by reference to which foreign affairs could be directed. He reasoned that because foreign affairs occupy a field of arbitrary and unforeseeable actions, neither citizens nor their representatives could expect to be consulted over their conduct. Locke reasoned as follows:

> For the Laws that concern Subjects one among another being to direct their actions, may well enough precede them. But what is done in reference to Foreigners, depending much upon their actions, and the variations of design and interest, must be left in great part to the Prudence of those who have this power committed to them, to be managed by the best of their skill, for the advantage of the Commonwealth.[2]

Foreign affairs have accordingly to be left to those who understand power politics and the workings of the diplomatic system.

Three centuries later, Britain's still liberally tinged mass democracy has found few effective ways of associating itself with the conduct of its affairs 'without'. The mutual unintelligibility of rulers and ruled when it comes to foreign affairs has deepened and become more thoroughly justified by the enfranchisement of the whole adult population. Among the motives for having a country of one's own, of being nationally self-determined, is the entitlement it bestows on those to whom it democratically belongs to busy themselves with what the majority considers of most compelling interest. Evidence suggests that for the multitude of citizens domestic affairs are not only more gripping than foreign policy, but that what is closest by and nearest to home is felt to be of greatest importance. Democracy authorizes as well as registers the primacy of civil over external affairs; of constitutional politics over power politics. Whether it is in deference to this democratically sanctioned preference, or for the reasons outlined by Locke, British governments do little to warn their electoral masters that disdain for foreign affairs may endanger the enjoyment of their private concerns. One way or another, the national interest 'without' is still assumed to be too recondite or too important to be entrusted to the localized desires of the sovereign people. This did not necessarily mean that because their authorization was not sought, the patriots who twice this century flocked to the country's armed forces, factories and farms in defence of their beloved homeland were being bamboozled. It more probably meant that the governed deferentially trusted governments to decide for them wherein lay their best interests. Although Locke might well have called this reliance of the ruled on the judgement of their elected rulers a form of 'tacit consent', the weakness of this form of justification is not confined to the way it evidently suits those in government.

The drawback of there being no 'democratic control of foreign policy' is that it provides few safeguards against the abuse by governments of the trust placed in them. Britain's relations with Europe make plain the ability of governments to keep the electorate uninformed of foreign affairs and then use the sops and slogans the public is fed on as justification for discounting its narrowly conceived opinions. Where in recent times it has become arguable that the national interest now lies in sharing government within the EU and above all in areas where 'salus populi or the people's safety' is at stake, it is an abuse of trust to pass off the EU with the pap that it remains an 'association of independent nation states' of no constitutional significance. Should the national interest now lie in an EU with effective powers of decision in foreign affairs, it should at least be explained that the ultimate justification of a 'surrender' of national authority is the need to safeguard Britain's future.

## VI

Shortly before his death in 1797, Burke berated his adopted fellow countrymen for having forgotten that 'because we have an important part of our very existence beyond our limits', they must 'stretch their thoughts beyond the pomoerium of England'.[3] Prompted by dramatic European developments set in motion by the French Revolution, from which he knew Britain could not remain unaffected, his thinking expressed a sense of why continental Europe mattered to Britain. He rightly saw that what Britain was, what it had become as a people, a state, an economy and empire, was inseparable from the civilization on which it drew and to which it contributed its own unmistakable self, in thought as in deed, in peace as well as war. Divorced from 'the Christian world and the republic of Europe', Britain would become unrecognizable to itself as well as to others. One may share none of Burke's attachments to the *ancien régime* while still applauding his feeling for Europe's imaginative and affective unity. Perhaps it has become necessary to labour that what an Irishman understood by Britain's 'very existence' referred not solely to levels of consumption, access to markets or national security, but to worth of being.

## Notes

1.    John Locke, *Two Treatises of Government*, ed. by Peter Laslett (Cambridge: Cambridge University Press, 1960), p. 411.
2.    Ibid.
3.    Edmund Burke, *Letters on a Regicide Peace* (London: Oxford Unversity Press, 1902), p.332.

# Index